Teaching and Learning through Reflective Practice

D1353023

Now in its second edition, *Teaching and Learning through Reflective Practice: A practical guide for positive action*, is a guide to enable all those involved in educational activities to learn through the practices of reflection. The book highlights the power that those responsible for teaching and learning have to appraise, understand and positively transform their teaching. Seeing the tutor/teacher as a reflective learner, the book emphasizes a strengths-based approach in which positivity, resilience, optimism and high performance can help invigorate teaching, enhance learning and allow teachers to reach their full potential. This approach busts the myth that reflection on problems and deficits is the only way to better performance.

The approach of this new edition is an 'appreciative' one. At its heart is the exploration and illustration of four reflective questions:

- What is working well?
- What needs changing?
- What are we learning?
- Where do we go from here?

With examples drawn from UK primary teacher education, coach education and vocational education, the book reveals how appreciative reflective conversations can be initiated and sustained. It also sets out a range of practical processes for amplifying success. This book will be a 'must have' for undergraduate and PGCE students on initial teacher training programmes and those wishing to increase their educational effectiveness. It will also interest practising teachers, teacher educators and all those on continuing professional development courses.

Tony Ghaye is an expert in positive psychology. He is Director of a not-for-profit social enterprise called Reflective Learning-UK (www.reflectivepractices.co.uk). He has experience as a school teacher, school leader and teacher educator. He is also Editor-in-Chief of the international, peer-reviewed journal *Reflective Practice* (Routledge).

Teaching and Learning through Reflective Practice

A practical guide for positive action

Second edition

Tony Ghaye

Routledge
Taylor & Francis Group

LONDON AND NEW YORK

First edition published as *Teaching and Learning through Critical Reflective Practice* in Great Britain by David Fulton Publishers 1998

Second edition published 2011
by Routledge
2 Park Square, Milton Park, Abingdon, Oxon OX14 4RN

Simultaneously published in the USA and Canada
by Routledge
711 Third Avenue, New York, NY 10017

Routledge is an imprint of the Taylor & Francis Group, an informa business

Copyright © 1998, 2011 Tony Ghaye

Note: The right of Tony Ghaye to be identified as the author of this work has been asserted by him in accordance with the Copyright, Designs and Patents Act 1988.

Typeset in Bembo by Wearset Ltd, Boldon, Tyne and Wear

British Library Cataloguing in Publication Data
A catalogue record for this book is available from the British Library

Library of Congress Cataloging-in-Publication Data
Ghaye, Tony.
Teaching and learning through reflective practice : a practical guide for positive action / Tony Ghaye. – 2nd ed.
p. cm.
Rev. ed. of: Teaching and learning through critical reflective practice / Anthony Ghaye and Kay Ghaye. 1998.
Includes bibliographical references and index.
1. Teaching. 2. Teachers–Training of. 3. Reflection (Philosophy) 4. Experiential learning.
5. Teachers–In-service training–Great Britain. 6. Teachers–Training of–Great Britain.
I. Ghaye, Tony. Teaching and learning through critical reflective practice. II. Title.
LB1025.3.G439 2011
371.102–dc22   2010029293

ISBN13: 978-0-415-57096-1 (hbk)
ISBN13: 978-0-415-57095-4 (pbk)
ISBN13: 978-0-203-83332-2 (ebk)

Dedication
To all those who strive to improve lives and livelihoods through strengths-based reflective approaches to teaching and learning.

Contents

Illustrations

Preface

Ask most people who are involved in education, in some way, what the term reflective practice means, and many may well reply, 'It's thinking about what you have done.' Most will acknowledge that reflection is important, and a lot might say that they don't really know how to do it, to get the best from it. This second edition is a practical guide to help educators with such needs. The book alerts the reader to some well-known caricatures of reflection and its practices. It then goes on to question them and explore other views. This is a broadening and building process. It begins with the customary view of reflection on 'problems', and broadens this to include reflection-on-strengths. So, in essence, it is a book that is intended to help you develop your understanding and skills of learning through reflection. The major difference between the first and second editions is that this second edition adds a strengths-based approach to teaching and learning through reflective practice. By this I mean it explores the power and potency of reflecting on successes, strengths and what went well, and offers this up to balance to the pervasive view that we reflect on our 'problems' and that reflective practices are, therefore, a solution looking for a problem.

This second edition complements the model of reflection-on-practice described in the first edition, with a strengths-based reflective learning framework and strategy. Taken together, I hope they help you to make sense of teaching and learning and enable you to be the best that you can be. Reflection and action are viewed as a continuous, creative and appreciative process. The book acknowledges that reflection-on-practice begins with a consideration of different things, most usually a consideration of problems. But I hope to show that reflection-on-strengths is equally important, and maybe more so! The book does not let you wander around hoping that you will bump into something that makes sense, but focuses attention particularly on professional values, practice, improvement and context.

One of the fundamental purposes of learning through reflection is to improve the quality of teaching and learning. Understanding the role of personal and professional values in this process is important. Values give educators a sense of professional identity. They also motivate them and provide them with reasons for teaching in the way that they do. The way values are put into practice is therefore explored. Confident, creative and competent teaching is also about reflecting systematically and rigorously on evidence derived from practice. How educators use evidence to reflect on the quality of teaching and learning is discussed. Reflection for improvement therefore needs to be evidence-based.

This is a book about the way positive emotions and focusing on strengths helps educators improve the way they think and act. This does not occur in a vacuum; it occurs in a changing context. So reflection is not just about self-improvement, team learning and workplace development, but also about understanding and questioning the contexts in which teaching and learning takes place. This can be done collectively and collaboratively.

Tony Ghaye
May, 2010

Acknowledgements

I acknowledge the following, who have helped me greatly in clarifying my thinking and practice in relation to strengths-based approaches to learning through reflection. They are:

Phil Chambers, Sue Lillyman, Sarah Lee, Shiphrah Mutungi, Ruggiera Sarcina, Simona Marchi, Bruna Lucattini, Debora Giannini, Massimo Tomassini, Galina Markova, Emma Ciceri, Antonella Barile, Elisa Cavicchiolo, Francesco Consoli, Hari Alexandrov, Antoaneta Mateeva, Furio Bednarz, Angela Bafokuzara, Anita Melander-Wikman, Birgitta Bergvall-Kåreborn, Rituu B. Nanda, Robinson Igwe, Karen Deeny, Ulrika Bergmark, Catrine Kostenius, Nona Lyons and participants in the 2009 World AI Conference: Creating a Positive Revolution for Sustainable Change, 16–19 November 2009, Soaltee Crowne Plaza Hotel, Kathmandu, Nepal.

Thanks also to Jules Holland, Senior Administrative Officer, Reflective Learning-UK for her help in preparing the manuscript for this second edition. I am also indebted to James Hobbs for his encouragement to write a second edition of this book.

Introduction

This second edition of the book is based upon six key ideas. These are as follows.

Key idea 1 Reflective practices help us understand the links between what we do (what we can call our practice) and how we might improve our effectiveness (by developing our practice). For example, reflective practices can help us understand the importance of high quality work, and provide ideas and options for developing this work. Reflection is therefore linked to practice (Figure 0.1). Through reflection, we can develop new insights and understandings that help us to improve our actions. Reflective practices are aimed at what you are really doing.

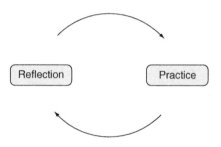

FIGURE 0.1 The link between reflection and practice

Key idea 2 Reflective practices also help us understand the links between feeling, thinking and doing. How we feel affects how we think. This affects what we actually do.

Key idea 3 Reflection is often described as 'structured' or organized thinking. So what might you think about? Maybe about your feelings, because your work is influenced by emotions (e.g., how you feel and how those you are working with are feeling). Your work is also guided by what you think and the context in which you practice, such as in a school.

Key idea 4 You can understand your practice by looking backwards – but work needs to be lived forwards. Looking back on your experiences and learning from them is important – but reflecting on the past can be limited by what we can remember and by what has happened. It is also important to reflect on the here and now – to reflect not only on what has happened or what we would like to happen, but on what's happening now. There are many other kinds of reflection.

Key idea 5   It is very important to use the power and potency of reflection to help you identify, develop and amplify what you *can* do, not just what you can't. It is important to reflect on your strengths. It is not always necessary to first analyse the problematic aspects of the situation/experience. What would it cost you to begin by looking at the successful aspects of the experience and to devote your energy to amplifying what went well? This might help you get rid of the negative feelings you may associate with reflection.

Key idea 6   Reflection can be triggered by many things. One thing is a question. It is important to know the difference between a deficit-based question (e.g., what went wrong) and a strengths-based question (e.g., what went well?). The latter can be called a 'positive question'. Strengths-based reflective practices draw upon the power of the positive question. Here are five examples of reflective questions:

1.   What am I doing? (awareness)
2.   How successful am I? (appreciation)
3.   What is a better way to do this? (imagine)
4.   What do I need to do to achieve this? (design)
5.   Is this what I should be doing? (judgement).

This second edition is also based upon five assumptions. These are as follows.

Assumption 1   The individual (or work group) has a level of commitment, an ability, and sees the need to reflect on what they do.

Assumption 2   The individual (or work group) is able to act to improve what they do, albeit in some circumstances in a limited way.

Assumption 3   The individual (or work group) is able (sometimes with help) to articulate the choice of action (or inaction) being taken. Reflection-with-action (see Table 1.1) assumes that we need to be clear about what particular kind of action we have in mind. There are different kinds of action. We can usefully think about five kinds:

- *Informed action*. This is about being clear about why you are acting (or not) in a particular manner. This kind of action is informed by your values.
- *Committed action*. This is being sure about what you are committed to doing.
- *Intentional action*. This is being clear about the purpose of your action (or inaction).
- *Sustainable action*. This is knowing how you can keep things going to achieve your intention(s).
- *Positive action*. This is acting in such a way that it serves to strengthen, build resilience and enhance human flourishing. It strengthens, not weakens, you.

Assumption 4   The individual (or work group) can explain (sometimes with help from others) and justify the outcome(s) of their actions.

Assumption 5 If the outcome is deemed to be 'good', then the individual or work group might develop this into some kind of habit or routine that works again and again. They may seek to amplify what is taken to be good.

Here are ten reflective questions that may help you think about the assumptions you make when engaging in reflective practices.

1. *Values:* How should I act?
2. *Expectations:* What ought I to do?
3. *Context:* What is actually possible here?
4. *Decisions:* Is my action justifiable?
5. *Options:* Could I have done anything better or differently?
6. *Judgement:* How far was this successful?
7. *Strength:* What is worth amplifying (getting more of, not less of) next time?
8. *Learning:* Who has learnt what?
9. *Voice:* Whose voice has been heard and whose has not?
10. *Knowledge:* Whose knowledge is worth knowing and why?

So reflective practices can help us with four kinds of learning. They are:

- *affective learning* – helping us learn through feeling and emotion;
- *cognitive learning* – helping us think about things differently, perhaps more creatively;
- *positive action learning* – helping us turn what we think and feel into action that is ethical, moral and strengthening;
- *Social learning* – helping us learn from and with others.

Here are six reflective questions to help you think through what you might use reflective practices to learn about.

1. What are the strengths and limitations of your current practice?
2. What do you need to keep doing well?
3. What are the things you need to change?
4. What is the best way for you to move forward?
5. How can you learn from success, no matter how small?
6. What does the evidence of positive development look like, and how far is this evidence trustworthy?

The reason for suggesting a range of reflective questions is that some say to me that they do not know what to reflect upon. Questions are one way to get the reflective process going. Below, I suggest another starting point. It is focusing on your passions, your proficiencies and your priorities.

- Reflect on your passions. Nothing motivates us more than our passions in life. Our passions motivate us like nothing else. In your working life, what are you passionate about? What do you love to do? A passion is something you care about a lot. If you focus on your passions, your practice is likely to grow in that direction.

- Reflect on your proficiencies. What are you good at doing? Everyone has gifts and talents. What are your strengths, as perceived by you (and others) and in particular work settings? To develop your practice, you need to know what you really love to do and what you really want to be good at doing. These can be tough decisions, because they mean you need to align your passions with your performance.

- Reflect on your priorities. Working on what you love to do, as often as you can, requires you to focus on your passions. Doing more of what you love to do means you have to be able to prioritize. You have to identify what's important, prioritize these things and then actualize, or do something about, each one. Reflecting carefully on your work, who you are working with, and where, makes prioritizing easier. You might usefully think about what you need to do immediately, and what you can leave until later. Another consideration is making a distinction between what you feel is important for you to develop, and what others feel you should work at developing or amplifying. You may also need to think about the difference between what you feel you could do and must do. The more specific you can be, the more likely you are to be successful in developing your practice.

Some Major Developments in Reflective Practice

Teaching and Learning through Reflective Practice: A practical guide for positive action aims to help you understand and take positive action about questions to do with:

- who you are;
- how you relate to and learn with others;
- what you can do (and don't do) to achieve, be successful and flourish;
- enhancing the quality of teaching and learning.

In order to get going on these four aims, I suggest it is important that I clarify a number of significant developments in learning through reflection, during the past ten years. Here are four of them.

Development 1: an expansion in our view of reflective practice

I begin with two clarificatory statements; one about reflection and the other about practice, as both are 'contested' terms. In the second edition of this book I'm going to begin with two conventional views of reflection, and then move on from there. Part of the process of reflection involves looking backwards to determine what we have succeeded in achieving already (or failed at doing), to get a sense of where we have come from and what our 'things to do' list looks like. Another part of the process, which is often given less attention, is looking forward, and therefore towards achieving our future goals. So, taken together, reflection can be said to involve both *projection* and *review*. These are pretty well known. But there are other elements of the process which are particularly significant. One is reflecting and responding in-the-moment. It is what is often called *improvisation*. In many aspects of human service work, like school teaching, management education, health care, social work, coaching and mentoring, and a range of other public services, improvisation is necessary. Arguably, it is at the heart of the creative process. Some people are generally wary of improvising (of deviating from a 'script') because they feel 'being creative' necessitates being original, or taking a risk, or having to make things up as they go along. This can be a bit scary.

Arguably, it is prudent to begin with some relatively more commonplace ways of thinking about reflective practice. The first is that there is more than one kind of reflective practice. Table 1.1 shows four important kinds that are often referred to in

TABLE 1.1 Four of the more common views of reflection

KINDS OF REFLECTION	MEANINGS
A. Reflection-IN-action	1. In a particular workplace 2. Thinking on your feet, improvisation
B. Reflection-ON-practice	1. After the event 2. On something significant
C. Reflection-FOR-action	1. For a reason or particular purpose 2. Planning what you are going to do
D. Reflection-WITH-action	1. Conscious future action 2. Action alone or with others

both practice and in the literature of reflection. Each kind of reflection does a different job. This is important to appreciate. In learning more about yourself, your work or workplace, and when trying to do something differently or better, you often have to be able to use more than one kind of reflection. In general, when people talk about reflection and its practices they have in their minds reflection-ON-practice. When we are teaching, chairing meetings and generally performing in some way, we often reflect-IN-action. We may not always be conscious of doing this. This kind of reflection may be automatic, habitual and intuitive. Reflection can also be done alone or with others. But (D) in Table 1.1 makes an explicit distinction between thinking alone and acting alone or in a work group/team/squad/faculty/department/unit and so on.

Understanding reflection and the practices of it soon takes you to the work of Donald Schön. There is a huge amount written about it. Schön (1983) wrote a very important book called *The Reflective Practitioner* (with a subtitle, 'How professionals think in action'). It is a book about the kinds of knowledge professionals need to do their job well. By implication, then, it is also a book about professional expertise. He talked about the importance of re-framing practice in order to make more sense of it. Re-framing means trying to see the same event from different viewpoints or perspectives – for example, from the viewpoint of a child, student, teacher, parent, carer, coach, mentor and so on.

Schön developed the ideas of reflection-IN-action and reflection-ON-practice. You could think about these two notions, described briefly a little earlier, like this:

1. *Reflection-in-action.* This has two meanings. First, it means reflection in a particular context or workplace – for example, in a classroom, an office, a hospital ward, a leisure centre, a home, a factory and so on. Additionally, it can mean thinking about what you are doing, while you are actually doing it. Some call this 'thinking on your feet'. Much of this can be unconscious; you may be unaware that you are doing it. For example, you ask a child a question, then read the expression on her face. You quickly see that she doesn't understand what you have said, so you re-phrase the question in your mind and ask it again. This happens quickly, in the heat of the moment. So reflection-in-action is about making on-the-spot adjustments to what you are doing, but in the midst of the action – not two or three days later. It is about improvisation.

2. *Reflection-on-practice.* This also has two meanings. It can mean reflecting after the event – say, a day or two later. This essentially involves looking back and going over things again. So this kind of reflection is linked with the notion of time. It's done after the event or an encounter with others. It can also mean focusing on something significant. This is where things can become a bit tricky. For example, what would your regard as a 'significant' encounter of incident? This implies that you have to be selective. The key thing is to ask yourself, 'What's significant in what I am experiencing and doing?' You might ask yourself, 'What's caught my eye and stayed in my memory?' You cannot reflect on everything! This is unwise, and not healthy or necessary.

Table 1.1 also shows two more kinds of reflection:

3. *Reflection-for-action.* This is fundamental. If you reflect on something you've done, been involved in or observed, presumably you are doing it for a particular reason. For example, you may want to understand it better, know more about it, change or improve it. These are all good reasons why you might reflect on your work or that of others. This kind of reflection is also about planning to take some (positive) steps to do something with what you've learned. This planning aspect is important, because there is a difference between planning for action and action itself. For example, you might see and imagine something being different or better, but actually putting these thoughts into practice, in a particular workplace, is quite different. Additionally, you might think of alternative ways of reducing the time 2-year-old children queue for the attention of a nursery nurse, for help with dressing-up activities, tying shoe laces, doing up zips and buttons. This is quite different from actually doing (or being able to do) something about reducing the queue. Planning-for-action is sometimes called 'anticipatory reflection' (van Manen 1991).
4. *Reflection-with-action.* This again has two meanings. First, it is actually about doing something. It is conscious action to develop your understanding or your skills. It is about weighing up what options you have, making a decision to act in a particular way and then doing it. The 'with' part also means acting alone or with others. There are limits to learning and acting alone. Often the power to change and improve something is better achieved by a group or team.

As I have mentioned, there is more than one kind of reflection. There are also many kinds of reflective practices. When I use the term 'practice', I take it to mean positive, purposeful action. The purpose may be many and varied, of course, but I confine it in this book to the purpose of 'bettering' or improving something. I link the ideas of *complexity* and *duration* with this view. Simply put, the more people are involved in or affected by the practice, the more complex it is likely to be. The greater the performance improvement we seek, the more complex the action and the longer it may take. When thinking about action, it is useful to consider the subtleties and different kinds of effort and thinking required. Redwood *et al.* (1999) set out ten major challenges when thinking about 'action'. They are shown in Table 1.2.

TABLE 1.2 Ten action challenges

Challenge 1: Plan for Action	All action needs to be guided by a plan
Challenge 2: Allocate for Action	Effective action needs to be resourced appropriately
Challenge 3: Lead for Action	Action leading to improvement needs to be well led, because much depends upon the exercise of power, influence and persuasion
Challenge 4: Strengthen for Action	Who or what needs to be strengthened, if action leading to improvement is to stand a chance?
Challenge 5: Mobilize for Action	Action needs enthusiasm and motivated people to initiate it and keep it going
Challenge 6: Clarify for Action	If you haven't explained to staff why they need to act differently, they are unlikely to change what they are currently doing
Challenge 7: Cultivate for Action	Better, rather than simply different, action requires an understanding of each person's gifts and talents
Challenge 8: Integrate for Action	Action for improvement often requires new and different ways of working to overcome functional barriers ('We do this, in this way here') and cultural barriers ('This is why we do what we do, everyday, with those we work with')
Challenge 9: Wire for Action	Some action requires the support of modern (information) technologies – fast, accurate, useable and well-managed information (knowledge) systems are required
Challenge 10: Re-energize for Action	Any action takes energy; energy management and renewal is important to combat fatigue

Source: Redwood *et al.* (1999).

In general, being able to achieve positive action and then to move forward is likely to be determined by at least six interrelated influences:

1. the nature of the feedback and pressure from students, parents, customers, clients, patients, and so on;
2. how safely, efficiently and effectively we feel we can learn new, and different, ways of working;
3. how understandable, and therefore compelling, the case is for new or preferred action towards a 'better' practice;
4. how long it took me/us before to complete something similar – this is about our practice memory;
5. the current resources available;
6. the present 'starting position' in relation to the desired goal.

Development 2: from deficits and towards strengths

Good reflective practitioners are good at observation. They observe with intense concentration in order to come to know what is going on in the (inter)actions or encounters in front of them and in which they are immersed. They observe and then notice, which is then the basis for reflection. So what is often noticed? Is it what is going wrong? Is it that which is less than desirable? And how does this affect any feedback process? Is this noticing about pinpointing 'problem/s' and trying to suggest how these might be 'fixed' in the hope that this feedback might enable those involved to 'go in the right direction'? Some argue that the best feedback is precise, and contains carefully selected detail. I would suggest that the best feedback is about being positive and also about being useful. By this, I mean using feedback (individually or collectively) to help those involved to reframe the current situation in such a way that it conveys a sense of positivity. It is feedback that liberates and energizes us to make a different, or even greater, effort to improve the current situation. It is also feedback that presents current limitations and constraints as exciting challenges. The key to this, I suggest, is receiving encouragement through the use of positive feedback. With regard to reflective practices in general, this is my view. When trying to improve work and working lives through reflection (of one kind or another), thinking and conversations often get stuck with vocabularies of human deficit, and in so doing fail to unlock the creative potential of those involved. Deficit-phrased questions lead to deficit-based conversations. These in turn lead to deficit-based actions. I show this in Figure 1.1.

When thinking about improving what you do, with and for others, you may need to change (or at least challenge) the view that asking deficit-type questions is the best way, under the circumstances, to begin such a process. Deficit-type questions are about what went wrong rather than went right. They are about problems rather than achievements, failures rather than successes. They are essentially about the kinds of things you feel you want to get rid of, to eliminate from your work, to fix. To answer them can require a considerable investment in human resources, all focused on removing things, or at least reducing their influence and impact. If we are not careful, an obsession with problems quickly becomes the problem! When we focus on problems, we begin to construct a world in which problems are central; they become the dominant realities that burden us every day. To ask questions about our failings is to create a world in which failing is focal. Deficit-based questions lead to deficit-based conversations, which in turn lead to deficit-based patterns of action. Yet we can flip this over and apply the same logic more positively. By asking ourselves positive questions, we may bring forth future action of far greater promise. Positive questions invite a different kind of conversation – one that brings with it the opportunity for positive action. I am not implying that we should ignore problems; I am advocating a balance in the kinds of questions we ask. Achieving and moving forward does not have to be only about getting rid of what

FIGURE 1.1 The deficit challenge

we don't want, namely problems. Conversations and actions do not have to be just about 'fixing' things that are going less well than we had hoped for or expected. It is unwise to perpetuate the belief that weaknesses can, indeed, simply be fixed. What benefit or usefulness is there in feeding back to those involved, through whatever process, only a description of what was not working – a description of error? Will this simply be discouraging? Recently there has been a slow but perceptible shift in our thinking about the role of reflective practice, away from being only about problem finding, problem solving and getting rid of 'unwanted' aspects of current practice. There has been a shift in attention and energy towards conversations about success, about understanding why particular aspects of our work are indeed successful, and how these joyful and celebratory aspects of practice can be further amplified and made more sustainable. First and foremost, this is about identifying and playing to your strengths. My argument is that if we change the question we ask, we have a chance to change the conversation. Change this, and we open up opportunities for different kinds of action. I suggest this is a fundamental concern for those undertaking reflective practices.

So one of the most significant developments in reflective practice recently is an appreciation that we grow in the direction in which we ask questions. For example, if we ask questions about our problems and about things that we feel have gone less well than we had expected, then we grow in that direction. If we ask questions about successes and fulfilment, then we grow in this direction. There are many kinds of question, and each one serves a different purpose. What-type questions usually ask for knowledge and information – for example, 'What are you good at doing?', 'What have you achieved today?', 'What do you love about your job?' How-type questions are usually associated with steps, methods, and solutions – for example, 'How can I?', 'How do I?', 'How should I?' Why-type questions are also important to ask, because they are linked with giving reasons for doing (or not doing) something. Sometimes we have to be a bit careful about asking why-type questions because they can be associated with the negative. Why me? Why now? Why should I? Why can't I? Why do people do that? Why is it always me? If we ask too many why-type questions, it can raise anxiety within us and cause us to worry. I am not saying that searching for reasons to act is not important; I am suggesting that, for those readers who are involved in practical action of one kind or another, we might usefully reflect upon trying to balance why-type with how-type questions.

One of the challenges to acting positively to our answers to how-type questions is procrastination. There are several types of this:

- not doing anything;
- doing the wrong thing;
- working on something you feel is more urgent (not necessarily more important).

To overcome procrastination, it might be useful to ask yourself five questions:

1. What is an important thing I have to do today?
2. Realistically, when will I get around to doing it?
3. What might get in the way?
4. So what do I need to change to enable me to tackle this important task/activity?
5. How could I reward myself for avoiding procrastination?

Try reflecting on the question, 'What do I really do in my work?' If you consider this, it is likely that three further questions come to mind. They are:

1. Who benefits from what you do, and in what ways?
2. How does this make them feel, and how do you know this?
3. How does this make you feel?

What kinds of positive questions could you ask about yourself as an educator? Might it be questions about the kinds of things you hope for – for example, how you might hope for more inspiration when doing your job, more job fulfilment, more responsibility; for more opportunities to be creative, do less paperwork, have better students, work with high-performing others, be successful, have more money, and so on? Additionally, I suggest it is important to think about what aspects of yourself are worth reflecting upon. For example:

1. *How you feel.* This can be a neglected area, as many of us jump straight into reflecting on how we are thinking. To reflect on how you feel requires a certain degree of emotional awareness and an ability to put words to feelings. This can be hard.
2. *How you think.* So how do you think about your working life? Do you know what is expected of you at work? How do you come to decisions? How far are you able to be focused, and when do you like to leave all your options open? Do you exercise mental discipline, do you love structure, and how do you cope with surprises? Are you a practical thinker, a strategic one, a big-picture person?
3. *How you relate.* How would you describe your relationships with your colleagues? Whom do you trust? Who do you confront or ignore?
4. *How you motivate yourself.* What motivates you to do the kinds of work you do? Are you a highly competitive person, an altruistic one, or a bit of both? How far do you feel you are motivated by the fact that you have the opportunity to do what you do best, every day? Does your motivation come from knowing that your line manager gives you recognition and praise for your good work? Is it because others with whom you work seem to care about you as a person, encourage you and say that your opinions matter? Or does the mission or purpose of the organization where you work make you feel as though your work is important?

Development 3: from fixing to flourishing

Why is it so tempting to try to fix people, including ourselves? For many years, those who use reflective practices have got drawn into using reflection to try to solve a problem. When doing so they have been working on a belief that by solving it, things will get better. On the face of things, this does not sound too unreasonable. But does this always happen? It is less likely to be the case if you work in an organization – like a school, for example – where there are lots of different people, procedures, systems and expectations. Sometimes the root cause of the problem is not close to you, within your practice or sphere of influence; it lies elsewhere in the 'system', and maybe outside your organization. Fixing something 'here' allows us to tick the box and to (temporarily) feel good. But the root cause of the problem might be over 'there'. So the problem comes back to haunt us, or we get a hybrid version of it coming back later!

This 'fix-it' type thinking generally means that to be successful and to get better, we must first identify our weaknesses and then fix them. This remedial approach to self-improvement is drummed into us from our first day in school through to our first performance appraisal. You may have a line manager who brings up, time and again, those few areas where you struggle, where you have always struggled, and you and your manager then cobble together another 'developmental plan' to try to shore up your weaknesses once and for all. A more hopeful way of looking at this is that by the time you reach the end of your career, you may have spent so much time fixing yourself that you might be well-nigh perfect! The best managers dislike this simplistic cause-and-effect relationship – one where you use the power of reflection to diligently shave off all your rough edges throughout your working life. There's a big message here, and one that requires a big decision from us. It is about the emphasis we place on reflective practices. There is a belief that if you keep working away on your weaknesses, problems, failures and those things you are not talented at doing, your persistence will pay off in the end. This second edition invites you to question this. Why? Because if the focus of your life is to turn your non-talents, such as empathy or strategic thinking, creativity or persuasiveness, into talents, then you may end up having a crushingly frustrating life!

Buckingham and Coffman (2005) state that your line manager may genuinely wish to bring out the best in you. But why should they (and you) choose to do so by focusing on trying to fix your weaknesses? Have you ever been in a conversation where you know you have many strengths, but others end up characterizing you by those few areas where you struggle? It's bizarre, but it happens! To turn this deficit-based thinking into something more fulfilling and enriching, I return to the idea of trying to frame positive questions. Why not reflect on these:

1. How would you describe success in your current role?
2. What do you actually do that makes you as good as you are? What does this tell you about your skills, knowledge and talents?
3. Which part of your current role do you enjoy the most? Why?
4. What would be the perfect role for you? Imagine you are in that role now. What are you doing? Why do you like it so much?

At this point in this second edition I wish to move from fixing to flourishing by raising the question, 'In what ways can reflective practices enhance human flourishing?' Underpinning this question is my assumption that to enhance human flourishing is important work. So in what ways is it important? Aristotle (384–322 BC) had much to say about this. Through his writing and teaching, Aristotle explained that the purpose of life is earthly flourishing, achieved via reason and the acquisition of virtue. Aristotle suggested that human beings should each try to use their abilities to their fullest potential, and should obtain fulfilment through the exercise of their realized capacities. Arguably, if human flourishing involves the intentional use of human potentialities, then these could include what an individual, a group, a team, an organization and a community may regard as their gifts, talents, abilities and virtues in order to pursue their freely and democratically chosen values and goals. Positive action could therefore be considered to be appropriate if it leads to the flourishing of the person (or people) performing the action.

I am also suggesting that the idea of human flourishing can encompass a wide variety of moral and ethical pursuits, the development of character traits such as being optimistic, meaningful and productive work, religious pursuits, community strengthening and altruistic activities, love, allegiance to persons and causes, self-efficacy, and so on. Some might regard all of these as relevant to the notion of well-being. Boniwell (2008:39) states that

> current theories of well-being seem to give a one-sided, rather bare picture of well-being. In fact what they seem to cover quite well is the notion of hedonism – striving for maximisation of pleasure – positive effect – and minimisation of pain – negative effect.

Another idea of well-being comes from Aristotle, and is called eudemonic well-being. This is a broad idea. He thought that true happiness could be attained through leading a virtuous life and, especially, doing what is worth doing. He argued that the realization of human potential was the ultimate human goal. So two questions arise: (1) in what ways is reflection a practice worth doing? and (2) in what ways do the practices of reflection contribute to the realization of human potential?

In this book I am advocating that the emphases set out in the first edition be complemented with a more strengths-based one – in other words, reflective practices that not only solve problems but also seek to enhance human flourishing. If we can shift the emphasis away from problems and more towards strengths, we may make a significant contribution to reducing depression, enabling people to do better at work, to stay healthier, to become more resilient and even to live longer! I have sketched out some possible foci of reflective practices that might enhance human flourishing in Figure 1.2.

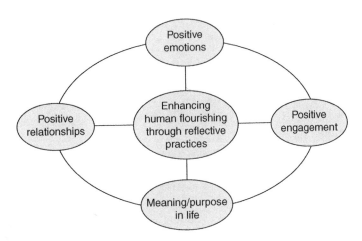

FIGURE 1.2 Reflective practices for enhancing human flourishing

One starting point is to consider the ways reflective practices help you to enhance your positive emotions, and those within work groups, teams, squads, departments, organizations and whole communities. These might be emotions like love, happiness, joy, contentment and accomplishment. Positive emotions can be about the past (gratitude), present (savouring) or future (hope). So how might you use the practices of reflection to build hope – for example, more hopeful learners? A consideration of the way reflective practices might enhance positive relationships can be linked with issues about the quality of interpersonal action, trust, honesty, openness and positive regard. The idea of using reflective practices to enhance positive engagement might take reflective practices into the arena of an activity that results in *flow*. This is a psychological state in which people are fully engaged in an intrinsically enjoyable and challenging activity (Csikszentmihalyi 1990). You might welcome this, because reflection can be associated with being a rather burdensome, time-consuming and traumatic experience. Positive engagement also opens up possibilities for reflective practices to explore work–life balance issues and, of course, your relationship with your organization. With regard to meaning and purpose in life and work, there is now a considerable and persuasive amount of research (RobertsonCooper 2008) that emphasizes how significant this is, especially in terms of psychological well-being. I suggest there is an important role for reflective practices to play in helping to enhance the meaning and purpose in your working life. Simply put, 'How far is your job meaningful – how far does it have some purpose?'

Development 4: from models to frameworks

Over the years, the processes of reflection have been associated with 'cycles' of one kind or another. Models of reflection have been characterized by their number and variety. While some are explicitly called 'models of reflection', others are more generally called 'models of learning'. Additionally, some require the learner to engage in reflection-on-practice in a sustained and continuous manner, while others include 'reflection' as part of a process which includes other actions or strategies – such as gathering data about practice (e.g., an audit) or as part of an inquiry into practice. Ghaye and Lillyman (2006a) summarize the commonalities of reflective models by suggesting that they can be seen from one or more of the following perspectives:

1. *a competency-based perspective*, in that they are to do with the development of a particular skill;
2. *a personalistic perspective*, in that they are to do with personal agendas, emotionality, self-study and individual enhancement through a greater sense of self-worth and identity;
3. *an experiential perspective*, in that they emphasize the active exploration of 'lived experience', one's own and the experiences of others; this requires that learners value their own experiences and have an openness that enables them to learn from the experiences of others;
4. *a transformatory perspective*, in that they are to do with asking questions that can challenge the status quo, challenge oppressive and disempowering workplace contexts, and focus on reducing or removing barriers to improvement.

An example of an early model is that provided by Smyth (1991). He developed a 'structured model' characterized by what he called 'a number of moments that can be linked to a series of questions' (Smyth 1991:113) thus:

1. DESCRIBE: what do I do?
2. INFORM: what does this description mean?
3. CONFRONT: how did I come to be like this?
4. RECONSTRUCT: how might I do things differently?

The third moment is often the most problematic, for it is here that practice has to be interrogated and questioned. It is where practice is given some legitimacy through a careful analysis of its genesis. As a way of providing more 'structure' to help in this confrontation process, Smyth offers a 'series of guiding questions that might include the following' (p. 116):

- What do my practices say about my assumptions, values and beliefs?
- Where did these ideas come from?
- What social practices are expressed in these ideas?
- What is it causes me to maintain my theories?
- What views of power do they embody?
- Whose interests seem to be served by my practices?
- What is that it acts to constrain my views of what is possible?

Arguably, understanding your practice better is no guarantee that it will indeed improve or strengthen in some way. Similarly, becoming more aware of the impediments to improving practice does not lead us on naturally to improving practice, if we are powerless to act to remove these impediments.

Another model often cited is that developed by Mezirow (1981). It spawned a number of other models that imply that reflection is, in some way, hierarchical or proceeded in stages. Mezirow's model is presented in seven levels, with 'reflectivity' at the base of the hierarchy and 'theoretical' at the top. These have specific meanings. However, as soon as reflection is modelled in this way, certain assumptions become apparent. The first is that different types or kinds of reflection can indeed be identified and described; the second is that one kind of reflection is more complex than the preceding one; the third is that this complexity is empirically verifiable; the fourth is that the benefits from reflection accrue by climbing the 'ladder' or ascending the hierarchy; and the fifth is that 'mastery' at one level is a prerequisite for moving onto the next level. The final assumption is that learning develops by some process of inclusion, in that the later levels encapsulate all that which has gone before.

Perhaps the most common way of structuring and supporting reflection has been by inviting the learner to engage in a reflective cycle. These models are principally based upon the idea that the reflective process is most appropriately described as a 'cycle', and that deepening awareness and increases in knowledge and skilfulness arise from repeated 'clockwise' movements around the reflective cycle. Gibbs (1988) provides a general cyclical model having six stopping points, with each point on the cycle being associated with a key question. With these so-called 'iterative' models, the ongoing nature of learning begins to be flagged up. Reflective cycles have an 'unfinished business' feel to them. Out of the stopping point, called an 'action plan', comes new and better future actions, and the impact of such plans is understood by again asking the leading question in the cycle – namely, 'what happened'?

Later in this book there is a re-statement of the 'enabling' model used in the first edition. What follows in this chapter is something designed to complement this enabling model. It is called a strengths-based reflective framework. Arguably, these kinds of framework have the potential to enhance human flourishing. Figure 1.3 shows how positive questions have been utilized. It emphasizes the process of appreciation; it requires an ability to engage in *appreciative reflection* and *appreciative action*. Appreciative reflection is a new form of reflection (Marchi and Ghaye 2011). This requires four basic kinds of appreciative intent:

1. *An appreciative intent towards knowing.* This is about, for example, recognizing our own gifts and the talents of others – focusing on what is and can be, rather than what isn't and can't be; on what is understood, rather than what is not. It is about being selectively attentive to the positive and essential.
2. *An appreciative intent towards relating.* This is about the active process of valuing and affirming the worth of others through interaction (e.g., good relations) and dialogue. It is about caring about growth-promoting and improvement-enhancing relationships.
3. *An appreciative intent towards action.* This is inspired by the positive intention for the betterment of self, group, organization and community. It is inspired by an ethic of care, and by social, cultural and organizational structures and processes that empower all involved to reach toward their highest potential.
4. *An appreciative intent towards organizing.* This is about organizing for the best individual, group, organization and community practices from an appreciative stance. It includes a commitment to trust-building amongst all those engaged in teaching and learning, team-working, getting ideas for better learning from everywhere, developing a 'readiness' for innovation (doing different things and doing things differently), becoming emotionally intelligent, and developing learning enriched conversational groups that build collective strength and wisdom to enable change for the better.

Responding to the four questions in Figure 1.3 also implies an understanding of and capability for appreciative action. Arguably, this involves the qualities of awareness, astuteness and alignment.

- *Awareness* concerns reflecting not only on what is, but also on what might be. It involves utilizing what it is we currently know as a creative springboard, to unleash our imagination in order to envision doing things differently. Having said this, individuals and organizations still have to exercise their judgement with regard to what is best, and for whom. A key question becomes, 'How can individuals and organizations improve their levels of awareness?' A good way to begin is to reflect upon our openness to experience, and the courage and opportunity we have to 'play' with new and different ways of relating, engaging and producing – in other words, the freedom we have (or otherwise) to explore new ways of relating. So how can we take or risk the time for such reflection and action?

- *Astuteness* is about our ability to interpret, organize and pragmatically use the fruits arising from awareness. Another way to express this is by using the word *implementation*. The particular form of reflective practice being described in this second edition is a strengths-based approach to improving practices (what we do) and policies (what shapes and governs what we do). So it follows that we need to be very astute in order to do this. Our political acuity and skilfulness at influencing others plays a big part in implementing something that may lead to building a better future. Astuteness is closely associated with empowerment, and our awareness of the influence of power and politics. The choice of implementation strategies is not a value-free choice, of course.

- *Alignment*: This focuses on the match (or alignment) between what we say and what we actually do. It also concerns the way individual values match with organizational or collective ones. Appreciative action of this kind is a way of understanding our personal relationship with others and with our work. When there is a good alignment, there is synergy between personal, organizational and/or work needs. This presupposes, of course, that we actually know what our organization stands for, and the direction in which our organization is moving.

Figure 1.3 invites you to reflect upon positive questions associated with:

1. appreciating
2. imagining
3. designing
4. acting.

The function of the 'Big R' is to remind us all that each question needs to be reflected upon. Depending upon your starting position, you can begin with a consideration of any one the four questions.

Figure 1.3 describes what I shall call the positive core of strength-based learning through reflection. As you can see from the figure, it has four intentions:

1. *To appreciate*. This is inspired by Schön (1983) and Dewey's (1933) work on the reflective practitioner, and more recently by work on appreciative enquiry (Cooperrider and Whitney 2005) and appreciative intelligence (Thatchenkery and Metzker 2006). In a more strengths-based reflective practice, it is an intention to appreciate and understand one's own and others' gifts, talents, limitations, self-worth, identity, role, responsibilities and accountability. It is an intention to develop a deeper understanding of one's own learning agenda, sense of self, self-knowledge, self-efficacy and purpose. The intention is to use the practices of reflection to deepen appreciations.

2. *To imagine*. The intention here is to use the practices of reflection to generate, manage and utilize knowledge, re-frame it, and then record this in some way. This is essentially done through reflective accounts and conversations of one kind or another; for example, through narratives, diaries, logs, portfolios, essays, problem-based learning assignments and case-based scenarios. The intention is to document learning about

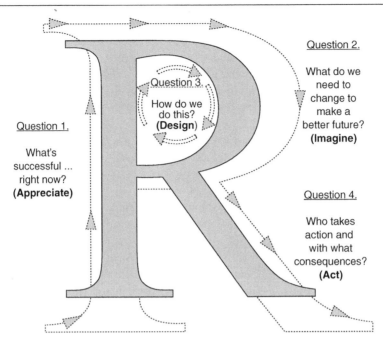

FIGURE 1.3 A strengths-based reflective framework (Ghaye *et al.* 2008)

what works, about what needs to change and in what way(s) – it's another way to improve practice. It is associated with seeing with fresh eyes. This intention weaves together new or different ways of thinking, talking and working. Doing this involves learning to 'let go' of some old feelings, thoughts and ways of working, and being able to 'welcome in' new and different ones.

3. *To design.* This intention can be influenced positively by intentions 1 and 2. It harnesses individual expertise and connects 'islands of innovation', bringing both together into a new wholeness of collective wisdom. Criticality and creativity are required, along with a preparedness to question conviction-laden practices and policies. Building collective wisdom is triggered by asking the practical question: 'How do we do this?' In some circumstances, it requires emotional literacy, political acuity and ethical courage.

4. *To act.* The intention here is to do, or achieve something, with this collective wisdom, bearing in mind that moving forward is only one option. Deciding to take no action, right now, might also be a positive step. What is crucial is that all involved document the decisions being made and the reasons for them. In moving forward we leave a 'footprint', a mark. If we do not record these 'footprints' in some way, we have no way of knowing where we have come from or how far we have travelled. Moving forward may be described and judged as incremental, or as a step–change.

In a practical sense, if the strengths-based reflective framework were to be applied at the individual, work group or team, and whole organizational levels, then the positive reflective questions in Table 1.3 might be useful.

TABLE 1.3 Using a strengths-based approach throughout the organization

MAIN FOCUS	THE INDIVIDUAL	THE WORK GROUP OR TEAM	THE WHOLE ORGANIZATION
What's successful … right now? (Appreciate)	What do you feel you do really well and why?	What are your team's talents and achievements? How can you play to your strengths?	What are your organization's major success stories? How can you contribute to them?
What do we need to change to make a better future? (Imagine)	What are some of your possibilities for improvement?	How can you ask appreciative questions to develop more strengths-based conversations amongst team members?	What options and alternatives do you have to increase performance and/or productivity?
How do we do this? (Design)	What are your core values? Why do you hold these?	What are your team's values? Why do you hold these?	What are your organization's values? What does it stand for?
Who takes action and with what consequences? (Act)	How far are you able to put your values into action?	How can you create more opportunities to do what you do best, every day?	How far is your performance aligned with mission?

This strengths-based reflective learning framework might look seductive and straightforward. In reality, it is pretty challenging. There are real and potential barriers to working through it, and to getting the most from it. I have set out some possible barriers in Table 1.4.

TABLE 1.4 Barrier-busting positive questions

BASIC INTENTIONS	POTENTIAL BARRIER TO REALIZING THE INTENTION	BARRIER-BUSTING POSITIVE QUESTIONS
1. To APPRECIATE	Failure to 'feel'	Think of an occasion when you felt valued by those you work with. What do you need to do to feel this way again?
2. To IMAGINE	Failure to 'see'	Think of a moment when you realized, 'Hey, there are other ways to do or understand this.' What do you need to do to experience this again?
3. To DESIGN	Failure to 'share'	Think of a time, at work, when you could meet, talk and learn with your colleagues. What do you need to do to create this time again?
4. To ACT	Failure to 'move'	Think of the last time when you were supported in your efforts to move your knowledge and skills forward. What do you need to do to achieve this kind of support again?

Reflective practice is an exploratory, purposeful, creative pursuit for better knowledge and understanding. If achieved, we then have to make a decision about how to put this new knowledge and understanding to good use. No one holds the copyright on what reflective practice 'is', 'might be' or 'ought to be'. No one has the final word on the practices of reflection, where and how to find them and what to do with them.

What I have tried to suggest so far in this second edition is that reflective practices can be used to build positivity and strength. They don't have to be used exclusively to tackle problems, and to 'fix' things. As I have tried to say, this does not have to be seen in either/or terms; both have their place. What I am proposing is reflection that enhances human insight, and practices which enable us to positively draw upon such insight to better understand our work, to amplify success, and to focus on doing more of what is valued.

Therefore, I argue that while we may agree that this is a central purpose of a reflective practice for positive action, we may also need to agree that the development of human insight and action that leads to building a better future for all can be achieved in different ways. For me, this means 'doing' a form of reflective practice that has the capacity to transform, is generative in style, and is thereby a hopeful practice that might positively contribute to building a better future for everyone.

In conclusion, the general view of reflection and its various practices that I will use in this book is as follows:

Reflection is skilled practice that uses experience, knowledge and inquiry processes to increase our capability to intervene, interpret, and act positively on successes, problems, issues, and significant questions. The use of particular reflective practices can reveal new insights and understandings about who we are and what we do. These practices can also reveal options, possibilities and avenues for positive and sustainable action. In this sense, then, one outcome of reflection is the creation of new, useable and hopefully better knowledge, to help build a better future for all.

2

Being a Reflective Practitioner

'I enter my first job knowing what I would *like* to achieve, but also knowing the likelihood of what I *will* achieve.'

(Sam Ansell, Final-year BA (QTS) student)

This was a comment made by a fourth-year student when reflecting on her final school experience placement. Note that she makes a difference between what she wants to achieve and what she thinks she will be able to accomplish. It is a comment from a reflective student who has a confident and developing sense of the kind of teacher she wants to be. Also in her initial teacher training she has learnt that schools can be very different as contexts for teaching and learning. Some of these contexts will be encouraging, stimulating and rewarding, while others will be much less so. Becoming a teacher and continuing our professional development is a challenging and complex business. Reflection-on-practice that is structured, challenging and supported is an essential part of this process.

So what does reflection-on-practice mean?

A group of 50 experienced teachers were asked to complete the phrase 'Reflection-on-practice means...' Some of their responses are listed in Table 2.1.

A conclusion from this is that these teachers thought that reflection-on-practice meant many different things. One comment was that it was something done by reflective practitioners. Another was that it involves reflecting on one's own teaching. There are many views on what reflection is (Bengtsson 1995), what reflective practitioners do, and the impact of reflection on the quality of teaching and learning. For example, some views on what reflection means are as follows. Note some of the things they have in common, such as what teachers think, feel and do. Reflection is:

- 'a way of being as a teacher' (Dewey 1933);
- 'intellectual and affective actions in which individuals engage to explore their experiences in order to lead to new understandings and appreciations. It may take place in isolation or in association with others' (Boud *et al.* 1985:19);
- 'a crucial element in the professional growth of teachers' (Calderhead and Gates 1993:1);
- 'a reaction against the view of teachers as technicians who ... merely carry out what others, removed from the classroom, want them to do' (Zeichner and Liston 1996:4);

TABLE 2.1 Reflection-on-practice means...

Navel-gazing	Learning from the day's chaos	Talking about what you do with others
Learning from experience	Reasoning	Remembering when
Being honest with yourself	Becoming more aware	Constructive criticism
Improving what you've done	Doing it after a lesson	Understanding your feelings
Re-assembling what you do	Questioning yourself	Letting go of personal prejudice
Something done by reflective practitioners	Gaining confidence in your work	Hard work
The latest bandwagon	What you do at college	Dwelling on mistakes
Justifying what you do	Personal growth	Helping you to see what you would or would not do again and why

- 'looking back and making sense of your practice, learning from this and using this learning to affect your future action. It is about making sense of your professional life' (Ghaye et al. 1996a:13);
- 'an intentional act of examining the rationale and justification of an action or belief (Tsang 1998:23).

The second edition of this book is intended to help develop your understanding and skill in reflecting-on-practice using a strengths-based approach (see Chapter 4). Reflection can occur before, during and after a teaching session. Reflection on what has been learnt from past encounters can be used to inform current planning. Reflection during the session is called 'reflection-in-action' (Schön 1983). This term is often used to describe quite unconscious behaviour, and is linked to phrases such as 'thinking on your feet' and being adaptable and responsive to a situation. Eraut (1995a) calls it rapid reflection because it occurs during our interactions with children and colleagues on the spur of the moment. Reflection after a session is called 'reflection-on-practice', and is another term used by Schön. It occurs after the event, when teachers look back on what has happened. Eraut calls this 'time-out reflection'. The different types of reflection can blend into each other, forming continuous cycles of reflection and action as teaching and learning progresses.

Many educators have benefited from learning through reflection, and have been called 'reflective practitioners'. Their teaching and their understanding of what is possible and what is less possible, their influence and its boundaries, have arisen from this process. Reflection-on-practice also helps educators make wise and principled decisions. It is about developing self-knowledge, the ability to 'see through' teaching and learning situations and understand the meaning of what is happening in particular organizational contexts. Engaging in the process of reflection is about being open to the possibility that practice can always be improved in some way. We can improve the way we nourish the 'good bits' and tackle the 'messy bits'. Reflection-on-practice refuses to let experience become a liability. In general, it takes experience and invites us to amplify the positives and re-frame the problematic aspects of it so that it becomes possible to change for the better. Reflection helps establish the improvement agenda for individuals and groups. It can provide educators with the courage and intellectual capacity to turn insight into improved action. With structure, challenge and support, the reflective process enables thinking and practice to move forward. Reflection-on-practice is not just about learning from experience in a private and solitary way; it is about knowledge production that has the potential to enlighten and empower those involved. In this sense, it is a creative process. It can help us envision, nourish and imagine improved teaching and learning situations. Reflection-on-practice is done by socially committed individuals and groups.

A few words of caution from the outset. As implied by Table 1.1, reflection-on-practice is a diverse process. It is much more than 'just thinking about what you do'. Reflection-on-practice is not a toolbox to 'help get you through'; neither can it be adequately described as a method. It is a blend of practice-with-principle. It is not always 'safe' but can be threatening as you question your practice and maybe the practices of others. It is about being professionally self-critical without being destructive and overly negative. It is not something to be 'bolted-on'. We are not a reflective practitioner one day a week and some other kind of educator for the rest of the time. Getting the most from reflecting-on-practice means having a consistently reflective approach to teaching and learning. It is a whole way of being; it cannot just be picked up and put down on a daily basis. A reflective practitioner is a professional practitioner. Reflection-on-practice is not private, self-indulgent 'navel-gazing'. It is not a process of self-victimization, but about taking a questioning stance towards what you do and what you organization stands for. It questions the means and ends of education. Reflection-on-practice should not be supported without challenge, for this is hollow. Neither should it be challenge without support, for this can be demoralizing. Ideally, it needs to be a judicious blend of sensitive support and constructive challenge.

Reflecting on Schön

Schön has made an important contribution to our understanding of reflective practice. In his book *The Reflective Practitioner* (1983) we find a number of key ideas, all of which are woven into this text. They are 'technical rationality', 'knowledge-in-action', 'reflection-in-action' and 'reflection-on-action'.

(a) Technical rationality

Schön's work contains a critique of technical rationality, which is linked to the ideas of practice being separated from theory and the teacher being a technician. Schön argues that technical rationality is a dominant way of viewing the relationships between the generation of knowledge and professional practice. Briefly, knowledge is generated in establishments of higher education, such as universities and research centres. This knowledge is 'theoretical', and is about how to achieve given ends. Schools, for example, are worlds of practice. The teachers' task is seen as applying this theoretical knowledge, from the universities or the 'academy', to solve their teaching problems. It is an application of theory to practice, and devalues the knowledge that teachers develop about and through their teaching. Teachers (and other educators) are viewed as technicians because they never question the values that underpin their practice and make them the kind of teachers they are. They never question the context in which they are teaching, and how this liberates and constrains what they do.

There are real problems with holding this technical-rational view. For example, first, the ends or products of education are rarely fixed but contested – people have different views about them. Second, we have to question the usefulness of knowledge that is produced out of the context to which it is to be applied. Third, the assumption that teaching problems can be solved just by applying someone else's knowledge to one's own practice is simplistic, and devalues the art and skilfulness of teaching particular children in particular settings. In this scenario, what are teachers to do when they find that, in trying to apply theory to their practice, the theory fails both to solve their teaching problems and explain their practice to them? In the busy worlds of classrooms and schools, for example, 'problems' are many and varied, and are often difficult to define and resolve. They cannot simply be solved by the application of theoretical knowledge. Schön turns this technical-rational view around, and talks about how reflection helps us to pose or 'frame' problems, how we should value and use the kind of knowledge that is embedded in our workplaces, generated by our practice and shared among teachers themselves. In the second edition of this book, I wish to complement Schön's emphasis on reflecting on 'problems' with a view of reflection that focuses upon strengths.

(b) Knowledge-in-action

Knowledge-in-action is another important Schönian idea, and is about the professional knowledge that we use in our daily practice. There are two parts to it. The first is that improving teaching and teacher development begins from a reflection on what we actually do, on our own teaching and experience. This reflection generates a rich and detailed knowledge base derived from practice. Our personal and collective teacher knowledge is drawn upon to transform and reconstruct what we do (Valli 1993). The second is that this knowledge is used by us in our teaching. It then becomes knowledge or 'knowing-in-action'. Our knowing is reflected in what we do, how we teach and encourage children to learn. Much of this knowing is often difficult to make verbally explicit (Schön 1987). The knowing is often described as unconscious, tacit, and even unarticulated commonsense, but it reveals itself in our teaching actions.

The idea of knowing-in-action is linked to a very different view of theory to that which is described in (a) above. It is a view that, as teachers and other educators, we do not just receive and apply someone else's theory to our practice, but hold and develop our own theories about practice. We have our own personally tailored 'theories' about what does and does not work for us in our teaching. We have theories about appropriate classroom management, effective teaching, meaningful learning, and so on. Teachers' work can be viewed in part as 'theory-guided practice'. Carr (1987) sets this out succinctly:

[S]ince all practice presupposes a more or less coherent set of assumptions and beliefs, it is, to this extent, always guided by a framework of theory. Thus, on this view, all practice … is 'theory-laden'. Practice is not opposed to theory, but is itself governed by an implicit theoretical framework which structures and guides the activities of those engaged in practical pursuits.

(Carr 1987:165)

Making theory of this kind explicit is important, and the chapters that follow should help you do this. Schön develops this idea in his work with Argyris when they describe their view of a 'theory-of-action' (Argyris and Schön 1992). This again comes in two parts: espoused theories, and theories-in-use. Our *espoused theories* are what we say or claim we do, or want to do. We find examples of this kind of theory in lists of lesson objectives and desirable learning outcomes, in school budgets, job descriptions, minutes of school meetings, in school brochures, and so on. *Theories-in-use*, on the other hand, are about what actually happens in practice (note the link here with 'knowing-in-action'). Teachers and other educators hold many theories of this kind. Normally, we can determine what these theories are by observing teachers at work; their existence manifests itself in the act of teaching. Reflection provides the basis for improvements in our espoused theories as well as our theories-in-use. The knowledge we have been describing in this section is value-laden, and the kind that teachers use to make sense of and to explain their everyday practice.

(c) Reflection-in-action

Reflection-in-action is the third major idea. Schön argued that it is central to the 'art' by which professionals handle and resolve their difficulties and concerns about practice. Reflection-in-action is a reflection on the adequacy of our 'knowing-in-action'. A 'surprise' usually triggers this process – for example, when we begin to realize that our existing stock of knowledge that we are using (our knowing-in-action, in other words) is no longer adequate in helping us teach in a competent and confident manner. Reflection-in-action, as the term suggests, occurs in the midst of action. It is based upon a rapid interpretation of the situation, where rapid decisions are required. Reflection-in-action guides further action. Eraut (1995a) looks at this in some detail, and in particular at how reflection needs to be further understood in relation to the notions of timeframe (when it occurs) and the context in which it occurs.

(d) Reflection-on-action

Reflection-on-action is a main focus of this book. It consists of reflection after the event, perhaps out of the workplace situation. It is a deliberate, conscious and public activity principally designed to improve future action. In Chapter 6, it is argued that this process of the generation of professional knowledge and the improvement of practice, through reflection of one kind or another, can be appropriately described as a practitioner research process. The reflective practitioner is a researcher. Reflective practice can be viewed as a research process in which the fruits of reflection are used to amplify strengths, and to challenge and reconstruct individual and collective teacher action.

Are definitions of reflective practice important?

As I guess you have become aware, there are many definitions available. Arguably, they are helpful if only because they illustrate the breadth of ideas and processes that have been caught up by the term. One definition rarely captures everything. It may not be wise to invest too much time in finding the perfect definition for yourself. You could always construct one. Here are some examples:

> Reflection is an active, persistent and careful consideration of any belief or supposed form of knowledge in the light of the grounds that support it and the further conclusions to which it tends.
>
> (Dewey 1933:118)

> critical reflection ... using the reflective process to look systematically and rigorously at our own practice. We all reflect on our practice to some extent, but how often do we employ those reflections to learn from our actions, to challenge established theory and, most importantly, to make a real difference to practice?
>
> (Rolfe et al. 2001:xi)

> Reflection, as a process, seems to lie somewhere around the notion of learning and thinking. We reflect in order to learn something, or we learn as a result of reflecting – so 'reflective learning' as a term simply emphasises the intention to learn as a result of reflection.
>
> (Moon 2004:80)

> Guided reflection is a process of self-enquiry to enable the practitioner to realise desirable and effective practice within a reflexive spiral of being and becoming ... Being in guided reflection groups is reminiscent of the 'campfire' approach to storytelling, reflecting on our own wisdom as practitioners, giving voice to our personal knowing, ideas and opinions, learning to dialogue, and working our stories into the caring-healing tradition of nursing and healthcare.
>
> (Johns 2002:3)

What is clear from these four statements is that reflective practice can be viewed as a catalyst for learning and a response to learning. You can, of course, choose to reflect on and learn from successful events in your work, or from failures and problems. Success and failure are two extremes.

The work of John Dewey

John Dewey (1933) argued that reflective processes cannot be separated from some sort of event called an 'experience'. So it follows that reflective practitioners use 'experience' as their raw material for learning. He also emphasized that not all experience educates. For example, can you remember living through events from which you emerged (apparently) unchanged? Have you ever felt that you have missed out and not learned lessons that others have learned, having gone through the same experience as you?

Dewey wrote that for learning to happen, an experience must include two key elements. The first is *continuity*. This means that to learn something, you need to be able to connect aspects of the new experience to what you already know. This may add to what you already know and can do. It may modify or improve it. The second is *interaction*. This means that to learn something, you need to be actively interacting with others in your workplace, continuously testing out and modifying what you are learning in the company of others. Dewey (1933) also argued that reflective practitioners learn by noticing and framing *problems of interest* in particular ways. He said that if you experience surprise or discomfort in your everyday work, the reflective process is triggered.

Dewey had a particular view of what constituted a 'problem'. Loughran (2006) develops Dewey's notion. He warns that although reflecting on problems is important, it should not be done at the expense of other aspects of our working life. He also states that using the word 'problem' has negative connotations, and conjures up images of mistakes and errors of judgement. Loughran helpfully re-defines a problem as 'a situation that attracts attention; something that is curious or puzzling; something that invites further consideration beyond that which might initially have been anticipated' (Loughran 2006:45). Dewey saw reflective thinking as a way to discover specific connections between actions and consequences. He believed that reflective thinking would help you learn from your experience and improve your problem-solving skills.

Further, Dewey argued that the reflective process consisted of several steps, including: (1) 'perplexity, confusion, doubt' due to the nature of the situation in which one finds oneself; (2) 'conjectural anticipation and tentative interpretation' of given elements or meanings of the situation and their possible consequences; (3) 'examination, inspection exploration, analysis of all attainable considerations' which may define and clarify a problem with which one is confronted; (4) 'elaboration of the tentative hypothesis suggestions'; and (5) deciding on 'a plan of action' or 'doing something' about a desired result (1973:494–506). Van Manen (1995) argues that a proper sequencing of such reflective steps makes up reflective experience, which in turn can lead to analysis and evaluation, and then to further reflective action.

The work of Jurgen Habermas

Jurgen Habermas (1974), like Dewey, also had plenty to say about reflection and experience. He saw reflective practices as a way of questioning experience and, in so doing, freeing the mind from unchallenged assumptions. He also saw reflection as a kind of investigatory process which has the potential to lead to personal enlightenment and emancipation. His work is also aligned with Schön's in the sense that he believed that knowledge is sought on the basis of self-interest:

> Yet in making the connection to action, Habermas did not see that knowledge generated by individual (critical) reflection was in itself sufficient for social action. He believed it was necessary to engage in discursive processes through which participants in the situation came to an authentic understanding of their situation.
>
> (O'Hanlon 1994:285)

The enabling model of reflection-on-practice from the first edition

The emphasis of the first edition was on the process of reflection-on-practice, what it might be taken to mean, how it might be done, with what intentions and interests in mind. It was also about knowing if reflection led to any valued outcomes. Two of these were improvements in teaching and learning. Reflection-on-practice was seen as a natural process of making sense of professional action; it was about using and learning from experience. Making sense of teaching was also about seeing the process of reflection as a meaning-making process. Arguably, not only is this necessary for good teaching, it is also a fundamental human necessity. Baumeister (1991) argues that we find meaning in life by trying to satisfy four needs. These are to do with the following.

1. *Purpose.* This is about doing things that are satisfying in themselves, such as walking the dog, displaying children's work in your classroom for others to appreciate, and listening to children sing in the school assembly. Additionally, it is about achieving certain goals and outcomes, such as a successful OFSTED inspection or being awarded a professional certificate or degree.
2. *Value.* This is about needs being satisfied by our ability to justify what we do and endow it with some legitimacy.
3. *Efficacy.* This need is satisfied by doing certain things associated with work, personal activities, projects and relationships. It is also satisfied by the understandings we feel we possess.
4. *Self-worth.* Satisfying this need is linked to our feelings of self-esteem and self-confidence in what we do and believe.

Reflection-on-practice helps us make sense of teaching and learning. Like some other things you will encounter in this book, sense-making sounds obvious and straight-forward, but is in fact a complex idea and process (Weick 1995). For example, sense-making is a process linked to the way we see ourselves. It is making sense of those things which serve to threaten our identity, reaffirm and repair it. Having to accept early retirement from headship, changing what and how you teach, or accepting that the promotion you really thought you deserved has gone to someone else can all threaten our sense of identity. Having a good evaluation of your lesson from a tutor or mentor while on school experience can often reaffirm it. Making sense is also about becoming more aware of the interaction between ourselves and the context in which we teach. The classroom is a particular context for teaching and learning. It is an environment that can be created and changed. But context also affects how we act – for example, in small and crowded classrooms, only certain non-table or desk-based activities are possible. Making sense is not just a process of having a private conversation with yourself about your teaching; it also involves coming to know through teacher talk and the sharing of experiences. It is an ongoing process which requires you to be good at noticing what is going on in your professional world. If events are noticed, then we have a chance of making sense of them. For example, we need to notice which child keeps talking, which grips a pencil incorrectly, which appears to enjoy reading, which is good at science experiments or talented at playing the recorder.

The first edition cohered around an enabling model for reflection-on-practice which was derived from, refined and used in the work, by both writers of the first book, with teachers and students (see Figure 2.1).

The model has four characteristics; it is:

1. *Cyclical.* Reflection and action form a continuous cyclical process. By engaging in the process, the idea is not to end up back at the beginning! More accurately, reflection-on-practice leads into new and better cycles.

2. *Flexible.* To be enabling, the model has to be flexible. It does not drag you mechanistically through a series of steps or stages; this is not how it was intended to work. There are two reasons for being flexible. First, we can begin to reflect on practice from different starting positions. For example, and more commonly, an educator might begin with a sense of frustration that she is unable to enhance the quality of children's mathematical experiences in the way she really wants, because of the many and different views on how this might best be done from her colleagues on the staff. Another educator might reflect on something that he tried out with his children (shared writing) and why it did not appear to work. Another educator might start with something she believes she wants (more equipment for her children to improve the quality of their science work) but cannot seem to get. Finally, another educator, in a small rural school, might want to reflect on the way he develops more effective relationships with neighbouring

FIGURE 2.1 Making sense of practice

schools, and partnerships with local business and commerce. The different starting points are related to the educator's values and strengths, on trying to move his or her practice forward, or on the school in the wider community.

The second reason for a flexible model is that it needs to be responsive to the way we learn. Improving teaching and learning does not proceed in a fixed and sequential way. For example, an educator might choose to reflect on a problematic aspect of her practice first. One thing she might learn is that she gives her children very few opportunities to be more autonomous as learners; she tends to direct, control and manage much of the children's learning for them. Armed with these insights, the educator might then have to reflect on her values and later, if changes in her practice are made, to reflect further on the nature of improvements in her teaching and in children's learning. Another educator might begin by a reflection on the context in which he teaches. The school might be located in a particularly impoverished socio-economic urban area. Links with parents might be poor, relationships with the community need developing, the school needs to boost its roll, more money needs to be found for staff development, and so on. From these reflections-on-context might emerge a consideration of the ways in which the context in which you work impacts on your personal practice. So values, practice, improvement and context are important points to reflect upon. The order in which this is done will vary from individual to individual, group to group, and organization to organization.

3. *Focused.* Flexibility does not mean wandering around in a morass of teaching problems and concerns hoping to bump into some kind of solution, at some point, that makes enough sense to get you out of the mess! Focus and direction are needed to enable meaningful learning to take place. Figure 2.1 should be regarded as a map. The 'model-as-a-map' idea means that it helps to direct and focus your attention. It enables you to find your way around, to see ways forward, to understand the educational terrain that needs to be explored. The model has four reflection–action foci; namely, values, practice, improvement and context. Educators are free to choose which to focus upon, depending on their interests, professional development agenda and ambitions.

4. *Holistic.* The model enables you to view teaching and learning holistically. It links professional values with practice, teaching with intentions for improving learning and with professional development. It reminds us that none of this operates in a vacuum, but in a changing and often uncertain context.

In the first edition, the chapters in the book related to each part of the model. After discussing the nature of reflection-on-practice, each of the subsequent chapters explored the four foci in the heart of the model. Within each of the four foci were three key ideas. These are shown in Figure 2.2.

It is important to understand the nature and importance of values (Figure 2.3). Our own values and those of others affect what we do. Values make us the kind of educator that we are. Our values are things we care about. Educators try to put their values into practice. For example, if a teacher values pupil discussion because she thinks it helps her children to learn more effectively, she will try to create opportunities for this to happen. Values give us reasons for doing things. We do not all hold the same values. Different

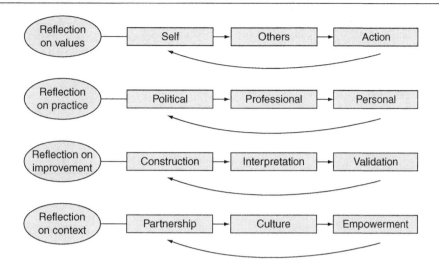

FIGURE 2.2 Reflection-on-practice: four foci

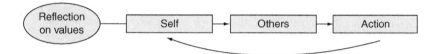

FIGURE 2.3 Focus: reflection-on-values

teachers, schools and governments can hold very different values, although in the recent general election in the UK, it was sometimes hard to discern this difference between political parties! Questions about the choice of particular values and the means to achieve valued outcomes make this whole topic of values 'contestable'. This focus links the values we might personally hold with those espoused by others. It then makes connections between values and practice. In this second edition, this chapter has been retained but expanded to include a leadership dimension. More specifically, I will be relating reflection-on-values to 'doing what you say you will do'. Arguably, this is the most important leadership lesson we can ever learn.

> [I]f you walk the talk, practice what you preach, stand up for your beliefs, put your money where your mouth is, follow through on your promises, do what you say you will do,... You will be more trusted, more powerful, more personally successful; have more loyal and committed people; and be more at peace with yourself.
>
> (Kouzes 2008:ix)

This is what Simons (2008) calls the integrity dividend, or what we get in return for behaving in ways that are consistent with our, and our organization's, values. Reflection is at the heart of this process.

Education is value-laden practice. Values help those involved in teaching and learning to make decisions on how to proceed. But there is also something else. Evidence

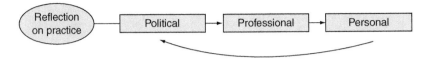

FIGURE 2.4 Focus: reflection-on-practice

helps educators to make wise and principled decisions. Confident and competent teaching requires teachers to reflect systematically and rigorously on evidence derived from practice. Reflective teaching and learning, then, is evidence-based. This particular focus links teaching, evidence and reflection with three things that influence them. These are political, professional and personal influences. In this second edition, reflection-on-practice is re-cast as a reflective inquiry process.

One of the fundamental purposes of reflection-on-practice is to improve the quality of teaching and learning (Figure 2.4). 'Improvement' is a slippery word; it can mean different things to different people. Change is not the same as improvement. Improvements in one aspect of teaching or school life can impair and hold back improvements elsewhere. Improvement is sometimes a trade-off between competing options. This particular focus disentangles improvements in teachers' thinking about their practice from improvements in practice itself. One does not always lead to the other. Understanding something as an improvement is seen to be a meaning-making process – in other words, we personally and collectively build or construct our understandings of improvement, and this is then linked to the idea of interpretation of reality. Finally, to be more confident that improvement, rather than change, has taken place, the processes of validation are presented. Self- and peer-validation are important features of this (Figure 2.5).

Improvements in thinking and practice are one thing; improvements in the context in which these are embedded are something else. In the first edition, the writers took a look at the way DfE Circular 14/93 (DfE 1993a) began to change the relationship institutions of higher education had with schools. It was a reflection on the way a government policy initiative impacted on local practice and, in particular, on the way initial teacher training courses must be planned and delivered in partnership with schools. Reflection-on-context is a critical look at the way the 'system' serves to influence, constrain or liberate educators. Reflective practices of one kind or another are relevant here, as they can question the big and complex issues of power, control, and the politics of education. Values can be exposed and questioned, and assumptions challenged. Contradictions between the rhetoric and partnership realities can be confronted. Partnership and the school's culture is linked to the notion of reflection for more empowered educators – that is, teachers and learners (Figure 2.6).

One of the central purposes of this second edition is to complement the chapters of the earlier book with an explicit strengths-based approach to learning through

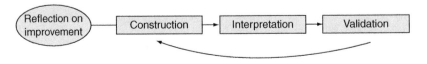

FIGURE 2.5 Focus: reflection-on-improvement

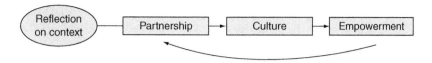

FIGURE 2.6 Focus: reflection-on-context

reflection. Developing more strengths-based teaching and learning in more strengths-based organizations means we have to change the kinds of reflective questions we have customarily been asking. So what do people do in strengths-based organizations that aim to deliver high quality teaching and learning? What do they feel, think, say and do? Without giving away too much of the richness of what follows later, the general strengths-based strategy upon which this book is based is shown in Table 2.2.

In conclusion, being a reflective practitioner, I suggest, means that we have to be cognizant of four things. They are experience, context, culture, and the processes of enactment. We could take these to mean the following.

1. *EXPERIENCE* plays a central role in learning through reflection. We can understand 'experience' as something that is lived, felt, reconstructed, reinterpreted, and understood. If we take a positive view on this, reflecting on particular experiences enables us to make sense and meaning of our encounters with others. Sense and meaning can be understood to be built-up, or 'constructed', through the use of reflective practices. This is very different from simply thinking that we can discover meaning, already nicely packaged-up and 'out there', somewhere in the workplace. Making sense and attributing meaning normally occurs in social contexts, such as in families, organizations and communities. Reflective practices can be used in any social context where we encounter each other.

2. These encounters and experiences occur in a *CONTEXT*. There are different ways to describe a context – for example, it might be a private or a public context,

TABLE 2.2 A strengths-based reflective strategy

Step one: Identify and Clarify (a) What do you believe are your strengths? (b) What would be a 'personal best' story where you felt you played to your strengths and performed well?
Step two: Affirming and Understanding (a) What do others know your strengths to be? (b) What kind of alignment is there between step one and step two?
Step three: Execute and Integrate (a) How far are you able to do what you do best, for the majority of your time, each day? (b) What needs to change to enable you to securely integrate doing what you do best into your everyday working life?
Step four: Amplification and Impact (a) How might you amplify your strengths and thereby eclipse your weaknesses? (b) When you feel able to play to your strengths, what impact does this have on your level of job satisfaction, your feelings toward your colleagues and sense of loyalty to your organization?

a current or an historical context, a home or a workplace context. Each context has social and often political aspects too. Sometimes these aspects are visible; at other times these aspects are rather more tricky to discern. In most contexts, there are people doing things like working, playing, making decisions and engaging in many other kinds of conscious and intentional activities. All activities require a level of motivation. More generally, a context can be regarded as a space for particular actions or, put another way, as a space for particular forms of participation, such as a team or a committee meeting. Space has both physical and psycho-emotional dimensions. There are:

- space-making actions (the 'where' of the physical space)
- space-taking actions (occupying space by right/invitation)
- space-shaping actions (knowing how to behave in this space, knowing the 'rules of the game').

When we *reflect in a context*, an important question is: 'How far does the space that has been created for participation constructively challenge, support or reproduce existing experiences, actions, structures and meanings?

3. In many workplaces, the dominant *CULTURE* is one of doing, with little time for reflection and, therefore, for workplace learning. In general, cultures of doing can be described in many ways – for example, as high- or low-performing. They can be characterized by busyness, pressure, targets and deadlines, or described as workplace cultures of appreciation, where everyone feels valued and respected, or as cultures of blame, where the languages of 'not being good enough', of poor performance, of inefficiency, and 'it's not my fault' dominate. An important question to reflect upon is, 'What aspects of workplace culture impact on organizational performance, and in what ways?' This question is important because organizations, in most fields, are often described as succeeding or failing on the merits of their actions alone, as if how we judge performance is only absolute rather than relative. There are determinants of performance which organizations are not able to control so easily. There are no guaranteed blueprints or formulae for organizational success. In general, we do know, from research and experience, that there are three important aspects of workplace culture that impact, positively and negatively, on organizational performance. These are:

- pleasure – how you feel about yourself and what you do;
- purpose – being able to engage in something you feel is worthwhile;
- fulfilment – achieving your goals and knowing you are doing well.

4. Reflection for *ENACTMENT* is the way the chosen reflective practices have enlightened and empowered individuals, groups and organizations, so that they feel more able to question and constructively challenge the existing 'state of affairs'. It also involves being sufficiently motivated, having the courage and clarity of thinking to act in a way that improves the situation and makes something 'better'. This again is putting a positive spin on things. Reflective practices can, of course, be used to prop up the status quo, to undermine people's confidence, to reveal weaknesses, to attribute blame, and much more!

Reflective practice is a label, used by some, that refers to the use of different methods which, arguably, offer the possibility of helping us make sense of the different encounters that we have with others in particular social contexts. My view is that reflective practice is much more than a method. This is why reflective learning may be a more inclusive and appropriate term. In certain circumstances, these methods may also help us see these encounters in new ways. I suggest that four generic reflective practices help achieve this. The first is a *self-reflective* or *collective-reflective* practice that chooses something significant to know more about or do something with, and which is directed and energized by interest and insight. The second generic reflective practice is the way individuals, groups and organizations *reflect on information* generated through the use of particular methods, like reflective journaling, mind mapping, drawings, storyboarding, scenario-based role-plays, and so on. This practice has the potential to reveal new meanings and views on particular encounters. It can present an opportunity for appreciating a different 'reading' of the situation. It can, of course, also confirm what is already felt and known. The third generic reflective practice is influenced by our capacity to openly *dialogue* with the information we have gathered through the use of particular methods. This means that the kind of sense we make of particular experiences, and the significance of the meanings we come to, are derived from a process of conversation and discussion with others. The fourth generic reflective practice is the way we use the above to enable us to *question* what it is that we claim we are coming to know. In this book, there is an emphasis on the power of the *positive question*. In reality, this means we need to make sure we balance the use of 'why-type' questions with 'how-type' ones. The word *why* is often associated with the negative. Why me? Why now? Why should I? Asking *why* too much is often a major contributor to worry, can be anxiety provoking and make people risk-averse. These are not good feelings to have, especially when working life might be requiring us to be quite the opposite – that is, confident, resilient and creative. Asking why-type questions rarely helps us worry less. Why can't I? Why do people do that? Why is it always me? Unlike *why*, the use of *how* is commonly associated with a solution and with moving on, hopefully, in some positive way. How can I? How do I? How should, might or could we? Asking how-type questions not only identifies solutions to problems, but can also open up positive action pathways. Such questions can also test readiness for potential change. I am not advocating replacing one type of question with another; rather, I am suggesting that it might be prudent to be aware of the need for balance.

3

Some Views of the Nature of Reflection-on-practice

This chapter begins with a look inside a primary school classroom. Charlotte, a newly qualified teacher, is about to finish her lesson with her class of 30 Year 5 children. It is through reflecting on her practice that Charlotte is able to learn from it. This particular practice incident allows us to begin to establish a vocabulary that teachers, as educators, might use when trying to talk meaningfully to each other about the nature and purposes of reflective practice.

Becoming a teacher and continuing your professional development thereafter is a challenging and complex business. Arguably, reflecting-on-practice is an essential part of this process. So, in this chapter there are a number of general principles that serve to characterize the practices of reflection. Also, at the heart of this process is the reflective conversation. This chapter sets out the characteristics of what might usefully be regarded as a truly reflective conversation, how it might be developed and nourished, and some of the things to be mindful of when engaging in conversations of this kind.

Look inside and see what's there

It is 10.30 am, and time for Charlotte to finish her lesson with her class of 30, ten-year old children. She has been working on the topic of canals. Charlotte recalls:

> After this morning's lesson, during playtime, I asked some of the children if they had learned anything from the lesson. Some politely conceded having learned something, others nothing. How can this be! Nothing! The most memorable response came from Billy when I asked, 'Well, what have you learned from the lesson, Billy?' His reply was, 'Eh, something Miss, But I can't remember what it was.'
>
> (Ghaye and Ghaye 1998:14)

Inside this primary school – in the playground, in fact – something interesting is happening. Charlotte, who is a newly qualified teacher, is reflecting on her lesson. Billy and the others are 'helping' her to do this. More specifically, Charlotte is reflecting on her teaching, and on what the children are saying to her about the learning that has gone on. You may think that Charlotte has been pretty courageous to ask her children a direct question of the kind, 'Well, what have you learnt from the lesson?' Alternatively, you may want to criticize her timing in asking the question, as the playground is wet and cold, and Billy is being strangled by his best friend Tom while trying to eat his way through a packet of Monster Munch crisps! Perhaps you may also think that Billy's response is rather typical, humorous, or even an expression of that ageless game some children play called 'guess what's inside the teacher's head'!

If we reflect on this small segment of primary-school life further, there is much, much more to learn. For in this example there are *people*, and there is *action*. Both are located in a *context* – in this case, a playground. The people involved have thoughts, feelings, hopes and desires. The action (that is, between Charlotte and Billy) is conversational in kind. Taken together, what we have here are some of the basic requirements for learning through reflection-on-practice.

Reflecting even more on this, and using different words this time, other things reveal themselves to us. Charlotte is trying to *account for herself*. She is trying to justify her practice by assessing the degree of alignment between her teaching intentions (or, more appropriately, 'desired learning outcomes') and some pupil feedback. Charlotte is also reflecting on her *experience* and drawing upon the experience of others (her pupils) in order to come to some understanding of the degree to which she might be able to claim that she has taught her lesson on canals in a competent and ethical manner. Charlotte is also showing a certain *disposition* to inquire into her practice. Part of this disposition evidences itself here in a question-and-answer form. The questions and answers are the beginning of a *dialogue*, or what we might call a reflective conversation, as she starts to tease apart what she has just taught in her lesson before playtime. What is also interesting is that those involved have made *sense* of the lesson, in different ways. Charlotte had a lesson plan; she acted in accordance with it. She communicated her plan, and her pupils *decoded* it. In decoding it, they were trying to make sense of what Charlotte was saying and of what they were expected to do. After the lesson, Charlotte made her own sense of it. She had *constructed* a set of personal meanings about it, some of which seem to sit more comfortably with the pupils' views of it than others!

So there are some big messages here. From a little, if we think about it in particular ways, we can learn a lot. Charlotte's playground behaviour is an example of a *reflective turn*. She is returning to look closely at that taken-for-granted feature of school life, the lesson. Some of her pupils' responses will inevitably challenge her taken-for-granted understandings about her teaching and her assumptions about what her pupils have learnt, or even claimed they have learnt! We can also link this playground action to three other ideas. First, Charlotte must have a reason for reflecting on her practice, because normally we reflect on practice to serve a particular purpose; reflection always serves certain interests. Second, Charlotte may well be able to improve what she does with her pupils because, through reflection, she has deepened her understanding of what she does, what and how her pupils learn, and the appropriateness of the learning context. This deeper and richer understanding may enable her to feel more *empowered to act*, in a particular direction, in the future. Finally, Charlotte may feel more enlightened as she weighs up the match between how she teaches, or thinks she teaches, and what her children learn, or think they have learnt. Put another way, the reflective conversation in the playground may act as a *bridge* between Charlotte's own '*theories*' about her teaching, and how far she puts these theories to use in her *practice*.

From this small example of an aspect of school life, some of the key words and vocabulary that customarily comprise a reflection on one's practice are to be found. In summary, the key words are:

- People (teachers, children and significant others);
- Action (that is intentional, there is a purpose to it);
- Context (this is where the action takes place and occurs over time; there are other ideas associated with context which will be discussed later);
- Accounting for ourselves (this has both a personal and professional dimension);
- Experience (what we have done and lived through – we reflect on this experience);
- Disposition (as a way of approaching the art of teaching);
- Dialogue (the different types of talk that goes on between teachers and their children, children and other children, teachers and teachers, and so on);
- Sense-making and decoding (this is where we use our powers of analysis, synthesis and evaluation to try to enhance our understanding of learning and teaching);
- Construction (the process of building meanings in order to help us to act in competent and ethical ways);
- Reflective turns (re-seeing, re-viewing and re-searching what it is we do in order to develop a more holistic view of things);
- Empowerment (positive feelings and a developed set of values that enable us to take wise and appropriate professional action);
- Theories (those things which we personally develop, or draw upon, from the work of others, that help to explain what we do).

What we shall do now is take this vocabulary, extend it, and turn the words into a set of general principles.

Some principles that characterize the practices of reflection

This is a book about the practice of teaching and learning and how we might reflect on it, in different ways, in order to strengthen and continuously improve:

- our thinking about what we do;
- the act of teaching and learning itself;
- the contexts in which teaching and learning take place.

It is also a book about the links between how we feel and what we do. Put another way, it seeks to set out how reflection can be used to elevate positive emotions. Why? My view on this is that appreciating the positive in ourselves and in our work does not simply *reflect* success, high performance and good health; it can also *produce* success, high performance and good health. I have devoted a new chapter to this (see Chapter 4). It can be related, for example, to the new National Curriculum for Primary schools in the UK, which seeks to create learning experiences for children where they all become:

i.   Successful learners who enjoy learning, make progress and achieve
ii.   Confident individuals who are able to live safe, healthy and fulfilling lives

iii.   Responsible citizens who make a positive contribution to society.
(Qualifications and Curriculum Development Agency 2010:12)

Here are ten principles that may serve to characterize some of the practices of reflection.

Principle 1

Reflective practice needs to be understood as a discourse (Fairclough 1998). A discourse can be understood as a set of meanings, statements, stories, and so on which produce a particular version of events. The reflective discourse, or conversation as we can call it in this book, is at the heart of the improvement process. Sometimes this conversation has the potential to disturb our professional identity and those things which give our teaching its shape, form and purpose. How can we ever claim to be able to consider doing something better if we are not prepared to be disturbed? Additionally, it is worth reminding ourselves that certain types of reflective conversation can disturb the status quo by questioning and challenging it. Developing and sustaining reflective conversations inside and between organizations, through the use of modern technologies, is fundamental to knowledge-sharing and knowledge management.

Principle 2

Reflective practice is fuelled and energized by experience (Weil and McGill 1990, Boud and Miller 1996, Boud *et al.* 1997). We have to reflect on something, and that something is our experience and all those things that it comprises. Most often, our natural default position is to reflect on those aspects of our work, or those encounters in the workplace, that are problematic, troublesome and unfulfilling in some way. But it does not have to be like this. We can reflect upon successes, try to get to the root causes of them, and then plan how to amplify them. We can use the practices of reflection to get an answer to the question, 'what do I/we want more of (success), rather than less of (problems)?' Things such as planning for learning, assessment and recording, learner management, teaching styles and strategies, and how teaching in the classroom is influenced by what is going on outside or at governors' and parents' meetings, from OFSTED inspection agendas and changes in National Curriculum policy. Reflection-on-practice takes experience, and interrogates it in particular ways.

Principle 3

Reflective practice is a process that involves a reflective turn. This means returning to look again at all our taken-for-granted values, professional understandings and practices. This focus on routines, rituals, on everyday occurrences that make up the bulk of a working day, is most important. Reflecting on practice is not about reflecting only on the extraordinary, the exceptional and the 'one-off'. In this 'turn', we can reflect on ourselves and the part we played in the particular practice incident. We can also think about the parts played by the significant others involved. In reflecting on ourselves and others, we are likely also to deepen our understanding of what it is we are looking at in terms of the practice incident itself. For example, we might understand more deeply incidents to do with managing challenging behaviour, differentiating work to suit a range of pupil abilities, and appropriate monitoring and recording of pupil progress.

Principle 4

Reflective practice is concerned with learning how to account for ourselves. This means learning how to describe, explain and justify our teaching. This is particularly important in the context of inspection, in the context of blame cultures and the need to be a socially responsible organization. It is important where both individual and collective teacher strengths and weaknesses are observed, and where practice is questioned. Part and parcel of being a professional means being able to account for one's practice.

Principle 5

Reflective practice can be understood as a disposition to inquiry. It is not just a collection of methods for eliciting evidence about practice. It is not a toolbox that consists of things such as critical incident analysis proformas, and guidelines on how to keep learning journals and conduct school experience debriefs. These are important, but should be seen as part of the bigger reflective process. Methods and a sound rationale for their use need to be developed. A rationale can be constructed if evidence-gathering methods are employed to serve more than short-term technical ends. This book tries to set out a powerful rationale for reflective practice that centres upon the idea of 'reflection as a disposition to enquiry'. The characteristics of this disposition are most often viewed as arriving at the present day via the work of John Dewey and Donald Schön. Having a disposition means that we view teaching and learning through reflective lenses, that we question it, look into it systematically, and continuously strive to learn from it. The overriding goal is to improve the quality of the educational relationships in each classroom, school and other learning environment. Clearly, then, we do need some kind of toolbox, or set of evidence-gathering methods, that works for us in the busy and complex worlds of classrooms, schools, colleges, universities and other learning environments. But we should be wary of those who reduce reflection to a set of techniques to be learnt and then applied to practice. Reflection-on-practice is about a whole way of seeing and being. It is about having a commitment to the development of a particular professional mindset that enables us to make even wiser and more ethical professional judgements.

Principle 6

Reflective practice is interest-serving. When we reflect, we are engaging in a process of knowledge creation. If we are committed to educational improvement, then, by implication, we are also committed to actually doing something positive and constructive with the knowledge that we create. We need to put the knowledge to work to achieve some desired and justifiable state. So we can argue that we do not simply reflect on what we do, but that we do so with certain purposes or interests in mind that need to be served. Different kinds of interest are served by the way we create and use this knowledge – for, example, the interests may be personal, professional, political and social. It is very important that we sort out in our minds what interests might (or actually will) be served through the reflective process.

Principle 7

Reflective practice is enacted by those who are critical thinkers (Barnett 1997). This can lead to personal and collective improvement through critical forms of reflective practice. Critical reflection-on-practice is essentially where educators acquire a language, a set of arguments, the skilfulness and power to transform the existing order of things, so as to improve the quality of learner's educational experiences. A critical form of reflection-on-practice can enable and empower educators to act in this way. Central to being critical is the ability to ask probing and challenging questions about what we do. These are often 'why-type' questions. Why do I teach like this? Why did I do it that way? Why has my teaching come to be the way it is? Why do I feel unable to live out my professional values in my everyday teaching? But, as I mentioned earlier, these need to be balanced by other types of question, especially how-type ones. Brookfield emphasizes the importance of this principle when he says, 'Being a critical thinker is part of what it means to be a developing person.... Without critical thinking ... our workplaces remain organized as they were twenty years ago' (Brookfield 1995:1).

Principle 8

Reflective practice is a way of decoding a symbolic landscape. Our everyday taken-for-granted worlds of teaching and learning, of schools, classrooms and other educational establishments, are symbolic landscapes. The symbolism is there for us to decode in every aspect of the environment in which teaching and learning takes place – for example, in the way classroom furniture is arranged, in the way modern technologies convey information, in what is displayed inside the school, in how people relate to each other, in what is rewarded, recorded and signified as being worthy. These symbols often go together to make up that phenomenon which is often called school culture. This is multi-layered, multi-faceted, and a significant influence on the quality of the learning environment. The symbols await professional decoding. Reflecting on practice helps us to discern the significance of this symbolism.

Principle 9

Reflective practice sits at the interface between notions of practice and theory. Reflective practitioners have a particular view of these two ideas. Through systematic and rigorous kinds of reflection-on-practice, educators are able to construct meaningful theories-of-action which are in a 'living' form (Whitehead 1993). They are 'living' in the sense that they are made up of reflective conversations and actual teaching episodes, created through retrospective thinking about practice and the public validation of accounts of it. Reflection-on-practice links the account (the 'theory') and the practice (teaching). Linking the two is a creative process.

Principle 10

Reflective practice occupies a position at the confluence or intersection of a number of ways of knowing. Postmodernism is the broad landscape within which this confluence is positioned. A postmodern way of knowing, namely social constructionism, provides some of the bedrock upon which this landscape is shaped (Burr 1995, Fosnot 1996). This important way of knowing helps reflective practitioners to construct understandings of the educative potency of their teaching, and helps them to interpret human action.

Summary of the principles

Reflective practice can usefully be understood as:

- a discourse;
- energized by experience;
- involving a reflective turn;
- a way of accounting for ourselves;
- a disposition to inquiry;
- interest-serving;
- being carried out by critical and creative thinkers;
- a way of decoding the symbolic landscapes of educational organizations;
- at the interface between practice and theory;
- a postmodernist way of knowing.

The reflective conversation

Becoming an educator and teaching in a confident, competent, creative and ethical manner is a challenging and complex learning process. Central to this process is our ability to reflect constructively, creatively and critically on our teaching intentions, the ends we have in mind, and the means we might use to achieve them. The reflective conversation is a medium through which we are able to learn from our educational experiences, and question the educational values that give a shape, form and purpose to what we do. This focus on values is the fundamental characteristic of a reflective conversation. It is one where educators interrogate, question and re-interpret the values that guide what they do, in the context in which they find themselves teaching. Without this quality, arguably, the conversation is not truly reflective but something else – for example, a conversation that is more technically focused. Just as some argue that not all thinking about teaching is reflective if there is no questioning of goals and values (Zeichner and Liston 1996:1), I would say that it is important to make an early distinction between what does or does not constitute a reflective conversation. Above all else, a reflective conversation is one that involves a discussion of values. A focus on values is at the heart of the personal and collective improvement process.

From the extensive literature that exists about the nature and use of conversations and dialogues that serve to introduce and induct us into the 'public discourse of teaching and learning' (Edwards 1996:143), I propose the following. Each point listed below can be seen as a distinguishing characteristic of a reflective conversation. Taken together, they form the basis of what educators might want to claim as being a truly reflective conversation. These characteristics might evidence themselves, more or less, in each conversation. Some are more easily 'heard' and looked for. Evidence of some is more easily grasped and perhaps recorded. If a reflective conversation is the centrepiece of the whole reflective process, then it seems appropriate to formulate our responses to questions such as 'So what is a reflective conversation?', 'How far would I recognize a reflective conversation if I heard one?' and 'How might I set about facilitating a conversation of this kind?'

1. I suggest that to be called a reflective conversation, there needs to be some consideration and questioning of the educational values that the teacher is committed to and tries to live out in his or her work with the children, staff and significant others that comprise the school as a community. Our professional values are those fundamentally important things that make us the kind of teacher that we are. They give our teaching its shape, form and purpose. Clarifying, justifying and trying to live these values out are things every teacher should strive to do. None of this is easy. Even quite experienced teachers have difficulties in articulating their values and addressing those things that get in the way of putting values into practice.

2. Reflective conversations may initially take the form of private 'conversations with self', but then they should be articulated in public company. In doing this, educators can try out the language they feel they need so that they can describe, explain and justify practice and, when appropriate, persuade, confront and encourage others to question their own practice too. The reflective conversation, then, is an opportunity for educators to reflect upon and to shape their own work and, in certain circumstances, to transform what they do, so as to improve the educational experiences of the learners in their care. But this characteristic has additional dimensions worth noting. Moving from the private to the public is often difficult because it implies attaching words to thoughts. Sometimes we stumble around for the most appropriate form of words, particularly if the reflective conversation is about a troublesome aspect of teaching which might involve other colleagues. We might not want to be unprofessional, so we pick our words carefully. This private-to-public characteristic is a process of moving from tacit and unconscious knowing (Polanyi 1958) to more conscious knowing. There can be occasions when, in trying to facilitate a reflective conversation, we sense that there is (or might be) a hidden agenda that might take quite a bit of teasing out. Sometimes this reveals itself when at the end (or what you think is the end) of the conversation, perhaps just as the teacher is about to leave, he or she turns and says, 'Oh yes, just one more thing…' We often have to be patient and allow time for the real agenda to be expressed. A final point about this characteristic: it can also be used to help us to appreciate what should rightly and properly remain private and confidential between two individuals, and what should be placed in the public domain because arguably it is in the educator's best interests and/or in the best interests of the learners and the organization.

3. The reflective conversation is a special kind of discourse that often takes the form of question and response. The questions can be of many kinds. Some have argued

(Smyth 1991, 1995), that there are some fundamental questions educators should ask if they wish to reveal the nature of the forces that serve to constrain or liberate them. In doing so, teachers give themselves the chance to tackle those things that get in the way of them being able, more fully, to live out their values in their practice. Some of these fundamental questions are:

- What is my teaching like?
- What is successful in my teaching?
- How do I know this?
- Why is it like this?
- How has it come to be this way?
- What are the effects of my teaching on those I am working with?
- What do I need to change to improve what I do?
- How might I do this?

The nature of the questions asked is important, for they need to enable those engaged in reflecting-on-practice to gain some sense of perspective on their teaching and the context in which it takes place. We grow in the direction in which we ask questions.

4. In a reflective conversation, the participants adopt a 'reflective posture'. This notion comes from the work of Paulo Freire (1972). He described the hallmarks of this posture as conversationalists examining their experience critically, questioning and interpreting it, and doing this in a public arena and not in isolation from others. There are limits to learning alone. This posture is not one that should be exclusively backward-looking, with the conversation being preoccupied with explorations and justifications of previous practice. Reflective conversations should also be forward-looking, and be conversations of both possibility and hope. Conversations of this kind contain not only what was thought and done, but also what might be or 'that which is not yet' (Ghaye and Wakefield 1993:x).

5. A reflective conversation is located in time and space. It is an artefact of the moment. It needs to be thought about and planned for, and time needs to be set aside for it. Additionally, the actual timing of a conversation of this kind affects what is, can and might be told. Often reflections soon after the event are very different from those which occur later, perhaps when 'things have cooled down' or simply when the 'teller' has had time to get things into some sort of perspective. Reflective moments need to be created so that conversations of this kind occur (Miller 1990). The 'space' is the physical, emotional and socio-political context in which the conversation is constructed. In its public form the space is occupied by at least two persons; the 'teller' and owner of the teaching experience, and a significant other. This twosome might be a student teacher and a tutor; or a student and a classroom teacher, a school mentor, a peer or friend. If one of the goals of a reflective conversation is the development of greater practical wisdom that can be realized in teaching, then the part played by the 'other' is crucial. Pendlebury (1995) calls this person the 'dialogical other', and describes his or her role as one that elicits the practical arguments and 'theories' that underpin the teacher's work. She goes on to describe the role of the dialogical other as having three parts to it.

The first is to help the teacher to reflect on aims and means, and to develop a particular course of action for the class or individual children. Leading on from this, the 'dialogical other' adopts a more critical role and challenges this planned course of action. The teacher then has to erect justifications and address any perceived weaknesses. Finally, and again through conversation, the 'other' facilitates the construction of an improved action plan, if indeed one is thought to be necessary and worthwhile. Pendlebury sees the role of the dialogical other in a particular way. It is supportive, and one that adds structure to the reflective conversation. But a note of caution. The purpose of a reflective conversation is not solely to focus on weaknesses and deficits; it is not an exercise in remediation. It is important to get things in balance. Although it is quite natural to want to focus on real and perceived weaknesses, and to know the difference – especially so if you happen to be a student in initial teacher training and on an assessed school experience! – it is just as important to use the reflective conversation to enable the 'teller' to focus upon those aspects of his or her teaching that are felt to be going well, to articulate the reasons for this, and to construct action plans to nourish and sustain the good things. This is using the practices of reflection to strengthen, broaden and build.

6. Teachers always have to make sense of their teaching in the situation in which it occurs. They have to make some sense of the perceived and actual impact their actions have on their children, and using language is a way of doing this. In reflective conversations, an important goal is to try and achieve a greater sense of clarity, rationality and certainty that teaching was done professionally and ethically, and what was learnt was worthwhile and meaningful. It is through reflective conversations that a greater sense of self and professional identity can be brought about. But this sense-making process is one which has to cope with the many possible meanings which can be attributed to any action within schools and classrooms. An important quality of a reflective conversation, then, is that making sense needs to be viewed as an active and creative process of jointly constructed interpretations (Newman and Holzman 1997). In professional development, and particularly in the context of becoming a qualified teacher, reflective conversations, seen as an act of collaborative meaning-making, are an important educational activity. Collaborative knowledge-building like this is the driving force for further learning. Through the communication, exploration, challenge and justification of the teacher's 'lived experiences', shifts in perspective, attitude and values may arise. It is through reflective conversations that our established and existing knowledge that guides our teaching can be undone and reorganized to increase its future educational worth. Knowledge generated through reflective conversations is a creative and constructivist process, and one 'that construes learning as an interpretative, recursive, building process by active learners interacting with the physical and social world' (Fosnot 1996:30).

7. The content of a reflective conversation consists of the significant aspects of the educator's experience. This is what is talked about. We have said that each conversation is located in both time and space; the same can be said of experience. Teaching experiences that are the substance of a reflective conversation do not exist in a social and personal vacuum. Experience is context-related. It is the context which shapes the experience, and therefore the learning that is possible. Boud and Miller (1996) have much to say about this.

Learning occurs within a framework of taken-for-granted assumptions about what is legitimate to do, to say and even think. It is influenced directly and indirectly by the power of others as well as by forces which constrain particip-ants' views of what is possible.

(Boud and Miller 1996:18)

Learning through reflective practice is centrally about acknowledging the impor-tance of working with experience – both positive and more difficult (or negative) experiences. In acknowledging this, we should be cautious of simply giving primacy to experience without taking into account the context in which, and through which, the experience has come about. Teaching experience should not be celebrated uncritically. In a reflective conversation it is important for the 'signi-ficant other' to affirm the student teacher's voice, for example, while simultan-eously encouraging the interrogation of such a voice. Teaching experiences can be distorted, self-fulfilling, liberating, suffocating, and so on. Simply having experi-ences to recount does not imply that they are reflected upon. They may be poorly understood and thought about uncritically. The bottom line is that a reflective conversation publicly demonstrates a preparedness to be open about the learning that arises from the experience of teaching. It also demonstrates a professional obli-gation to continue to develop one's practical knowledge. Through conversations of the kind I am suggesting, future teaching possibilities are potentially opened up to us, biases and blind spots can be detected and addressed, and the whole 'value-ladenness' of the practice of teaching examined.

8. The final quality of a reflective conversation is linked with the notions of enlight-enment and empowerment. I made the point earlier that it is through conversa-tions of this kind that educators' experiences can be interrogated, reconstructed and reorganized. An important objective of the process is to try to add meaning to what the educator claims to know. This is a vital ingredient for the continual enhancement of professional practice. Some educators find this process threatening, as their espoused values and values-in-action are questioned, especially if they con-clude that improvement is needed. This is why who teachers choose to engage with in this process is an important decision. Students in initial teacher training may not have such an opportunity to choose – tutors may be assigned to them, for example. Higher-education staff involved in school experience supervision and school mentors might usefully be conversant with the principles of, and skilful in, deploying the processes that enable truly reflective conversations to develop. Reflective conversations can be empowering. But it takes skill to make this a lived experience for all involved.

To help to see this process in this light, the conversation has to be a positive experi-ence: we have to 'get something out of it'. Reflective conversations that are empower-ing enable educators to name, define and construct their own 'realities'. They enable educators to sustain themselves. They nourish their sense of professional dignity. They enable educators to express, in their own way, their authentic concerns. The notions of enlightenment and empowerment through reflective conversations are well put by Elliott (1987), when he argues that teachers should have more opportunities to reflect systematically on, and to confront, their thinking and practices. Elliott argues that the best way to improve practice lies not so much in trying to control people's behaviours as in helping them to control their own by becoming more aware of what they are doing.

The reflective conversation is central to the process of professional improvement and lifelong learning. It counts for nothing and contributes little to enabling educators to become reflective practitioners if the conversation does not value educators' own practical theories and lived experiences. It counts for nothing if it does not address the purposes of education in the spirit of openness and constructive critique.

Summary of the reflective conversation

A reflective conversation has the following characteristics:

- it provides a focus on educational values;
- it moves from the private to the public;
- it takes a question-and-answer form;
- it looks back to what has been;
- it looks forward to what will be;
- it is located in time and space;
- it makes sense of teaching and learning;
- it interrogates educators' experiences;
- it has the potential to enlighten and empower.

There are a number of things to be mindful of when committing oneself to and engaging in reflective conversations. Some of the most prevalent are as follows.

- To give conversations of a reflective kind time to emerge, they need to be worked at, persevered with and nurtured.
- There needs to be some empathy between the 'teller' and 'facilitator'; each one needs to understand the function of the conversation and the role of the other.
- Reflecting-on-practice through conversations is a skilful business which involves feelings, thinking, and how these evidence themselves in teaching actions. Some facilitators might need to be trained in this skill.
- It is important that the facilitator does more listening than telling, more guiding, helping and enabling than prescribing and directing.
- There should be some appropriate balance in the conversation between more introspective and contemplative moments, and being able to feel that the conversation is going somewhere and that it has a momentum. Time is unlikely to be an infinite resource for either the teller or the facilitator. What counts as an appropriate ending to such a conversation is a crucial issue.
- It is important that both parties understand what the 'ground rules' are for such conversations, particularly in relation to ethical, moral, legal and professional issues. Reflective conversations are about people and practice. They can be charged with emotion, judgemental, and potentially defamatory. If records of conversations of this kind are kept, then it is important that the nature of the record is agreed

between both parties, together with where it is stored and who has the right to access it. It is therefore just as well if both parties are clear about issues to do with defamation, litigation, privacy and confidentiality, rights to know, professional misconduct, and the like.

Relationships that strengthen the reflective conversation

A reflective conversation is not a private conversation that you have with yourself; it is a public one enacted with others. This may be with a tutor, mentor, coach, and so on. It may be in a one-to-one situation, in a triadic relationship, or in a bigger group that is brought together with a shared understanding of its purpose.

Six essential qualities of positive relationships were identified during the research and development of the Mobius Model (Demarest *et al.* 2004), which, I suggest, is highly relevant if you are wishing to generate a more strengths-based conversational process. In summary, the six Mobius qualities are:

1. *Mutual understanding.* This exists when each person feels understood and also understands the other(s). It is important to note that mutual understanding is not the same as agreement. We can understand others without necessarily agreeing with them.
2. *Possibility.* This exists when everyone recognizes something new that is desirable and seems realistic to create.
3. *Commitment.* This exists when there is agreement to priorities among the goals and values that will direct action.
4. *Capability.* This exists when there is agreement to a way to fulfil the commitments to which everyone has agreed.
5. *Responsibility.* This exists when there is agreement to expectations about what each person, team department, and so on, will do to carry out the commitments.
6. *Acknowledgement.* This exists when there is mutual recognition of what has been accomplished, and what is still missing, for the commitments to be fully realized.

Mutual understanding

Mutual understanding means each person is understood and understands the others. It is present when each person confirms that he or she feels understood by and also understands everyone else. When it is present, people will say what they really think or feel about the subject of the reflective conversation. They value and learn from the differences among themselves. When others speak, they listen and expect to learn. When mutual understanding is missing, people feel misunderstood and disrespected, and don't trust each other. Differences among people are ignored or become the cause of disagreements. People are reluctant to say what they really think or feel, and they may keep relevant information to themselves. They expect others to listen to and learn from them, but they themselves do not expect to listen to or learn from others.

When those participating in a reflective conversation listen for understanding, they seek to contribute to mutual understanding by listening, taking in and appreciating the information and perspectives contained in others' points of view, and then saying what their understanding is, to confirm that they have understood. When we engage in this kind of conversation, we expect to be understood by the others, but not necessarily agreed with. For many people, particularly in settings where taking action to get results is highly valued, staying engaged in listening in this way is very challenging. We want to have our say. Different kinds of conversations are needed for developing effective and satisfying relationships. In working and living together, things work out better when we reach an understanding of others before setting goals, planning, and taking action that we expect others to commit to as well. In the Mobius Model, reaching understanding of one another occurs before these other activities because it provides the underpinning for them.

Possibility

Possibility means everyone recognizes that there is something desirable (and positive) that could be created through the reflective conversation. When possibility is present, people focus on what they want to create, not what they want to avoid. What they want more of, not less of. They welcome new ideas, see challenges as opportunities, and discuss and respect differences without attacking people. They proceed from the belief that things can be made better, that challenges can be met, and that issues can be resolved. Put another way, they adopt a hopeful, optimistic and positive attitude.

When possibility is missing, people focus on what they want to avoid. They are not interested in and may resist new ideas, and they are reluctant to make suggestions because they fear their proposals will get shot down. They believe that there is little or no possibility of making things better, meeting challenges, resolving issues, or being understood. They are often deeply invested in defending their point of view that things can't get better.

When considering new possibilities for their practice and their organization, it is common, as I have mentioned before, for people to begin by focusing on what's wrong. Shifting 'what's wrong' statements into descriptions of 'what's right' or 'what's missing' is a key strategy to creating possibility. This shift in a conversation for possibility is comparable to listening for understanding in a conversation for mutual understanding, and can be equally challenging to initiate and sustain.

For example, 'What's really wrong around here is that no one cares if we do a good job or not!' is a 'what's wrong' statement. But what if you were to ask, 'What's missing that, if it were present, would make this a great place to work?' This is still in the realm of deficits, but with a positive spin. What if you asked, 'Think of a time when things were much better here. What one thing, were it to happen again, would make a significant and positive difference to how you feel? So what needs to change to make this happen?' The complaint about no one caring might be restated, 'What's missing is someone acknowledging what we've accomplished, about feeling valued and respected.'

When trying to imagine new possibilities, people may note the obstacles they see, the reasons why 'it' couldn't be possible. When this happens, asking 'What if?' can help move the focus from seeing barriers to perceiving new opportunities. For example, in response to the statement 'We don't have enough resources to do anything creative around here', ask 'What would we achieve if we could get the resources?' Recognition of new possibilities paves the way for commitment because something that is both desirable and feasible is now acknowledged. Compliance or 'go-along' behaviour, not true commitment, occurs when people are asked to undertake an effort they do not see as advantageous or realistic; one that they do not view as possible.

Commitment

Commitment means that there is agreement to priorities among the goals and values that will direct action toward making possibilities real. Goals are hoped for and valued circumstances intended to exist at some specific time in the future. Values are conditions that we want to exist at all times in our relationships. There are three basic statements of commitment: yes, no, and I'll let you know later. When commitment is present – say, for example, to improve an aspect of your work or workplace – goals and values are spelled out and agreed on *before* taking action. These are then used to direct action, allocate resources, and measure progress and success. When commitment is missing, people are not clear about and may not share the same goals and values. So they may be working toward disparate ends, or toward no particular goals or values at all. Unable to agree on priorities, they lack a clear basis for measuring success.

Another common response is to focus on what is not wanted rather than what is wanted. This is another expression of deficit-based thinking and action that I mentioned earlier. It is a natural default position for some. For example, 'I wish we'd stop all this arguing and bickering' reflects what is *not* wanted. To transform this statement into a possible goal, we might ask, 'What would it look like if […] were gone?' In other words, 'What would it look like if the arguing and bickering stopped?' In this situation, a statement of what is wanted would be, 'Well, if we didn't argue and disagree so much, it would be more pleasant to work here, and we'd get more work done.'

Commitment clarifies priorities and sets us up for positive action. Once choices have been made, it is natural to ask *how* the commitments can be carried out. The work of capability is to create a way to fulfil commitments and to garner the necessary resources. Trying to plan before everyone reaches a common commitment can lead to focusing on the wrong things, to frustration later, and to the inappropriate use of scarce resources.

Capability

Capability means that people have agreed how to combine knowledge, skills and resources in innovative ways that enable all commitments to be met. When capability is present, people believe that they have, or can develop, a way to meet any challenge. They are willing to try, to learn from their mistakes, and to incorporate what they learn into current and future efforts. They like to roll up their sleeves and bring new ideas to life.

When capability is missing, people are less interested in, and may resist, trying new things because they think things are okay the way they are, or they are afraid of making mistakes. They may feel incapable of making things better. Capability is essentially a positive planning phase.

Responsibility

Responsibility means that everyone knows who is going to do what by when. It is the carrying out of the positive action plan to meet the commitments. When it is present, people know what they are expected to do and what others are to do, and they do it. As individuals and as a group, they find satisfaction in doing a good job. And they talk openly about it if something doesn't get done. Even though responsibilities have been spelled out and committed to, people's tasks are not set in stone or inflexible. Responsibilities can be established anew when the situation changes, and people willingly work outside their specific responsibilities when they help someone else. When responsibility is missing, people are not clear about what they are expected to do, and so all the things necessary to carrying out the plan don't get done. People don't always do their part.

Acknowledgement

Acknowledgement is recognizing what has been accomplished in terms of reaching the commitments, and what remains to be done for the commitments to be complete. When it is present, both individuals and the whole group know where there is agreement, and where there are differing perceptions about how well things are going and what still needs attention. Differing perceptions are openly accepted and considered, and there is a willingness to move ahead and address those things seen as missing. When acknowledgement is missing, people may not know how they are doing, even if they are doing quite well. This may be associated with an absence of using reflective practices wisely and prudently. It may also be because those involved do not take time to consider that there are differing views of the status quo, and of progress. The basic practices for creating acknowledgement are the use of three questions:

1.   What have we achieved so far?
2.   What still needs to be done?
3.   Where should future efforts be directed?

Some more things that 'get in the way'

I have tried to stress that a reflective conversation does not happen by magic. It takes skilfulness and commitment. There are many things that can 'get in the way' of the experience being useful and fulfilling. Here are some things that can get in the way, and that all involved might usefully be mindful of. I have couched them in a deficit-based way. They are:

- *Passivity*. This means not acting in situations that need action. This includes doing nothing, uncritically accepting goals and suggestions made by others, becoming paralysed regarding action, or even becoming aggressive (shutting down or letting off steam).
- *Learned helplessness*. This helplessness means those involved feel they can do nothing to change or improve the situation. There are degrees of helplessness, ranging from statements such as 'I'm not up to this' to feelings of deep inadequacy often

coupled with a depressive state. Those involved can feel that educational improve-ment is not in their control, is outside of their sphere of influence, and is not within their immediate experience.

- *Disabling self-talk.* This is where those participating in a reflective conversation talk themselves out of things and into passivity. Conversations slide into an obsession with problems and obstacles. The vocabulary style used is 'It won't work' and 'We can't do it.'

- *Vicious (not virtuous) cycles.* Here, plans do not go well. The future does not unfold from the present in the expected way. Those involved feel knocked back, and begin to feel they are losing a sense of self-worth. They lose heart and confidence in their plan for change. This spirals individuals and groups downwards into a mindset of defeat, negativity and even depression. They lose their sense of optimism.

- *Feeling that things are falling apart.* Sometimes those involved have a tendency to give up on action they have initiated. Action to implement a positive plan for change can begin strongly, but then dwindle and stop. Plans seem realistic and achievable, and begin with enthusiasm. Then implementation becomes tedious. What seemed easy at the start now seems to be quite difficult. Those involved seem to flounder. They get discouraged, and may give up without the appropriate kinds of support. In other words, the improvement or positive action plan is not sustainable.

- *Choosing not to change.* Some of those involved in reflective conversations develop new understandings and awareness of themselves, others, their work and their workplace. They appreciate what their strengths are, try to play to them, and develop new ones. They also appreciate what they need to do in order to change the current situation to make things even better. However, they choose not to act. They do not want to 'pay the price' called for by committing fully to the action. This can be attitudinal, or related to values, confidence, and running out of steam or energy.

I will just say a little more about the two important ideas of having energy and a sense of optimism, for both are essential ingredients to a fulfilling reflective conversation. I will frame them within Loehr and Schwartz's (2005) notion of being fully engaged – more specifically, being fully engaged with reflective practices. Loehr and Schwartz (2005) explain that it is energy, not time, that is the fundamental currency for moving forward positively. In other words, using reflective practices to build further success and continuously improve is about energy, not time management. This message can come as quite a shock to some. To be fully engaged, they argue, we must be physically ener-gized, emotionally connected, mentally focused, and spiritually aligned with a purpose beyond our immediate self-interest. Loehr and Schwartz (2005) set out four key man-agement principles that they believe are at the heart of any change process, and that are highly relevant here:

1. Full engagement requires drawing on four separate but related sources of energy: physical, emotional, mental and spiritual.
2. Because energy capacity diminishes both with overuse and with underuse, we must balance energy expenditure with intermittent energy renewal. In other words, we

need recovery breaks. We need to take time out. We shouldn't just try to keep going, as our batteries, at some point, will go flat!

3. To amplify our strengths and continuously improve, we must push beyond our normal limits, training in the same systematic way that elite athletes do. Have you ever thought about this?

4. Positive energy rituals (highly specific routines for managing energy) are the key to full engagement and sustained high performance. This is more than taking the odd coffee break.

When Loehr and Schwartz (2005) talk about the different kinds of energy we may need to improve educational experiences, they mean;

- *Emotional energy* – energy generated by the positive feelings of mutual appreciation experienced by colleagues as they engage in teaching and learning.
- *Physical energy* – the amount of physical energy that can be devoted to interacting and strategizing, especially given that many of us, in any one day, are juggling numerous commitments.
- *Mental energy* – the way we find the mental energy to stay focused, for long enough, and without distraction from other duties, to feel we are actually achieving something and moving forward.
- *Spiritual energy* – energy derived through interacting with others in an appreciative, safe and supportive context, from a deep sense of an alignment of what we say with what we do, and that our work has some positive meaning and purpose.

Drawing from the perspective of positive psychology, Seligman (2006) reminds us how important *learned helplessness* and *explanatory style* are to understanding working life (e.g., our educational practice) as successes or failures of personal control. Learned helplessness is the 'giving up' reaction, the quitting response that follows from the belief that whatever you do doesn't matter. Explanatory style is the manner in which you habitually explain to yourself why events happen. An optimistic explanatory style stops helplessness, whereas a pessimistic explanatory style spreads helplessness. Your way of explaining events to yourself determines how helpless you can become, or how energized. In a very cogent way, Seligman (2006) argues that there is one particularly self-defeating way to think; namely, making personal, permanent and pervasive explanations for bad events. Pessimists believe that bad events will last a long time, will undermine everything they do, and are their own fault. Just as we can learn to be helpless, so too can we learn to be optimistic. For those who enter into a reflective conversation, I would urge them to do so with a sense of optimism.

Strengths-based reflective conversations

When you and your line manager discuss your performance, what do you spend the most time talking about – strengths or weaknesses? If asked, 'Which will help you be most successful, building on your strengths or fixing your weaknesses', what would you say? What would help you be more successful in your life, knowing what your weaknesses are and attempting to improve your weaknesses, or knowing what your strengths are and attempting to build on your strengths? I had a very interesting experience recently when I was attending a parents' meeting, where teachers were discussing the examination grades of the students in their class – interesting in the sense that even if a student achieved two A grades and two B grades, most of the time was spent talking about the one F grade! I'm not saying that teachers and parents (as well as the student involved) should ignore the F grade, any more than you should ignore your own weaknesses. But what was highly significant was the weight of consideration and time given over to a discussion of the one exam the student had 'failed'. The assumption that everyone seemed to be making was that this was a good use of time – that focusing on the failure was right and proper, as if all the great work and effort the student had done to achieve the top grades would simply look after itself! Is this wise?

One purpose of a more strengths-based reflective conversation is to enable all involved to work in ways that allow them to identify and to use their strengths. This means being able to do what they do best, every day, at work. This has positive implications for performance, and can provide a more pleasant and happier working life. One definition of a 'strength' can be drawn from the research of Chris Peterson and Martin Seligman (2004), as well as from the work of The Gallup Organization (Rath, 2007). From their work, an area of strength is an area in which you are able to consistently perform at a very high level, which energizes you, and which you perceive as producing a positive experience. It derives from one's natural talents or capabilities, and is ultimately displayed in organizational settings through the actions of people. A few examples of the many possible strengths include communicating, creating, analysing, being strategic, providing perspective, being fair, being curious, appreciating, adapting, being honest, and showing courage.

Identifying, using and developing strengths is not as straightforward, alas, as it may seem. In a reflective conversation, those involved might usefully be aware of three fundamental things that can affect the outcomes of it:

1. *Self-awareness*. It is important to develop a realistic view of how other people perceive you, rather than relying on your own view of yourself and your capabilities, wherever that sits on the continuum ranging from self-deprecation (running yourself down) to self-aggrandisement (bigging yourself up). This involves seeking feedback from those people whose judgement you trust, as well as using empathy to anticipate other people's reactions to what you say – not least about yourself. Self-awareness is the foundation stone on which self-esteem and self-efficacy rest.

2. *Self-motivation*. Motivation is the force which causes a person to act in order to achieve a goal, and then to sustain that action until successful. Resilient people are self-starting; they don't rely on others to motivate them. While they might procrastinate a little, or reflect on the best way of approaching a task, they get on and do things, reasonably quickly. They can then sustain that action until the job is done.

3. *Self-affirmation*. In building self-esteem and self-efficacy, it is not enough merely to create success; you must also give yourself credit for having done so. And you should aim to become the supervisor of your own self-improvement and development programme. This gets to the core of reflective learning.

In practical terms, when engaging in a reflective conversation we may have to choose between asking two more kinds of question: deficit-based or strength-based. In

TABLE 3.1 Different questions, different conversations

DEFICIT-BASED QUESTIONS	STRENGTHS-BASED QUESTIONS
1. What's the problem?	1. What was a success?
Response:	Response:
2. What were the causes of the problem?	2. What contributed to the success?
Response:	Response:
3. What needs to stop in order to 'fix' the problem?	3. What do you need to keep doing to create further success?
Response:	Response:
4. What is one behaviour you will need to get rid of, and how far can you do it?	4. What is one behaviour you need to amplify, and how will you do this?
Response:	Response:

reality, it might be a combination of both. Much might depend upon the purpose of the conversation. These alternatives are shown in Table 3.1.

I suggest that for more strengths-based reflective conversations, those engaged in it might usefully have a repertoire of positive questions. These are three that I have found I use a lot, and that serve to open up significant conversations:

- Think about a really positive experience for you when you felt appreciated and respected at work. What contributed to this?
- Think about a really positive experience for you when you felt you were able to cope well with your work. What contributed to this?
- Think about a really positive experience for you when you felt that different ways of doing things were valued. What contributed to this?

How to cultivate a culture within the workplace where failure, lack of success or poor performance doesn't destabilize progress is a major challenge for many of us, and may well dominate some reflective conversations. So how can a reflective conversation keep all involved on a positive learning trajectory? This is a big question!

Fundamentally, the overall purpose of reflection and its practices needs to be clear to all involved. Arguably, it is to enhance our awareness of ourselves, the impact that our actions may have on others, and the way we might be the best we can be, each day. When we talk about reflective practice, we cannot escape the interdependency of the interests it serves, the issues it addresses and the approaches it uses. For example:

1. The range of theoretical frameworks and practices often referred to in the literature underscores the notion that 'reflective practice' is an eclectic and hybrid field.
2. The different purposes of reflective practice and the different interests that it serves reflect both critical and creative (more of the former, normally) processes at work.

3. The knowledge and understanding that arises from reflective conversations can (and should) be constructively 'put under pressure'.
4. The practices of reflection do not only have to be paper-and-pencil type practices; they can also embrace a wide spectrum of meaning-making practices – for example, from the visual and creative arts.
5. There are often unanticipated outcomes of reflection and possibilities created for us to think about what we don't know and do, as well as enhancing and amplifying what we do know, and can do well.

Types of reflective conversation

Different kinds of reflection can give rise to different kinds of conversation. Much depends on the kinds of questions we ask. What follows are examples of reflective conversations which illustrate this point. Each example of a conversation is a way of making sense of the experience of teaching and learning. They are based the work of Ghaye and Ghaye (1998) with students and teachers. The main issues at stake here are as follows. The first is that reflective conversations have to be developed. Their quality varies, and this can be as a result of many things – such as how used the participants are to learning through conversations of this kind, and how much experience of teaching the 'teller' has. Not surprisingly, then, reflective conversations can exhibit different characteristics. Not all are penetrative, positive, constructively critical, forward-looking, felt to be empowering, and the like. It takes a while for them to mature into this form. Some conversations may be rooted, anchored and even locked into elaborate descriptions of 'what is', or perceived to be, rather than anything else. The conversations that follow show some of these different qualities. Earlier, I stated that such conversations are value-laden. In each of the conversations that follow, there is a values dimension. Sometimes it is more clearly and explicitly discernable than in other conversations. Although I discuss values in the next chapter, it might be worth stating here that knowing then articulating and justifying our professional values is a challenging business. In the following conversations, two things should become apparent: that teaching and learning is a value-laden activity, and that some teachers are more conscious of their values and of trying to live them out in their daily work than others.

Three further points of clarification: first, different conversations held over a period of time can show evidence of the same or different kinds of reflection-on-practice. Second, within the same conversation – say, between a student teacher and her tutor – there may be evidence of one dominant kind or of different kinds of reflection. Part of the tutor's skill is to detect these different kinds of reflection and then to enable the student to appreciate the dominance of one or more when talking about their experiences. An additional role for the tutor is try to get the student to draw upon other kinds of reflection, depending upon the context and the purpose of the conversation as it unfurls. Third, it is unwise to see these reflections as being mutually exclusive and as tight, almost watertight, compartments. I am not implying that any kind of reflective hierarchy exists, either. A reflective conversation is a fluid and dynamic phenomenon. It is important to appreciate that as it develops, reflections-on-practice might naturally evidence more or less of one kind, or quality, of reflection or another. So another central message that is emerging in this book is that reflection-on-practice is much, much more than that encapsulated by the often-stated cliché, 'Reflection is just simply thinking about what you do!'

A lesson with Amy

Amy is a third-year student on an honours degree course in Primary Education. She is working in a mixed Year 3/4 class of 32 children. She has been with the class for two weeks. This is her first full week of teaching the whole class, and she is looking forward to the challenge.

Amy has planned and carefully thought through an English lesson. Her desirable learning outcomes are clearly stated in her plans, and she is confident that the lesson will go smoothly. Her National Curriculum focus is 'literacy', with a particular emphasis on writing for a specific audience. She is also hoping to address speaking and listening skills. During the lesson, Amy will be observed by her tutor. She will then have the opportunity to discuss her teaching afterwards. The intention is for the tutor and student to engage in a reflective conversation.

The particular activity which Amy has planned involves the children working in groups of four, writing a collaborative story for a child in a Key Stage 1 class. The children have already met their 'audience', and have discussed the types of story that each child enjoys reading. Amy has looked at a variety of books with her class, and discussed page layout, illustrations and vocabulary. She feels very satisfied with her preliminary work, and is confident that her children are now ready to begin to write their story.

She introduces the lesson to the whole class and then divides them into groups of mixed ability, each group including children from both Years 3 and 4. Amy gives each group a large piece of paper and a pen, and encourages them to 'brainstorm' and write their ideas on the paper. After 20 minutes, she feels they should be thinking about beginning to write the story. Each group has to get one child to act as a scribe. By the end of the lesson, Amy hopes that each group will have agreed both the content and structure of the story.

Once Amy has explained the purpose of the lesson and how she wants the children to work, she tries not to intervene in each group's work. She monitors the noise level, positions herself at the teacher's desk, and decides to take the opportunity to hear individual children read. She calls them to her, one by one, glancing up from time to time to monitor the group work. She deduces from this that the children are busy, that discussions are taking place, that most of the children appear to be 'on task' and that there seems to be a positive working atmosphere in the classroom. Amy is therefore pleased that her tutor is observing a well-organized, cooperative group work activity.

After 20 minutes, Amy reminds the children that they should now be choosing a member of the group to act as scribe. They have a further 40 minutes to put their collective ideas into a story form. She continues to hear children read, and responds when the children ask for help. From time to time she moves around the classroom and pauses to check that each group is busy. The noise level is occasionally rather high, and so Amy asks them to work more quietly. Throughout the lesson, her tutor takes the opportunity to speak to some of the children and observe each group. Amy's School Experience file is read, and her tutor writes comments in it.

Five minutes before the end of the lesson, Amy asks the children to stop working and to tidy up. They are told that they will be able to continue with their stories the next day. The class responds sensibly, and waits for the dinner bell to ring. At lunch-time, Amy has the opportunity to discuss the lesson with her tutor and to look through the children's work.

A reflective conversation with Amy

What follows are extracts of the conversation that Amy had with her tutor. It was tape-recorded so that Amy could reflect on it further if she so wished. The extracts that have been selected illustrate one particular kind of reflection which is a personal, comprehensive and retrospective account of teaching. It is essentially a description of a lesson, or part of it. Few justifications are offered for the way in which Amy teaches. It serves to place teaching in a context, and therefore contains reference to what was taught, where, when and with whom. Conversations that are predominantly descriptive reflections-on-practice may also have a sense of history about them as the 'teller' refers to past events. These may be what she has done before with her present class or with other classes. This kind of reflection is the teller's view of what happened. In this case, it is Amy's version of events.

In order to help Amy to learn from her experience, her tutor asks her a series of questions. The purpose of these questions is to gently 'deconstruct' Amy's teaching. This deconstruction involves pulling it apart, sensitively and patiently, in order to explore it. Deconstruct does not mean destroy; on the contrary, the tutor's intention is to try to enable Amy to become more aware of what she is doing and why her teaching is the way it is. As I have said, this can be a time-consuming process, and may not be fully or satisfactorily achieved in the context of an immediate post-lesson conversation and just before the tutor rushes off to the next school and other students. Reflective conversations require much skilfulness on the part of the tutor, and a preparedness, by Amy, to engage in such a conversation, openly and positively with her tutor. I am now beginning to touch upon some of the 'big ideas' of John Dewey (1933) when he argued that reflective teaching requires attitudes of open-mindedness, responsibility and whole-heartedness.

Five of the questions that Amy's tutor asked have been selected. Each one can be taken as an invitation to Amy to reflect on what she has taught.

TUTOR: Amy, I noticed that you structured your lesson to involve the children work-ing in mixed-ability groups. Why did you decide to do this?

AMY: I thought it would make a change for the children to work in groups with Years 3 and 4 together. I tried this on my last teaching practice and it seemed to work well. So it seemed commonsense to give it a go again on this practice. They don't have many opportunities to work on a group task and so I decided that I would plan an activity which would help them to work together.

TUTOR: Your plans show clearly what your learning outcomes would look like. How far do you feel you have achieved them?

AMY: I think the class knew what was expected of them and I can see that they have all produced something. They've put their ideas on paper and they seem to have made an attempt to start the story. They seemed to be getting on with it in the right sort of way.

TUTOR: How do you see your role in today's lesson?

AMY: I wanted the children to work on their own as much as possible. I don't think they need the teacher interfering all the time because it can put them off. So I decided to listen to readers because I've seen the class teacher take opportunities to do this whenever she can. I've seen how she does it.

TUTOR: How successful do you think you were at monitoring the children's learning?

AMY: Well, I kept an eye on the class and I made sure they were all busy. There was a bit too much noise at times and so I tried to quieten them down. I think it worked. They all looked interested in the activity and there was lots of discussion, especially between Emma and Nicky who don't normally get on well.

TUTOR: What have you learned from the lesson?

AMY: I think the children can work together in groups but maybe I could organize the classroom better. I think four in a group is fine. I'd do this again I think. I was pretty happy with it.

Created conversations

Earlier, I mentioned that the quality of reflective conversations is related to the kinds of question we may ask. For example, deficit-based questions can lead to deficit-based conversations, and so on. But there is a possibility that the same question can be answered in a number of different ways. In order to illustrate this, a number of other (possible) conversations that Amy might have had with her tutor that day are given below. I have taken the same five tutor questions, referring to the same lesson, so that you can compare the conversations more easily. These created conversations act as evidence to show the different (and additional) ways Amy might have reflected on her lesson. Many things can affect the nature of Amy's answer – for example, how she is feeling, her relationship with her tutor, issues of mutual understanding, expectations, and much more. What I am saying is that I feel we are capable of offering different kinds of explanation and using different kinds of reflection, even though one kind may dominate from time to time. With experience, those involved are likely to become more aware of this possibility and therefore more able to construct a context that enables the quality of the reflection to be enhanced. This is where it is important to enact the Mobius qualities.

When reading this second conversation through, a number of different qualities emerge. This conversation contains an explicit emotional element. Amy makes a demonstrable link between descriptions of her teaching and her personal feelings about it. As a teacher, it is only natural to have both positive and relatively more negative feelings about yourself, about other colleagues, and about the school in which teaching and learning take place. Reflective conversations of this kind convey such things as passion, joy, aggression, puzzlement, sadness and appreciation. The conversation links together teacher thinking and feelings.

TUTOR: Amy, I noticed that you structured your lesson to involve the children working in mixed-ability groups. Why did you decide to do this?'

AMY: I feel very strongly that these children need to work in groups from time to time. Each child has a different strength, and I feel that the rest of the group should appreciate that. I like children to learn from each other, so I tried to give them the opportunity. It pleased me to see children cooperating at this age and I wanted to give them a chance.

TUTOR: Your plans show clearly what your learning outcomes would look like. How far do you feel you have achieved them?

AMY: Well, I feel very satisfied with the outcomes. It's a shame that they can't carry on this afternoon. I was pleased that they cooperated. I felt I coped OK with the readers and at keeping one eye on the rest of the class. I wondered if the 'brain-storming' bit might get out of hand, but I needn't have worried because they came up with some good ideas.

TUTOR: How do you see your role in today's lesson?

AMY: I must admit to being very comfortable in my role. More comfortable than I thought I might, actually. I really wanted the children to be able to get on inde-pendently, to talk amongst themselves and decide how they would write the story. I really didn't want to intervene in case I inhibited them. I feel quite strongly about this. I like listening to the children read, helping and encouraging them. I was a little worried that it could have gone wrong because they do depend on me, too much I feel.

TUTOR: How successful do you think you were at monitoring the children's learning?

AMY: Well, I did feel pleased with the way the lesson progressed. It went according to plan. No real hiccups, I thought, that made me panic. The noise did concern me a bit, though. I think they enjoyed the lesson, and when that happens I enjoy it too.

TUTOR: What have you learned from the lesson?

AMY: That the children are keen to try out new ideas and like to work in different groups. That they can have fun when they are in school and still be learning something at the same time. That I can organize a lesson like this and actually enjoy it too! Yes, it was a good experience, I thought.

The first two types of conversation are retrospective, personal accounts, essentially descriptive in nature and associated with feelings about how well teaching was felt to have gone. They are egocentric in the sense that they are Amy's own view of things. In the next created conversation, further qualities evidence themselves. Here, Amy clearly relates her view of the world, and her (re)construction of classroom reality, to that of others. She is open to alternative perspectives. What makes this a different kind of con-versation from the two previously is that Amy offers, through the process of reflection-on-practice, clear justifications for practice derived and synthesized from her own and other people's views of things. Amy reflects in such a way that she brings forward evid-ence in order to authenticate and justify her practice. So this kind of reflection has some important qualities. It is reflection that generates practical knowledge that is 'posi-tioned'. By this, I mean it is knowledge that is positioned or aligned in relation to some wider and more complex picture. This picture would include the experience of other teachers, the professional literature in the form of journals, books and magazines, and practitioner research. Amy is able to critique what she claims to know, and, in doing, so new possibilities for action arise out of new insights.

TUTOR: Amy, I noticed that you structured your lesson to involve the children working in mixed-ability groups. Why did you decide to do this?

AMY: This is something that I've wanted to try for a long time. I've read about the different ways of grouping children, and I've seen some really good lessons by other teachers who believe in mixed-ability group work. I thought I was ready to give it a go, especially after talking with the class teacher about the mix of abilities in each group. I'm not sure that I got the mix right for every group, though. It's not quite as straightforward as some books make it out to be!

TUTOR: Your plans show clearly what your learning outcomes would look like. How far do you feel you have achieved them?

AMY: I need to spend some more time looking at what the children have produced, but I know that at least one group did achieve the targets and they have now written a good story outline. It's got a clear beginning, middle and end. That's one success, but I'm wondering if they would have achieved more for someone else, like their own teacher. I'll ask her later. Some of the children said they enjoyed the lesson, but I must admit I was disappointed by others' efforts. There are definitely things I need to work on.

TUTOR: How do you see your role in today's lesson?

AMY: To be honest, I was in a bit of a dilemma with this one. I wasn't sure whether to mingle with the children throughout the lesson or whether to follow my teacher's example and listen to some children read. Bearing in mind the time that it takes to do this, I'm not sure which is a more effective use of my time. Too much control by me, and the children don't think for themselves and get dependent. Too little control, and some of them start floundering while a few others just exploit it and try to mess around.

TUTOR: How successful do you think you were at monitoring the children's learning?

AMY: Well, I have seen this lesson taught in a similar way by a teacher in my previous school. She seemed to have it down to a fine art, all the children worked really well and she knew what each group was doing. I'm not sure that I did actually monitor them carefully enough. Perhaps they are not as independent as I thought they would be at this age. Or maybe it's just different for them and they need to adjust to my way of teaching.

TUTOR: What have you learned from the lesson?

AMY: The most important thing is that this activity is a lot more difficult to put into practice than I imagined. It seemed a simple idea, but planning took ages. And you have to expect some of the children to disagree with each other or want to write their own stories without using everyone else's ideas. It's OK in theory but…! Also they said that they haven't had much experience of this way of working, you know in teacher-less and more cooperative-type group work. The class teacher doesn't do much of it. She told me so. They need practice at it. I think I'm much more aware of what I need to do now.

In the following reflective conversation, Amy articulates things that are not present in the other three conversations. Here, Amy articulates the links between learning from her teaching experience, and future action. This kind of reflection is not only a process of looking backwards but also, more significantly, a process that is forward-looking. It takes the learning that has arisen from other kinds of reflective conversations and begins to put it to work. Here, she is beginning to organize past learning, future intentions and teaching rationales in the form of an articulated positive plan for action. Such plans show how imagined solutions to improve teaching are justified in terms of moving individual or collective practice forward. This kind of reflection also makes clear the part others might play in enhancing future practice. The past is not irrelevant. What has been learnt is paramount. The challenge is putting this learning into improving practice.

TUTOR: Amy, I noticed that you structured your lesson to involve the children in mixed ability groups. Why did you decide to do this?

AMY: Well, I thought the children needed an opportunity to work in a different learning situation and with children who they do not normally choose to work with. I thought this would be a good learning experience for them. I've only been with the class for two weeks, so I am still getting to know them. I don't think each group was as carefully balanced as it might have been. Next time, I think I need to make sure that each group has at least one competent writer in it, someone who enjoys drawing, and a balance, where possible, of boys and girls. I don't know the children's characters well enough yet, but I think I know what changes to make next time.

TUTOR: Your plans show clearly what your learning outcomes would look like. How far do you feel you have achieved them?

AMY: This is difficult to assess at the moment. I know that some groups took far too long on the first part. I'm not sure that I can just expect them to 'brainstorm' unguided, in 20 minutes, and get all the ideas down on paper. I think I might structure that a bit more next time. Also, the big paper and felt-tip pens were a novelty to many, it seemed. Maybe we could have more of a whole-class discussion first or maybe, in the groups, individuals or pairs could write their ideas down on separate pieces of paper. Then they could all be placed in the middle of the table, read out and then they could try to agree on the best four or five. I'm semi-pleased with the outcomes, but I also think I'll have to sort out how I can help the group with Jamie in it to start to write the beginning of their story. They can't decide.

TUTOR: How do you see your role in today's lesson?

AMY: I deliberately planned to give particular children some quality reading time while the others were working. I did not intend to keep them away from their groups for too long in case they felt they missed too much. It didn't work as well as I'd hoped. Some were reluctant to leave the group to come out to read. Others stayed longer than I had planned. When Sophie and Ben went back to their group, they were greeted with a bit of hostility. They couldn't get back into it. Sometimes I also had a queue at the desk of those asking for help. Then I thought I should get up and move around. Next time I'm going to try to manage the middle part of my lesson better. If I have to juggle different roles then I don't want to get stressed out or lose control of the class.

TUTOR: How successful do you think you were at monitoring the children's learning?

AMY: They knew that although I was listening to readers, I was also keeping an eye on them. In future I think I would stop the class, from time to time, and ask for one person to update me on the progress of each group. That way I would know if they were keeping on task. The noise level did get up a bit. Well, it was too noisy at times. I've got to stop the 'nagging' bit. You know, always saying 'come on, work more quietly please'. I'm aware of this, and I think I need to make my expectations clearer. I might give some of the children a chance to catch up at playtime if they want to. I'm going to work some of this into my next lesson and see if things improve.

TUTOR: What have you learned from the lesson?

AMY: I've definitely learned that, despite how carefully you plan and how well you prepare, things can still go wrong or not run as smoothly as you would like. I need to be more realistic, and appreciate that every day will have its ups and downs. I think I also need to be prepared to adapt my plans. This is a big thing with me, having a clear plan and yet being able to be flexible. I'm going to talk to my class teacher about this. She knows the children, and I need to build some of this experience into my planning.

In the final reflective conversation, Amy adopts a questioning tone. Amy begins to question accepted routines, classroom practices and school rituals. Here, 'why-type' questions are being asked and answered. They are asked with reference to the teaching of individuals and groups of teachers. In doing so, the status quo is being challenged. Criticism should not be confused with cynicism, destruction and negativity. Critical reflection has the intention of being creative and constructive. In this created conversation, Amy's values that guide her teaching are exposed, questioned and not taken for granted. Assumptions made about effective teaching and effective schools are opened up to debate and critique. Contradictions between what is perceived to be educational rhetoric and teaching realities are confronted. This can be quite threatening for some.

A more critical form of reflection-on-practice cannot be meaningfully undertaken without an understanding of and a willingness to confront the big and complex issues of power and politics in schools. It is a kind of reflection that is about the individual teacher, the individual as part of the whole school culture, and how teaching might be transformed in order to improve the quality of the educational relationships. What is important is to understand how the quality of individual action is influenced, constrained or liberated by 'local' structures and the 'system' within which the teacher works. Teachers are not 'free agents' to do just as they please. Teachers work within local, regional, national and international systems which serve to guide and influence what they do and provide opportunities for growth and development. These systems, which are, for example, political, cultural, economic and professional in kind, can also serve to constrain, devalue, marginalize and disempower teachers.

TUTOR: Amy, I noticed that you structured your lesson to involve the children working in mixed-ability groups. Why did you decide to do this?

AMY: This is a teaching strategy that I've used successfully with children before. I've noticed that the practice in this school does not usually encourage mixed-ability grouping. But the class teacher was willing to let me try, so I'll have to keep her in touch with how it's going. I believe that children should have the opportunity to work together, to collaborate and share their skills with other children, because as they get older they will have to work with different people and get on with them.

TUTOR: Your plans show clearly what your learning outcomes would look like. How far do you feel you have achieved them?

AMY: Well, all that stuff about leadership, giving children clear roles and responsibilities and independence to be creative is important. Some might say, 'Well, I don't think the children have done much today!' Some groups haven't got a lot written down, but I would argue that they have in fact been really busy, thinking and discussing. I'd argue that learning doesn't necessarily have to find its way into the children's folders at the end of each lesson. I believe that process is as important as product. But I do feel that the school puts me under pressure to produce something for parents. I feel I've achieved something perhaps that I didn't expect. That all learning outcomes are not visible and concrete, and if you go for that all the time, you have to compromise on other things.

TUTOR: How do you see your role in today's lesson?

AMY: It was a combination of teacher direction, at the beginning, with independent work in groups. I'm aware that listening to children read while the others are working might be criticized by some teachers. I'm in a bit of a difficult situation. The school expects every child to be listened to, on an individual basis, once a week, and I knew that I was running behind schedule. The school's reading policy is clear on this. Also, my reading records have to be completed by Friday. This is a pressure so I decided to fit in some more readers. I'm sure there is a better way to manage this expectation, especially now that we have the literacy hour. I'm not happy with how I help children to read, and the system just adds to the pressure. Reading is given priority in this school. I'm not sure that I agree with it. I'm not sure I did the right thing. I want to be fair to all the children.

TUTOR: How successful do you think you were at monitoring the children's learning?

AMY: I think I could have monitored things more closely. But I bet everyone says this. I don't know. Well, your question makes me think, about my management, the noise level, leaving them to get on and the rest. Am I contradicting myself? It seems that I want everything, doesn't it? I believe independent working is good for the children, but with direction. That I want a quiet classroom but I can't insist on one, don't want to, and especially if I want the children to work independently. I believe that the children should be given lots of opportunities to discuss things, talk through things in their own way, and yet I'm also anxious that they have something down, you know, something to show for it.

TUTOR: What have you learned from the lesson?

AMY: I think I was over-ambitious and that I needed to support and encourage all the children more. I think I should have taken opportunities to get the children to share their work with the rest of the class as they progressed, because I really believe that children should learn from each other, should listen and ask each other sensible questions. These are lifelong skills, after all, aren't they? Trying to get them working effectively in groups, in this school and on teaching practice is all a bit ambitious, I think. But I'm still going to try. The children aren't used to group work. I know what I believe in, but actually putting it into practice on TP is more than about you. If the school or class teacher is not supportive, then you have to be prepared to say one thing and not be able to put it into practice. You've got to get the teacher and the children on your side. If the teacher is a bit awkward or sees what you do as threatening, then you've got to explain why you want to try something out. Sometimes this takes a lot of guts. Sometimes you have to be prepared to make compromises. With my group work, I'm trying to emphasize children's self-discipline and collaboration. But the teacher thinks there's no discipline because they're all doing their own things and because I'm not in the role of authority figure.

A Strengths-based Reflective Practice

Towards strengths-based thinking

This chapter really gets to the essence of the second edition. It is about describing, explaining and justifying a new kind of reflective practice – one that explicitly emphasizes reflecting on strengths so as to identify them, play to them and develop new ones. This is a pretty tough task, as many of us are programmed to reflect upon problems and weaknesses rather than strengths and successes. A major message in the second edition of this book is that reflection that only focuses on fixing weaknesses is a mistake and a misallocation of time and energy. I am suggesting that, to help people become the best they can be, we also need to reflect on the positives, and use reflection and its practices to identify, develop and amplify their gifts, talents and strengths. The point of this chapter is simple. It is about balance. I am not advocating replacing a one-sided perspective of reflection being a solution looking for a problem, – an obsession with what is wrong – with another one-sided perspective – an exclusive focus on what is right. This is misguided and simplistic. I am trying to go beyond this swinging pendulum kind of reflective practice by advocating an approach to individual growth which recognizes that both strengths *and* weaknesses have an appropriate place in learning and development. A focus on reflection for strength-building takes us into some new, interesting and humanly significant areas, such as those to do with

FIGURE 4.1 Using reflection in a strengths-based way

excellence, creativity, resilience and optimal functioning. When people are performing in roles in which they play to their strengths, studies show that performance and satisfaction increase, productivity improves and they have a greater chance of achieving their full potential (Buckingham and Clifton, 2001). This is a radical departure from the long-held view that to enable someone to perform at his or her best, you work as hard as you can at trying to overcome their weaknesses. This view is evidenced by the fact that only 20 per cent of employees in companies across the globe feel their strengths are in play on a daily basis (Buckingham and Clifton, 2001). So my argument here is that it is a great investment, in time and other resources, to use reflective practices to develop strengths and to build workplaces where these strengths can be used for the majority of our time, each day.

So how might this turn itself into a set of suggestions for using reflective practices? In Figure 4.1, I set out four such practical purposes.

How might we begin to reflect on strengths? Here are some starting suggestions.

1. What was your best day at work in the past three months? What were you doing? Why was it the 'best day?' How far do you think you could re-experience it?
2. What was your worst day at work in the past three months? What was going on? Why did it drain or weaken you so much? What frustrated or bored you?
3. What's the best relationship you have ever had with a colleague? What made it so good?
4. What's the best recognition you have ever had? From whom, and why?
5. When did you learn the most? What was going on?

What is a strength?

It isn't as easy as it may seem to define a strength. Is it about what we do best, what we do better than other people, and/or what we do better than others *which is also aligned* with what organizations need from us as employees? The startling fact is that most of us don't know our strengths – we can't list them easily, we don't know how many we have, and we often get embarrassed when invited to talk about them. But we are acutely aware of our weaknesses. So perhaps it is worth considering how reflective practices can help us find our strengths, build on our strengths, fashion our work around particular strengths, and find a workplace and a role that enables us to play to your strengths (see Table 2.2). How might a strength-based reflective practice enable you to make your strengths even stronger?

Kaiser (2009) argues that we need to be clear about how we define a strength. Simply stated, strengths might be those talents, skills and competencies you personally have and do best. But there is more to defining strengths than this! For example, we could look at strengths in at least two ways. One is what measurement experts call an ipsative way. This refers to what you personally are best at, independent of how good you are compared to other people. This can play an important part in how successful you are at work. The second way to look at strengths is to compare your strengths to relevant, and other, people. This is often called a 'normative' comparison, because it considers how strong you are *relative* to an appropriate norm group – for example, those doing similar kinds of work, such as teaching in a school. Another way to refer to these two ways of defining a strength is 'personal best' and 'competitive', respectively. I develop the notion of personal best into the reflected best-self later.

Let's take the notion of personal best for a moment. There are at least four ways to think about this: (1) your personal best, which may or may not be enough to succeed; (2) competitive strength, where your skills are stronger than most of your competitors; (3) distinctively competitive strengths, which distinguish you from everybody else but may not be the keys to success in your job, role or career; and (4) competitive and aligned strengths, which, arguably, are the best bet in long-term career success. So one thing we can take away from these definitions is that if you plan to succeed by focusing on your strengths, it would be prudent to try to make sure you do more than just discover and build on your personal-best strengths! You will also need strengths that enable you to stand out compared to your peers (competitive strengths).

Playing to your strengths

It is all too easy to think that success is just the opposite of failure, and many do! So we study divorce to learn about marriage, we study unhappy customers to learn about the happy ones, we study frustrated employees to learn how to engage employees, we study depression and psychosis to learn about joy. We study the behaviours of naughty children to learn about good behaviour. Only recently, and patchily, have we begun to flip this over and study successful organizations to learn about success. It is all too easy to get ourselves into a frame of mind where good is seen as the opposite of bad, so if you want good you should study bad and invert it. But if we do this, surely all we can hope for is 'not bad'? Studying depressed educators teaches us a lot about depression, but does it tell us anything about joy? Some who advocate reflective practices that focus on problems and mistakes argue that by doing so we can learn from our mistakes. But maybe not! What we may be able to claim is that we learn about the characteristics of mistakes, from mistakes. In what ways do we learn about success from studying failure? I'm not sure. Another thought. How many organizations that you know would you describe as strengths-based? For example, can you name a strengths-based school?

So a key question at the heart of this second edition is this: 'What do you think will help you be most successful in your work and get most fulfilment from it – building your strengths or fixing your weaknesses?' Maybe it's a bit of both. If you gave these choices to a colleague, what do you think they'd say? If they work in a target-driven, high-performance oriented, externally assessed and inspected organization, where resources are becoming scarcer, I think I know what they'd say. Fix our weaknesses. Use reflective practices to get rid of the things we don't do well, and hopefully things will get better. When somebody uses the cliché 'people are our greatest assets', they don't mean that; they mean people's *strengths* are our greatest asset. If you are a school leader, for example, there is not much point in engaging new and talented people, who are also expensive, and then getting them positions in the organization where they don't play to their strengths ... much. How often do you feel you play to your strengths? Once a week? How would you move from once a week to most of the time? Think for a moment about the most successful and most fulfilled people you know, or work with. How much time do they spend using their strengths? Do they seem to spend most of their time doing activities that invigorate them? Well, if you have anybody in mind, it may be prudent to reflect on the fact that what they do doesn't happen by accident. More realistically, it happens because incrementally, week by week, somehow they manage to make the best of their job into most of their job. So I am suggesting that we try to work out a way where reflective practices are used to deliberately tilt the world toward the best of you, so that you can be the best you can, most of the time.

Discovering your strengths

A strange obstacle stands in the way of enabling us to positively embrace and develop our strengths. It's a negative attitude some of us have regarding hearing good news. Many of us are impatient with affirmation, with positive feedback and with compliments. Some regard this as simply a feel-good experience; it is criticism that is truly useful. It is the sting of failure that motivates us. It is reflecting on problems, and getting rid of them, that is the serious work to be done. In Table 4.1 there is a series of ten questions that help you discover your strengths. Try completing them alone, and then share your results with a colleague.

I gave some of these questions to a group of experienced people who were working on a European Union funded project called 'Reflect-OR', which aimed to enhance the quality of education for vocational and career guidance workers. Table 4.2 shows some of the strengths the group disclosed.

TABLE 4.1 Discovering your strengths

STRENGTH STATEMENT	RESPONSE
A major strength of mine is...	
When I get to use this strength I am specifically...	
When I am doing an activity that strengthens (not weakens) me I FEEL...	
When I am doing an activity that strengthens (not weakens) me I THINK...	
When I am doing an activity that strengthens (not weakens) me I WANT TO...	
What FEEDBACK, if any, have you received about your strengths?	
What needs to change to enable you to use your strengths more often?	
What needs to change to enable those you work with, to use their strengths more often?	
What needs to change to enable those in your organization, to use their strengths more often?	
How could you measure/track how much you use your strengths?	

TABLE 4.2 The disclosure of strengths

A major strength of mine is...   • The capacity of appreciating others' richness and peculiarities   • Creativity on developing methodologies and tools   • To find new paths and opening visions   • Enthusiasm for new positive things; ability to listen to and support others; need to share and discuss my experiences   • Using strengths-based approaches   • Energy for facilitating decision-making processes   • A participative attitude, a very strong conviction that 'we' is better than 'I'   • Being curious, open, self-confident (I've still never found what I'm looking for)   • Vision   • Attentive to others needs
When I get to use this strength at work, I am specifically...   • Succeeding in listening to others and catch the richness of their experience and values   • Facilitating workshops with practitioners   • Involved in reconsidering our practice, with more insight   • Encouraging colleagues or participants; analysing the relational dynamics; learning from the feedback and implementing this in my work task   • Reflecting   • Thinking about objectives and aims to be reached, and facilitating a sharing process   • Trying to involve all the group, I try to ask everyone's opinions (and keep them really in mind). I recognize other's points of strength   • Leading the group towards new challenges and perspectives   • Trying to help shared understanding   • Being empathic
When I am doing an activity that strengthens (not weakens) me I FEEL...   • Richer, more open-minded   • Responsible, excited, happy   • Excited   • Happiness, mutuality, sense of belonging and mission   • Empowered   • Useful, appreciated and with plenty of energy, open-minded   • Like a complete puzzle, transparent with myself and with others, I feel that I learned something. I feel generative   • I'm learning a lot   • Positively engaged   • Free

Positivity as a strength

I wonder what you might get out of a kind of reflective practice that enables you to develop strategies and methods that help you to experience positive emotions. Positivity comes in many flavours. It can also be fragile. It is possible for you to experience it, but it depends on how you think. Like all emotions, positive ones arise from the way you interpret ideas, actions and events as they unfold. How far are you aware that you have the power to turn positivity on and off for yourself?

■ Experiment with this. Turn positivity **ON** right now. Ask yourself:
   a. What's right about my current circumstances?

    b.   What makes me lucky to be here?

    c.   What aspect of my current circumstances is a gift to be treasured?

- Now turn positivity **OFF**. Ask yourself these positivity-spoiling questions:

    a.   What's wrong here, right now?

    b.   Why do I feel so fed up?

    c.   Who can I blame for this?

Fredrickson and Joiner talk about the power of positivity and the use of positive emotions (Fredrickson, 2001, Fredrickson and Joiner, 2002).

Fredrickson's (2001) *broaden-and-build theory* is a major, guiding theoretical framework for this second edition. The broaden-and-build theory describes the form and function of a number of positive emotions, including joy, interest, contentment and love. A key proposition is that these positive emotions *broaden* an individual's momentary thought-action repertoire. This means when we feel positive, we are generally more open-minded, more receptive to new ideas, more adaptive and more flexible. For example, joy sparks the urge to play, interest sparks the urge to explore, contentment sparks the urge to savour, and love sparks a recurring cycle of each of these urges within safe, close relationships. The broadened mindsets arising from these positive emotions are contrasted to the narrowed mindsets sparked by many negative emotions (i.e., specific action tendencies, such as to attack or flee). In other words, when we feel more negative we feel much less prepared and able to consider alternatives, to 'play' with ideas and to consider options. A second key proposition of this theory concerns the consequences of these broadened mindsets. By broadening an individual's momentary thought-action repertoire – whether through play, exploration or similar activities – positive emotions promote discovery of novel and creative actions, ideas and social bonds, which in turn build that individual's personal resources and ability to be resilient. These can range from physical and intellectual resources to social and psychological ones. Importantly, these resources function as reserves that can be drawn on later to improve the prospect of successful coping, survival and good health. These resources are shown in Figure 4.2. There is an important knock-on effect going on here. As positivity grows, so does our ability to be more open-minded and wholehearted in what we do. With this positive mindset comes a greater ability to actually try things out, to experiment, and to improve what we do. Fredrickson (2009) argues that we can actually work at increasing our sense of positivity, and that it also:

- makes us feel good;
- changes how our mind works;
- can transform our future;
- puts the brakes on negativity.

More specifically, Fredrickson (2004:1367) argues that

> positive emotions signal optimal functioning, but this is far from their whole story
> ... positive emotions also produce optimal functioning, not just within the present,
> pleasant moment, but over the long term as well. The bottom-line message is that
> people should cultivate positive emotions in themselves and in those around them.

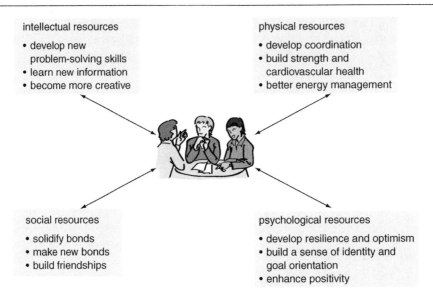

intellectual resources

- develop new
  problem-solving skills
- learn new information
- become more creative

physical resources

- develop coordination
- build strength and
  cardiovascular health
- better energy management

social resources

- solidify bonds
- make new bonds
- build friendships

psychological resources

- develop resilience and optimism
- build a sense of identity and
  goal orientation
- enhance positivity

FIGURE 4.2 Positivity and the the development of human resources? (Source: Fredrickson 2001)

Positivity is linked with self-regard. This means how we see ourselves. It is certainly something to reflect upon, especially as some feel that reflective practices tend to make them feel nervous if they are to self-disclose in some way. Neale *et al.* (2009), in the context of emotionally intelligent coaching, developed a very useful series of short and powerful questionnaires that enables us to reflect upon our sense of self-regard. In Table 4.3, we find an illustration of their work. Work out your score and then show this to a friend or colleague. What do they think?

TABLE 4.3 A self-regard questionnaire

QUESTIONS	5 ☺☺	4 ☺	3 AVERAGE	2 ☹	1 ☹☹
I regularly think positive thoughts about myself					
I tend to be optimistic					
I am comfortable saying 'no' to people and giving an honest explanation					
I take time to 'take in' and reflect on positive feedback other people give me					
I rarely, if ever, look to blame others					
I do not avoid conflict, but embrace it with assertive, positive behaviour					
I rarely, if ever, criticize my physical appearance					
I rarely, if ever, wish I was someone else					

Total score (out of 40) _____
Source: Neale *et al.* 2009.

Self-regard is linked with self-esteem, which in turn is associated with our feelings of self-worth. Self-efficacy is also another important part of building your strengths. It relates to your belief in your ability to achieve your aims. Two questions help to make the distinction between self-esteem and self-efficacy clear. For example, 'What am I worth?' is clearly a different question from 'How likely is it that I will succeed?'

Building a personal positive portfolio

I am trying to make a case for a reflective practice that strikes a balance between reflecting on problems, and practices that help to build strengths such as positivity. In this

TABLE 4.4 Ten positive emotions for your positive portfolio

Reflect upon and then include items that evoke **JOY**. 1. When have you felt safe, relaxed and joyful, glad about what was happening at that moment? 2. When have things really gone your way, perhaps even better than you expected?
Reflect upon and then include items that evoke **GRATITUDE**. 1. When have you felt grateful or thankful, deeply appreciative of someone or something? 2. When has someone gone out of their way to do something good for you?
Reflect upon and then include items that evoke **CALMNESS**. 1. When have you felt fully at peace, truly content with your life at that point? 2. When does your body feel completely relaxed, with all your physical tensions melted away?
Reflect upon and then include items that evoke **INTEREST**. 1. When have you felt intensely open and alive, as you concentrate on something that fascinates you? 2. When have you felt an intense desire to explore and learn more about something of real interest to you?
Reflect upon, and then include items that evoke **HOPE**. 1. When you have felt hopeful and optimistic, encouraged by the possibilities of something good happening? 2. When have you been faced with uncertainty, but still somehow believed that things would change for the better?
Reflect upon and then include items that evoke **PRIDE**. 1. When have you felt most proud of yourself and your achievements?. 2. When have you achieved something great through your own efforts?
Reflect upon and then include items that evoke **AMUSEMENT**. 1. What really amuses you? 2. When have you, and others, infected each other with laughter?
Reflect upon and then include items that evoke **INSPIRATION**. 1. What has caused you to make even more effort to achieve something you never thought you could? 2. When have you seen someone perform, or act, better than you ever imagined possible?
Reflect upon and then include items that evoke **AWE**. 1. When have you felt overwhelmed by greatness, or by beauty on a BIG scale? 2. When have you felt part of something much larger than yourself?
Reflect upon and then include items that evoke **LOVE**. 1. When do you most readily feel the warmth of love between you and another? 2. When does a relationship of yours evoke one of the other forms of positivity – joy, gratitude, calmness (serenity), interest, hope, pride, amusement, inspiration, or awe?

way, this kind of reflective practice celebrates the elevation of positive emotions. So why not try to build your personal positive portfolio? (Melander-Wikman and Ghaye 2010). You might structure the process around ten forms of positivity. You might like to think of them as ten positive emotions. One or more might be the focus of your portfolio. In Table 4.4, each positive emotion is illustrated with two questions to get you reflecting. Write notes to yourself as you answer them. What memories and images come to mind? After you've pulled together some ideas, think about how you might go on a 'treasure hunt' – for example, to find the best photos, words, sounds and objects to create each section in your portfolio. Perhaps a song or video clip would evoke a very positive feeling; or perhaps a scent, a taste or a tactile sensation. Think about how you might create your portfolio with care and creativity. Remember:

1. Your personal positive portfolio is a gift to yourself.
2. You may feel more comfortable with some forms of positivity than others!
3. You don't have to build a personal positive portfolio that includes all ten emotions in Table 4.4. You might be inspired to start with a small selection. But try to develop an appreciation of the reason(s) for your choice.
4. In certain circumstances, it might be a good idea to talk about the content of your portfolio with others, to share the content and to exchange portfolios.

Positivity and job satisfaction

Positivity, as a strength, is also linked with job satisfaction. When people use their strengths in their job, most of the time, it is not surprising that they feel more positive about work. They get more pleasure from it, and find it more meaningful. So two key reflective questions become, 'What percentage of last week did you spend doing things that you really like to do?' Or 'What percentage of last week did you spend playing to your strengths?' Answering these two questions mean that you have been able to identify how and where particular strengths that you feel you have can be used in your current role. If you draw a blank with this, you may wish to reflect upon these questions: 'How far are there missed opportunities, in your current role, where you could, in different circumstances, spend more time using particular strengths?' Or 'What new situations can you put yourself in, at work, to use particular strengths that you possess?' Or, finally, 'How could you expand your current role to make better use of particular strengths?'

Buckingham (2007) talks a lot about job satisfaction. He suggests that it is linked with the twin strategy of playing to your strengths *and* cutting out your weaknesses. If you can't cut them out, can't fix them, then perhaps, with practice, you might be able to contain them. The worst thing is hearing yourself say, 'I wish never to have to do this type of activity again.'

> While it may feel like your entire job is contaminated, that's probably not true. In reality, just a few activities are ruining your days, corrupting everything else in your job. By identifying, naming and tagging them (that is problems or weaknesses) you restore them to their actual size: little puffs of annoyance, not a radioactive haze.
>
> (Buckingham 2007:156)

Buckingham (2007) suggests four practical actions to stop or to contain your weaknesses:

1. **S**top doing the activity and see if anyone notices or cares
2. **T**eam up with someone who is strengthened by the very activity that weakens you
3. **O**ffer up one of your strengths, and gradually steer your job toward this strength and away from the weakness
4. **P**erceive your weakness for a different perspective.

(Buckingham 2007:175)

In this chapter of the book I am trying to set out a new kind of reflective practice that is more strengths-based. In doing so, I am inviting you to reflect upon the links you may have, in your working life, between positive feelings (like job satisfaction) and your actual performance or practice. Neale *et al.* (2009) devised a clever way to reflect upon links such as these. They developed a simple but powerful 2×2 matrix as a catalyst that enables us to reflect, in a systematic way, on the links between job satisfaction and level of performance. This is shown in Figure 4.3.

Now take a look at Figure 4.4. Reflect on your current job. Where would you place yourself in this blank matrix and why?

Reflection-for-resilience

Resilience is a strength, so it is worth reflecting upon. At work you may have noticed that some colleagues are simply less fazed by setbacks than others; clearly show more resilience, whatever life throws at them, than others. People like this are able to learn

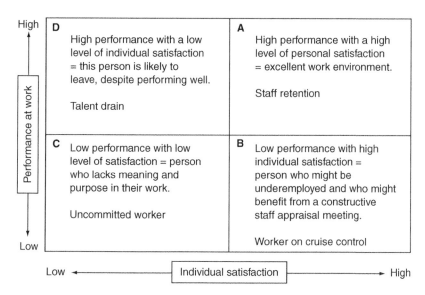

FIGURE 4.3 The links between individual job satisfaction and performance at work (after Neale *et al.* 2009:132)

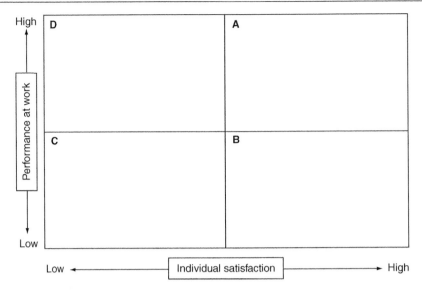

FIGURE 4.4 Your job satisfaction and performance at work (after Neale *et al.* 2009:132)

from their experience, be adaptable and flexible according to the demands of their work environment, are energized rather than drained by crises and problems, and other people actively choose to collaborate with them (Clarke and Nicholson 2010). Some people are more resilient than others, but why? Why do some people seem better able to bounce back from whatever life throws at them than others? We know that individuals respond differently to different events. So what's the key? Some people seem more able to exploit the positive events in their life. Some are proactive problem-solvers. Some have a tendency to tackle issues rather than avoid them. Some people seem to have a radar system that provides them with information regarding the need to change. Some seem able to keep things in perspective and see beyond the immediate pressures of their everyday working life. And, crucially, some know where to look for assistance. Arguably, these are some of the characteristics of resilient people. Reflection and strengths-based practices can play an important role in building resilience. One way to think about resilience is as the ability not to see failure (or failing) as something to dwell on, but rather as an opportunity to learn from and to move forward, accepting that failure is a part of life. If this sounds a bit negative, here is another view. We could argue that resilience is based on two things: (1) a belief in and commitment to what you're doing, and (2) confidence that you can make things better. There are at least four implications of taking this view. I suggest they are:

1. being comfortable with who you are;
2. being clear about your values;
3. having other interests which provides a source of relief, even escape, and that help you get a sense of perspective on things;
4. having drive and determination, matched with realistic optimism – in life and work, we can't win all the battles!

A further view of resilience as a strength is that it is about keeping going in stressful situations, about bouncing back and not allowing yourself to become bogged down.

Reflection on your level of self-esteem

In order to demonstrate resilience, you need a reasonably high level of self-esteem. You have to feel a sense of self-worth and self-regard in order to have a belief in your own abilities (self-efficacy). Without this, most of us struggle to find the necessary confidence and drive to bounce back from challenging situations and to be the best that we can each working day. Having high self-esteem, and especially if it is a stable resource for you, is a strength – so again, it is worth reflecting upon. Some psychologists say that high but fragile levels of self-esteem lead to narcissism, or excessive self-love based on ego. This is a danger. Self-esteem, as a strength, also implies a degree of contentment – a capacity for happiness, not necessarily with your work environment, but with yourself. This helps you to avoid taking things personally, and enables you to forgive others more readily. Self-esteem is also associated with having a protective sense of perspective, which counteracts the tendency for paranoid thinking to develop ('Why is it only me that this happens to?') and encourages the process of bouncing back ('What am I going to do to make this situation better?'). Self-esteem can help us be more resilient, so it is worth reflecting on.

Reflection on your level of self-efficacy

So, why is self-efficacy important when it comes to resilience? Well, first and foremost, in order to demonstrate resilience you need a challenging situation to deal with. People with high self-efficacy are more likely to be excited by challenges and view difficult tasks or situations as diversions rather than roadblocks. They are not knocked off course easily. Undaunted by the unknown, they take broad view of the task in hand in order to establish the best way forward. And they demonstrate significant tenacity in dealing with problems. People with low self-efficacy, on the other hand, assume that tasks are harder than they are. They worry about encountering failure, rather than focusing on achieving success. They may prepare thoroughly, but since they tend to take a narrow (and sometimes short-sighted) view of a challenge, their planning is not always focused on the right priorities (Clarke and Nicholson 2010). So how do you feel about your level of self-efficacy?

A strengths-based reflective practice can help you build a positive view of yourself. In doing so, it is important to look for evidence of success, to celebrate this, and work hard to get things in perspective, treating a minor setback as just that – a setback – not a permanent roadblock to development. Using this as your foundation, you might benefit from building your sense of self, through strengths-based reflective practices, in terms of three key elements:

1. self-awareness
2. self-motivation
3. self-affirmation.

Self-awareness

A reflective practice, of the kind I am describing in this chapter, can be used to help you develop a realistic view of how other people perceive you, rather than relying on your own view of yourself and your capabilities. There is a practice called the *reflected best-self* that helps with this, and which I discuss a little later. The reflected best-self (RBS) helps you place yourself, realistically on the continuum ranging from self-deprecation (running yourself down) to self-aggrandisement (bigging yourself up). The RBS involves seeking feedback from those people whose judgement you trust, as well as using empathy to anticipate other people's reactions to what you say – not least about yourself. Self-awareness is the foundation stone on which self-esteem and self-efficacy rest.

Self-motivation

Self-motivation is another strength. How much do you have? It is the force which causes us to act in order to achieve a goal, and then to sustain that action until successful. Resilient people are self-starting. They don't rely on others to motivate them. Would you describe yourself in this way? While we might procrastinate a little, or reflect on the best way of approaching a task, those who have this strength get on and do things, reasonably quickly. They can then sustain the positive action until the job is done.

Self-affirmation

In building self-esteem and self-efficacy, it is not enough merely to create success; you must also give yourself credit for having done so. This is often a hard thing for us to acknowledge. So how do you give yourself credit? How to you praise yourself? This is not an act of self-indulgence, unless greatly overdone. It is a way of saying to yourself, well done, good job, and you should be proud of what you have achieved. In work-places where there is a real culture of appreciation, this affirmation can come naturally from colleagues. When was the last time your line manager came up to you and said, 'Well done, good job, you should be proud of what you have done?'

Developing your resilience through reflection

One of the first things we have to do is to ask ourselves the question, 'In what situations do I feel in/out of control?' In the busy worlds where teaching and learning take place, knowing what you can and can't control becomes critical. What needs to be controlled and what doesn't, what should be controlled and what can be left alone, are also important. For example, what does the term 'classroom control' actually mean? One of the most basic reasons why taking control, appropriately and in certain circumstances, increases your resilience is that if you feel you are not in the driving seat, you may find it more difficult to reach the various levers you need, in the future, to get back on course following a setback. For example, student teachers are often urged to 'take control' early on in their school placement experience, thereby setting their standards. The thinking goes that if they do this, they may have fewer problems with class-room control later. Is this a myth or a reality, I wonder? There is an important difference between *feeling* in control at work, and not necessarily *exercising* control. However, refusing to take control, or considering yourself helpless, is a vicious and depressive circle that can be learnt, just as choosing to take control can also be learnt. This is what Martin Seligman (2006) called 'learned helplessness' – the idea that some-one feels unable to exert influence or control, even when any obstacles to doing so have been removed. Being able to take control is one way of boosting your self-confidence and optimism. Here are five more:

1. *Think or talk things through.* Many people like to reflect alone and calmly analyse the facts of the situation, without allowing emotion to cloud their judgement. Some people find that it helps to write everything down, like in a reflective journal, perhaps under headings, continually asking the question, 'what can I learn from this'? They might believe that this is the reflective method for them. Others, however, recognize the benefits of talking things through, either with those who have been directly involved in the issue or with someone more impartial. This could be a trusted confidant or a friend. There are limits to learning alone.

2. *Get good at managing conflict.* Resilient people manage conflict well. They have the strength of character not to take criticism and differences of opinion personally (unless, of course, the comments *are* intended to be personal). They also have the wisdom to know what needs to be done – do they need to confront the conflict, or is it best to let things go, if only for a while? Being able to reflect positively on a conflict situation is a strength. In such situations, it is important to know how assertive you feel you need to be, and how cooperative. It is absolutely imperative to reflect upon your personal threshold, how much pressure you can take, what type of challenge is likely to increase your stress to an uncomfortable level, and what the warning signs are.

3. *Visualize success.* A key characteristic of resilient people is that they create their own vision of success. Merely being in possession of this vision helps them to achieve their goals because it provides a clear sense of where they're headed, and enables them subconsciously to work towards it. But it must be based on what is currently possible. Resilient people recognize that there is a fine line between goals or ambi-tions being stretching, and them being unrealistic. They know where to draw this line.

4. *Build a strength network.* It is a strength, not a weakness, to ask for help. So how good are you at doing this? Do you know when to reach out and ask others for help? How far do you have a clear idea of who the best person would be to turn to, in any particular situation? What would it take to build a strength network? What would each person in this network offer you and others? Try to map it out.

5. *Practice the flip-it process.* Heppell (2009) wrote a very practical and useful book called *Flip it: How to get the best out of everything.* Arguably, it should be on all read-ing lists for reflective practitioners who wish to use more strengths-based practices. 'Flipping it' is a process which simply involves turning things over with the inten-tion to try to see them differently. Literally flipping it! Turning what's wrong into what's right; turning a mistake into an opportunity to learn something positive;

TABLE 4.5 Flipping it as a reflective practice

I AM THINKING	I FLIPPED IT
I am the victim of my personal history	• I can take control of my own destiny – and will
There's so much to do, it's not even worth trying	• Let me break the problem down and work out which parts can be tackled now
I only get one shot at this	•
There's only one a right answer to this	•
I am on my own when I do this	•
This isn't fair	• There's no point complaining, I need to get on and put things right
I'm not very practical	•
Why don't they understand?	•
I don't think this is going to be successful	•
I need to fix my weaknesses	•

turning thoughts like 'I'm not good at working to deadlines' into 'I can organize my time better so that I prioritize the important things over the urgent ones.' Flipping it is allied to the process of re-framing. In Table 4.5, I have combined, modified and extended the work of Heppell (2009) and Clarke and Nicholson (2010). See how far you can fill in the blanks. How might you extend the table with your own thoughts?

Building your reflected best-self (RBS) portrait

Being a 'great' teacher, coach, mentor or leader is a value-laden term. In Ghaye *et al.* (2009) we suggested that it is not simply about being extraordinary, being in a position of honour or glory, or even being successful in other people's eyes. We suggested that the essence of this is being *true-to-self*. Central to this is acting with integrity and care. The term the 'best-self' (Glickman 2002) describes knowing and acting in this way. This, of course, is not at all easy. It requires at least the *discovery* of what 'the best' means to those involved (e.g., the students, team, organization); an *attitude* that stops those involved from settling for second best (this is different from doing the best we can in the prevailing circumstances); the *ability* to optimize collective (educational) wisdom, talent, resources and motivation; and the *determination* to avoid self-sabotage by only addressing what's not working and thinking that the sting of criticism is the only way to performance improvement. We know that when the stakes are high we often pay keen attention to negative feedback, and all those involved get drawn into deficit-based conversations. It is a paradox of human psychology that while we remember criticism, we respond well to praise. Arguably, the former can make us nervous, fearful, defensive and anxious. This, of course, can in a way be motivating. The latter can produce confidence and *broaden* our momentary thought–action repertoire (Fredrickson and Branigan 2005). Praise can spark the urge to perform harder, better and differently. It can help build resilience. The broadened mindset that arises from positive feedback and strengths-based reflective conversations can be contrasted with the narrowed mindset sparked by many negative emotions and deficit-based feedback (i.e., specific action tendencies such as attack or flee, and feelings such as anxiety and anger). There is a second proposition that concerns the consequences of broadening an individual's momentary thought–action repertoire. It is that a strengths-based reflective practice to improve performance can encourage the doing of things differently and can promote more meaningful social bonds between teacher and learner. This can, in turn, *build* the learner's personal resources. So what can we take from this? Maybe positive emotions should not just be end-states in themselves. Positive emotions need to be engendered through strengths-based reflective practices, and these also provide a means to achieve improvements in performance. Additionally, I suggest, there are four mutually supportive 'enablers' that all those involved in performance improvement and better learning need to develop. They are the ability to build and sustain:

- a *positive atmosphere* amongst all those involved, based upon feelings such as optimism and enjoyment;
- *positive relationships* built upon trust, courage, empowerment and high-quality connections/networks (Cassidy *et al.* 2009);
- *positive communication* fuelled by 'best-self' and appreciative feedback;
- *positive meaning* so that everyone involved knows and understands the direction of travel.

When reflecting upon these enablers, it is important to ask the question, 'positive to whom?' Those who advocate more strengths-based approaches to learning through reflection (Seligman 2002, Chaffee 2005, Ghaye *et al.* 2008) focus on improving performance and learning by focusing on the positives, understanding what success means to those involved, understanding the root causes of successful action, and then amplifying the positive aspects of it.

So what is this important process of the 'reflected best-self?' Coe (2009:3) talks about the best-self in this way: 'Aiming for excellence is not so much about gratifying the ego (beating everyone else for the sake of it) as the desire to see how far you can get, how much you can do – to become the best you can be.' The notion of the reflected best-self is an expansion of this. For all those involved in improving performance and the quality of educational experiences, reflecting on those moments when you felt that your best-self was brought to light, affirmed by others and put into practice, is an important part of developing a 'portrait' of who you are (and what you do) when at your personal best. Self and team reflection-on-practice is a process where these portraits can be made explicit and awareness developed about how and why these portraits change over time. These best-self portraits serve both as an anchor and a beacon, a personal touchstone of who you are, and a guide for who you can become (e.g., a university graduate, a winner, a great teacher). The notion of the reflected best-self emanates from work at the University of Michigan. It is actively informed by positive psychology (Seligman and Csikszentmihalyi 2000), by research which shows how individuals change their conceptions of themselves through socially embedded experiences and resources (Tice and Wallace 2003), and by research on the relational context in which individuals find themselves (Bradbury and Lichtenstein 2000, Dutton and Heaphy

2003). This has a major effect on how we define and feel about ourselves. The prefix word, 'reflected', is hugely significant, as it emphasizes that the portrait is based on perceptions of how others perceive us. These 'others' may be family members, peers, team mates, teachers, coaches, managers, and so on. This conception goes beyond the 'Snow White' approach to reflective practice, which starts and ends with looking at oneself in a mirror and asking, 'Mirror, mirror on the wall, who is the best (teacher) of them all?' The word 'best' is positively aligned with many strengths-based approaches to performance improvement (Ghaye *et al.*, 2008), and refers to the gifts and talents that educators, for example, bring to a particular situation (e.g., in preparing students for their exams, giving a consoling word after a poor performance). The reflected best-self portrait is not a response to the question, 'When I am at my best I...', but a response to the question answered by others – namely, 'When I see you at your best you...' It is the things we do, or exude, when at our best and as perceived by others. Of course, others' perceptions of us may not always be the 'truth' on the matter. Socio-cultural norms and rules, workplace cultures, learned behaviours and often humility can inhibit people's willingness to ask others to identify sources of strength. It can be uncomfortable to ask others, 'What do you think I'm best at?', or 'What am I doing when you think I am being the best I can be'?

Choose a good friend or trusted colleague. Then ask *yourself*:

1.   When I am at my best I...

Now ask your friend or colleague:

2.   When you see me at my best, what am I doing?

Now compare your two responses. What are you learning?

A 'jolt' can change your reflected best-self portrait. A jolt has two meanings. There is a challenging jolt and an appreciative jolt. Simply put, a jolt is an experience which causes us to consciously pause (if only momentarily) and reflect upon a current encounter or experience. In that moment, which may happen in the blink of an eye, some kind of conscious learning occurs. It's a moment where something is confirmed or a routine is disrupted; a moment when the way we are thinking about ourselves (e.g., as good teachers, or an exam failure) is challenged. A jolt therefore should not necessarily connote something negative. It might be a positive experience that jogs us out of a routine and prompts us to think about ourselves in new ways. The timing of jolts is often crucial in the way they prompt changes in the RBS portrait. If we have low levels of self-esteem, for example, jolts can be dismissed as irrelevant and unnecessary. Some jolts (such as the sudden change of teacher) can be met with a sense of anxiety, fear and dread with a sense of relief and optimism by some students.

Figure 4.5 shows how jolts work in practice. It is illustrated with an example from coach education (Ghaye *et al.* 2009). The vertical axis describes two *kinds* of jolt: a jolt as a *challenge*, and an *appreciative* jolt. In this instance, the former is a structured and planned-for opportunity. The latter is spontaneous, and often helps build self-esteem and self-efficacy. The horizontal axis describes the *context* (or situation) in which the jolt may be experienced, referring to *formal* and *informal* jolts. The former is organiza-

Kinds of jolt

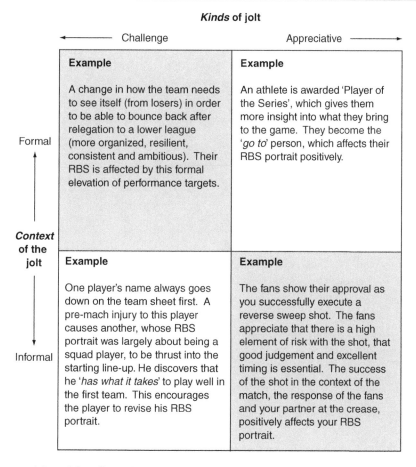

FIGURE 4.5 Jolts and the reflected best-self

tionally sanctioned and approved – for example, by school rules or norms. The latter arise unexpectedly, out of the blue.

Now take a look at Figure 4.6. Reflect on your current job. See how far you can complete the figure with examples drawn from your own practice and encounters with others. What have been the significant 'jolts' to your reflected best-self portrait?

Reflection-for-optimism

Do you feel you tend to lean towards the 'glass half empty' mindset, rather than the 'glass half full'? Do you tend to see the silver lining? Do you feel you are generally more pessimistic than optimistic? Like resilience, optimism can be regarded as a strength. So this is worth reflecting upon. Optimism is one of the most important characteristics of resilient people. It is really important to try to look on the bright side of things, to try to feel hopeful when things seem to be going wrong. Knowing your strengths and playing to them as much as you can nourishes a feeling of optimism. It is possible to learn to be optimistic.

Kinds of jolt

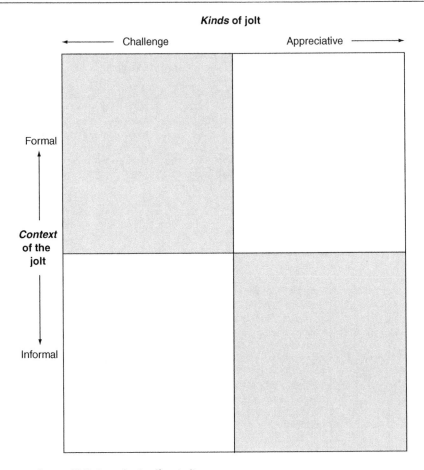

FIGURE 4.6 Personal jolts to my best-self portrait

> Optimists believe that things are getting better all the time, and not necessarily just for themselves, but for others close to them and for society in general. Optimists are therefore likely to view change positively, and to be more confident about what the future holds – and that they will be able to cope with it.
>
> (Clarke and Nicholson 2010:49–50).

Optimism can also enhance your self-belief and promote a 'can-do' attitude. And, as I have suggested earlier in this second edition, positive thinking can encourage positive action. So optimism is an energizing force, while pessimism tends to be a debilitating one. We do, however, have to be a little careful about being optimistic. Optimism can be a powerful and positive force when it is pragmatic, but it can turn into something less desirable. For example, misplaced or blind optimism (based on fantasy rather than grounded in reality) and overdone optimism (a refusal to abandon a positive view when the evidence on which it was based turns out to be ill-founded) are not good qualities.

Can strengths become weaknesses?

Arguably, for effective teaching and learning, and also in the context of lifelong learning, there is a need to have a repertoire of *different* strengths to be successful, as circumstances change over time. It is possible to overuse existing strengths, when they are no longer the ones needed in this situation. For example, I once had a teacher who wrote beautifully on a chalk-board and on flip-chart paper with felt-tip pens. She could do wonderful drawings with coloured chalk sticks. With the advent of computers and interactive whiteboards, she found that her existing strengths (using chalk and, later, A1-sized flip-chart paper) became redundant. The situation she found herself in required a different skill set. Kaiser (2009:45) puts it this way:

> How might things have been different had they acquired new strengths along the way rather than clinging to, and over-relying on, what had made them successful in the past? As situations change, the development of new strengths (and often the letting go of old ones), may be required. People are inclined to stick with their strengths (and the more successful they are, the more likely people are to stay with doing what they know).

The moral of this story is that playing people to our strengths might look like an effective strategy until the situation changes and the old strengths no longer serve us well. If everything remained the same – ourselves, our colleagues, our workplace – then whatever set of strengths was effective in that situation would never need to change. It would be a sensible strategy to focus on those strengths and reinforce them. But things change over time, so different strengths are necessary to successfully meet the different kinds of challenges that confront us in teaching and learning. In Figure 4.7, I have set out some strengths that you may feel you have. On the left-hand side of Figure 4.7, I have suggested how a strength, in a different set of circumstances, might be perceived as a weakness. Focus on those strengths that take your eye. What circumstances do you think give rise to the strength being seen as a weakness?

McCall and Lombardo (1983), Judge *et al.* (2002), Hodges and Clifton (2004) and Cucina and Vasilopoulos (2005) all warn against developing and then sticking to a set of strengths, especially in the context of change. They illustrate this with reference to the very laudable professional quality of conscientiousness. They argue that some believe that conscientiousness is the most important personality characteristic driving job performance. Conscientiousness is important in stable environments, where consistency is valuable. They go on to suggest that conscientious people tend to be rigid and inflexible, and adapt poorly to change.

A strengths-based reflective practice for teaching and learning

At this point in the chapter I wish to bring everything together, regarding a more strengths-based kind of reflective practice, in diagrammatic form. What follows are four linked diagrams which I hope provide a summary and enrichment of the main points in this chapter. I also hope they are self-explanatory. Each figure develops the previous one – so, for example, Figure 4.9 develops the content of Figure 4.8 and encapsulates

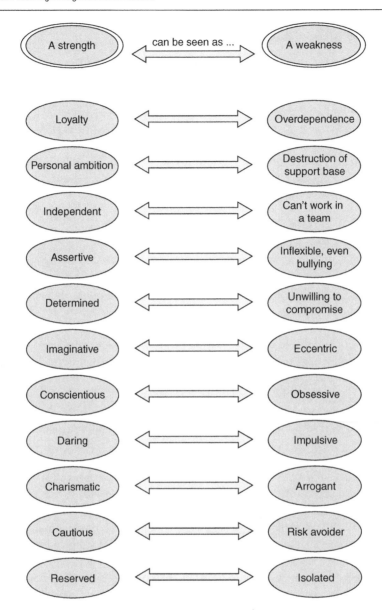

FIGURE 4.7 Can strengths become weaknesses?

the content of Figure 4.8 within it. Figure 4.8 focuses on the learner. Figure 4.9 focuses on the significance of reflecting on feelings and behaviours. Figure 4.10 re-states positivity as a strength and looks at the flip-side – that of de-motivation and disengagement. Finally, Figure 4.11 looks at how to amplify strengths and reduce deficits through reflection.

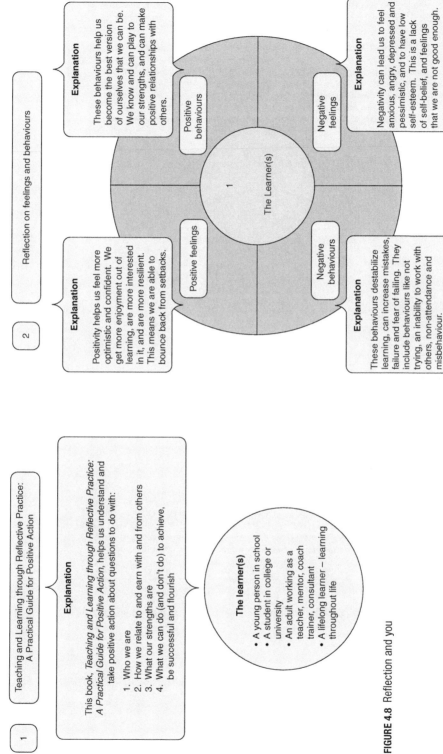

Reflection on feelings and behaviours

1

Teaching and Learning through Reflective Practice:
A Practical Guide for Positive Action

Explanation

This book, *Teaching and Learning through Reflective Practice:
A Practical Guide for Positive Action*, helps us understand and
take positive action about questions to do with:

1. Who we are
2. How we relate to and earn with and from others
3. What our strengths are
4. What we can do (and don't do) to achieve,
   be successful and flourish

The learner(s)

- A young person in school
- A student in college or
  university
- An adult working as a
  teacher, mentor, coach
  trainer, consultant
- A lifelong learner – learning
  throughout life

FIGURE 4.8 Reflection and you

2

The Learner(s)

1

Explanation

These behaviours help us
become the best version
of ourselves that we can be.
We know and can play to
our strengths, and can make
positive relationships with
others.

Explanation

Positivity helps us feel more
optimistic and confident. We
get more enjoyment out of
learning, and are more interested
in it, and are more resilient.
This means we are able to
bounce back from setbacks.

Positive
behaviours

Positive feelings

Negative
feelings

Negative
behaviours

Explanation

Negativity can lead us to feel
anxious, angry, depressed and
pessimistic, and to have low
self-esteem. This is a lack
of self-belief, and feelings
that we are not good enough.

Explanation

These behaviours destabilize
learning, can increase mistakes,
failure and fear of failing. They
include behaviours like not
trying, an inability to work with
others, non-attendance and
misbehaviour.

FIGURE 4.9 Reflection on feelings and behaviours

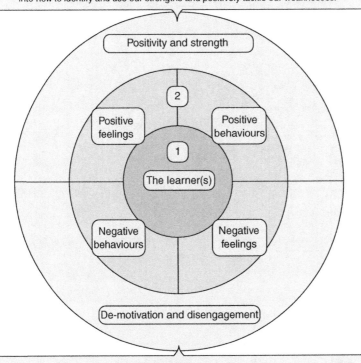

Reflection on positivity and strength, de-motivation and disengagement

Explanation
This includes reflection on how positive emotions and behaviours help to broaden our ideas about possible future actions, make us more receptive to alternative ideas and ways of doing things, and more creative. Positivity (both as a frame of mind and as a process of sensing and building on possibilities), linked with learning that strengthens (not weakens) us, helps us know what we are good at, what we love to do and how to tackle our weaknesses in the best way. More strength-based reflective practices can give us insight into how to identify and use our strengths and positively tackle our weaknesses.

Positivity and strength

2

Positive feelings

Positive behaviours

1

The learner(s)

Negative behaviours

Negative feelings

De-motivation and disengagement

Explanation
This includes reflection on the causes of failure or poor performance, on who was not good enough, on what was too difficult, unfair or not controllable. When learners' self-esteem is dependent upon others' perception of their cleverness, or their own view of their competence, every experience is something to be feared. It is feared because the learners' self-esteem is always at risk. Learners become avoidance-oriented, not success-focused. This can lead to demotivation and disengagement.

FIGURE 4.10 Reflection on positivity and strength, de-motivation and disengagement

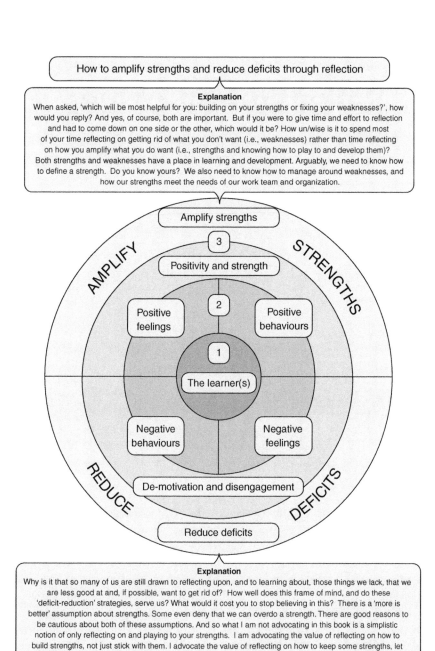

How to amplify strengths and reduce deficits through reflection

Explanation
When asked, 'which will be most helpful for you: building on your strengths or fixing your weaknesses?', how would you reply? And yes, of course, both are important. But if you were to give time and effort to reflection and had to come down on one side or the other, which would it be? How un/wise is it to spend most of your time reflecting on getting rid of what you don't want (i.e., weaknesses) rather than time reflecting on how you amplify what you do want (i.e., strengths and knowing how to play to and develop them)? Both strengths and weaknesses have a place in learning and development. Arguably, we need to know how to define a strength. Do you know yours? We also need to know how to manage around weaknesses, and how our strengths meet the needs of our work team and organization.

Amplify strengths

AMPLIFY

STRENGTHS

3

Positivity and strength

2

Positive feelings

Positive behaviours

1

The learner(s)

Negative behaviours

Negative feelings

REDUCE

DEFICITS

De-motivation and disengagement

Reduce deficits

Explanation
Why is it that so many of us are still drawn to reflecting upon, and to learning about, those things we lack, that we are less good at and, if possible, want to get rid of? How well does this frame of mind, and do these 'deficit-reduction' strategies, serve us? What would it cost you to stop believing in this? There is a 'more is better' assumption about strengths. Some even deny that we can overdo a strength. There are good reasons to be cautious about both of these assumptions. And so what I am not advocating in this book is a simplistic notion of only reflecting on and playing to your strengths. I am advocating the value of reflecting on how to build strengths, not just stick with them. I advocate the value of reflecting on how to keep some strengths, let others go and develop new ones. This is consistent with the view that we can learn, do grow and will change. Reflective practices are the catalyst for this.

FIGURE 4.11 How to amplify and reduce deficits through reflection

5

Reflection-on-values

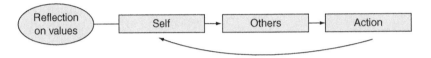

FIGURE 5.1 Reflection-on-values

What kind of teacher am I?

This is a challenging question. You should not be drawn into thinking that this is a simple, obvious and straightforward one to answer. To answer it, we have to be honest with ourselves and have an ability to reflect on what we do and why we teach in a particular way. Describing what we do is a good starting point; after this we need to move on to trying to explain and then justify our teaching, both to ourselves and to others when called upon to do so. Our values play a key role in this process.

Throughout our teaching careers we think and behave in certain ways and believe in certain things, such as how far our teaching can be called 'educational', about what we can offer children and what our capabilities are. What we do, think, and feel about teaching constitute our sense of professional identity. We can reveal and communicate this identity when we address and articulate an answer to the question, 'So what kind of teacher am I?' To begin to tackle this question, we need to look at what we do. Sometimes teachers talk in specific terms – for example, 'I am a specialist in teaching English and I am very confident in assessing and diagnosing children's reading skills through the use of miscue analysis with my Year 2 class.' At other times teachers may convey what they do in more general terms – for example, 'I try to give every child in my Year 2 class the opportunity to achieve their full potential.'

Describing what we do is a good starting point in exploring the issue of being a professional. In doing this, we are often making the tacit explicit (Polanyi 1962, Day 1991). This is a process where we make the things that give our teaching its shape, direction and purpose more conscious, more knowable, and therefore more open to inspection and critique. If we reflect on these descriptions of practice, we give ourselves the chance to learn from our experiences of teaching. This can help to move our practice forward.

If we look at our own teaching, or if others observe what we do, we should expect them to see an effort being made to put into practice what we value. We might not always achieve this to our full satisfaction; knowing our values is therefore very important. But this process of knowing is not always an easy one. Often this knowing remains rather unconscious. We often hear teachers say 'we do what we do but we are not that good at articulating why we do it that way'. Our professional values therefore provide us with reasons for teaching in particular ways.

Whilst working at the University of Worcester, Ghaye and Ghaye (1998) asked all final-year primary school students to undertake an assignment where they had to respond to the question: 'What kind of teacher do I want to be?' In this account, they had to state and justify their professional values. They subjected the scripts of 140 students to content analysis, and found that many values were being expressed and in many forms. These values were to do with things such as being enthusiastic and stimulating; being tolerant, fair and respectful; praising and encouraging children; and so on. Five common value 'clusters' emerged which arguably gave this cohort its sense of purpose and professional identity:

1. *Developing a sense of community* – for example, consideration for other people, trust, honesty, cooperative learning, belonging and togetherness;
2. *Exercising care and compassion* – for example, with regard to enhancing pupils' self-esteem, being fair and genuine, and making pupils feel secure through clear rules and routines;
3. *Fostering pupil self-determination and participation* – for example, through developing autonomous learning, self-reliance and a sense of pupil empowerment;
4. *Respect for human diversity* – for example, pupils being valued as individuals and treated as equals, curriculum differentiation, pupil identity and rights, interpersonal acceptance;
5. *Professional demeanour* – for example, being committed, passionate, reflective, enthusiastic, motivating, approachable, trustworthy and a good listener.

Interestingly, some of these values are scrutinized as part of OFSTED inspections and the way schools help to develop pupils' 'attitudes, behaviour and personal development'. For example, inspectors look out for the extent to which pupils:

- behave well in and around school, are courteous and trustworthy and show respect for property;
- form constructive relationships with one another, with teachers and other adults and work collaboratively when required;
- show respect for other people's feelings, values and beliefs ... show initiative .... willing to take responsibility (OFSTED 1995a:17).

In clarifying your allegiance to your professional values, you might find that you are in a state of 'dynamic equilibrium'. By this I mean that you do not become attached to one set of unchanging values, but that your values tend to move around and become modified as you develop more experience and insight, and as the contexts in which you work change. As we search for greater self-understanding, more robust rationales for what we do and greater consistency in trying to live our values out in our teaching, a sense that all our values are static and fixed entities may be far from our lived reality. Our values can and do change. This is quite natural. At the point of career entry, arguably, student teachers need to have a set of personally-owned professional values that they can articulate and defend, and know how to respond in school when encountering others who hold conflicting and alternative values equally as strongly as themselves.

> We cannot base our work together for the common good on reticence, embarrassment and incoherent mumbling, yet this is the state into which the discussion of morals and values has descended in many parts of Western society today. The main culprit is the popular cultural assumption that to try to define something as good and right in an absolute sense is an unwarranted and potentially oppressive incursion into a domain which should be purely private. What is right is simply what feels right to me. What is good is simply a matter of individual opinion.
>
> (Carey 1997:3)

In order to be called professional and to be convincing about what we do, we have to reflect on what we are doing and be appropriately responsive to what is happening around us in our classroom and school. However, it is no good for teachers to simply say that they are doing a good job; proclaiming this is not enough. Good practice needs to be demonstrated. The art of teaching is one that needs constant renewal and reworking. In order that it does not disintegrate, it is imperative that this process coheres around a set of educational values that can be justified by being held under constant review and communicated clearly and convincingly. A teacher's values should be derived from the nature of what constitutes effective and ethical practice. To reach this position, we have to understand and question the purposes of education.

> The assumed relationship between values and practice stands in need, then, of considerable qualification and refinement ... The values implicit in ... practice have to be actively sought out and acknowledged. From this perspective, teaching is a profession only insofar as the educational values it espouses in theory are professed in – and through – its practice. The prime task for teachers as professionals, therefore, is to work out their educational values, not in isolation and abstraction but in collaboration with colleagues and amid the complexities of school life.
>
> (Nixon 1995:220)

Teresa is an experienced teacher who has created a description (Lehane 1992) of some of her work with children who have profound and multiple learning difficulties. She expresses her values in the following way:

> VALUE 1: 'I believe children's experience of school should be happy and positive. To profoundly handicapped children, the education system and the classroom can be fairly meaningless ideas.'
> VALUE 2: 'I want children to achieve. Before 1970 they were considered 'ineducable' and excluded from the education system ... I am committed to the children's progress and education as opposed to care alone.'

VALUE 3: 'I also believe in the child-centred interactive approach where children are encouraged to follow their own interests and wishes through play and inter-action, and where education aims to enhance experience and personal growth rather than simply building up skills or knowledge.'

Teresa's values illustrate why she works with children in the way she does. Our profes-sional values therefore provide us with reasons for teaching in particular ways. The fol-lowing scenario in Teresa's classroom describes her practice and her reflections on the way she relates to one particular child.

Kevin is nine years old. Teresa introduces her account with a brief sketch of him – a sketch which she radically redraws after reflecting on her teaching and asking herself a modified Smyth (1991) question. She does not think it appropriate to ask the initial question suggested by Smyth – namely, 'What do I do?' – but, in the context of her teaching, she argues that the question 'What do *we* do?' is more appropriate and power-ful. This is Teresa's early thumbnail sketch of Kevin.

Kevin is 9 years old and cortically blind but walks with help and splashes around the swimming pool with armbands. Kevin can communicate and although his speech is limited and repetitive he makes relationships with his carers. Kevin needs and demands a great deal of attention. He explores the environment with his hands but is unaware of his own strength, cheerfully destroying playthings. Kevin needs help to feed himself with a spoon. He is doubly incontinent and epileptic.

In one account of part of her work with Kevin, called 'one wet Tuesday afternoon', Teresa describes how she is trying to teach Kevin to locate and move towards the sound of an audible ball. Teresa placed a video camera on a tripod in the corner of her classroom. She often videotaped some of her teaching so that she could reflect upon it later, interrogate it, and get a better sense of herself as a teacher. Teresa later reflected on her teaching, and called the account that she wrote from watching the videotape, 'Missing the best bits'. Here is an extract from that account.

Missing the best bits

Work with Kevin starts abruptly with me announcing, 'We'll go and find your ball.' … When he then moves from crouching to a high kneeling position I say, 'good kneeling', but on reflection Kevin's action looked like a communicative ges-ture of joining in than mere motor action. Later when the toy organ stops working and I say so, Kevin says 'oh dear' … again I missed it perhaps because Kevin often says this as a catchphrase. However on this occasion the words were meaningful and deserved a response to underline the fact.

I omit to let Kevin feel the ball at the start of the activity, one of his few ways of working out what is going on. Kevin successfully locates the ball. I reward him with an enthusiastic, 'good boy, well done' but did not reinforce the meaning of the situation by saying what he had done. The task is only one of seeking, not of doing anything with the ball.

I missed opportunities to engage Kevin's attention and activity. When guiding him to the ball I could have asked him to give me his hand rather than just grasping it. I do not control background noise for a task in which audibility is crucial and I leave Tim (and James) without input for minutes at a time. When moving away for a few moments to 'troubleshoot' I do not explain this to Kevin and leave and return unannounced, potentially unnerving for a blind child.

There is a beautiful clip of film where Kevin and James interact with each other, a notoriously rare event for children with profound and multiple learning difficulties. To my shame, although I am working with Tim, I clearly see this happening and yet I take no affirming action and intervene simply to take control when the contact becomes rough. This effectively ends the interaction.

The contact begins with Kevin trying to further inflate a silver balloon (the inside of a wine box). Kevin rustles it. James snatches at and rustles it and then Kevin rustles it again and pulls it away. James shrieks and then Kevin pats him on the back, pulling the smaller child towards him. I could intervene sensitively at a number of points, for example I could encourage James to echo the pat on the back. Instead I simply pull the two boys slightly apart with the words, 'stop fighting'. On continued replaying of the video it can be seen that after initially pulling James, Kevin says, 'be careful', as if telling himself and then becomes gentler an instant before I intervene.

(Lehane 1992:55–6)

There is much to learn from this account. It is only through a commitment to reflect on her teaching that Teresa is able to become more aware that she is, in her words, 'missing the best bits'! Her account shows us how Teresa is putting some of the principles described in Chapter 3 into practice. For example, through reflection she is becoming aware that she could look at her practice in different ways. She knows that what she does with her children will serve certain interests, such as educational and personal ones. She is looking at videotapes of her own teaching which enable her to ask questions about what she is doing, or thinks she is doing. Teresa is also convinced that by doing these things she might see her teaching in new and different ways and, as a consequence of this, reshape and rebuild aspects of it so that she becomes even more effective in her work.

Later in her account Teresa explains how reflection on her teaching is helped by wearing different spectacles, or reflective lenses. She gives her spectacles different names because they do different things for her. There are, for example, her 'painful questions specs' that she uses to ask herself reflective questions such as 'What am I doing there?', 'Why am I doing it that way?' and 'How did it come to be like that?' She uses these glasses when she confronts herself and her own teaching. Then there are what she calls her 'professional values specs'. When she sees what she is doing with these on, she is looking particularly at the way she is trying to put her values into practice. Questions of value arise in almost every educational decision that we make. Our professional values then make us the kind of teacher that we are. They help us to answer the questions, 'What kind of teacher am I?' or 'What kind of teacher do I want to be?'

If you have experience of teaching children with profound and multiple learning difficulties, or if children with special educational needs are being included in your 'mainstream' school, you may empathize with Teresa's values. But because values are a very personal thing, you should not be surprised to find that different teachers have different values and that they hold these for certain reasons. It is unwise to assume that just because school staff work together, they share the same underlying values. The fact that they are different people with different backgrounds, expectations and career aspirations means that they may see the purposes of education as fulfilling different needs. Teachers have different perspectives on the purposes and processes of education. They therefore have different priorities, which leads to differences in values. The same can be said for each school, each Local Education Authority, and different governments. Expressing our values is one thing; the way values are perceived, interpreted and actioned by individual teachers and schools is something else. Haydon (1997) puts this point well when he says, 'the difficulty often faced by teachers lies not in outlining the values which a school stands for, but in recognising precisely what this endorsement will mean in practice, particularly if some of the values do not sit comfortably together' (Haydon 1997:11). An additional challenge for teachers is justifying particular values as being appropriate, ethical, moral and professional, given the context in which they work.

So what do you do?

Creating descriptions of our teaching fulfils two fundamental purposes. First, it creates a 'text' that we can interrogate by reflecting on it. Reflection has the power to change something that we might not fully understand or have control and influence over into something with more personal clarity, coherence and meaning. Second, the descriptions provide us with evidence of the values which form a rationale for our teaching. Most of us need some help to come to know our teaching in new and more meaningful ways. There are many reflective strategies and techniques available to us which I will present in detail later. One useful approach worth mentioning here is described by Boud *et al.* (1985). Their approach to learning through reflection-on-practice begins with a description of a teaching incident. This is followed by a series of steps which are designed to help us enhance our future practice. To get the most from their approach, we need to understand four key ideas around which the learning process coheres. These are:

- *association* – making links between the ideas and feelings we have about the teaching incident we are describing;
- *integration* – making sense of these associations in some way;
- *validation* – trying out these new ways of seeing and understanding teaching;
- *appropriation* – taking on board and retaining ownership of these new insights and learning so that we can use them to inform our future teaching.

Boud *et al.* state that practice can be explored by following these six steps:

1. Making a clear, succinct *description* of an incident from your teaching. What to describe is always a tricky issue. Finding something professionally significant is the important thing. As I have already mentioned, it does not have to be something in your practice that 'went wrong'! This step is about *returning to the experience*.

2. Giving an indication of how you felt about the incident and the *feelings* of any others involved (e.g., children, other staff, teaching assistants) as far as you are aware of them and can express them. This step is about *attending to feelings*.

3. Trying to make some sense of what you did and how you felt about it by *connecting* this incident to your previous knowledge and experience of similar incidents. This is about *associations*.

4. Being aware of any new teaching *ideas, insights or changes in values* that may be emerging as a consequence of linking and synthesizing aspects of this incident with your previous knowledge and teaching experience. This is about *integration*.

5. *Testing out* your new ideas. Develop an appropriate action plan (e.g., a lesson plan, units or schemes of work, planning for progression, and so on) and try to improve your teaching by putting your new insights into practice. This step is to do with *the process of validation*.

6. *Integrating and securing* your new ideas and insights into your practice so that they may serve to guide and give added justification to your future teaching. This step is about *appropriation*.

Boud *et al.* (1985) serve to remind us that knowing our practice is centrally about learning to reflect upon it, and that this process of reflection involves both looking back (returning to experience) and looking forwards. This means using our new understandings and appreciations to improve our future teaching. This is a most important point, as reflection is often caricatured as only a backward-looking process. Reflection-on-practice, as stated earlier, gives rise to many consequences. One of these is to inform and improve future action. Implicit in this statement, of course, is the assumption that we have a degree of control and ownership over what we do in school.

But what we do is principally influenced by three things. The first, and most fundamental, is our developing *sense of self*. This is made up of our personal histories of joys, achievements and sadnesses, as well as our future intentions and ambitions. Reflection of this kind emphasizes the centrality of professional experience in the process of 'understanding the self'. As teachers, we experience the world of school through our own particular forms of consciousness. Often 'we are conscious not only of a world about us but also of a world within of inner thoughts, feelings and reflections' (Stevens 1996:18). Reflection-on-practice does require us to remember things. Through reflective journal writing, significant-incident or encounter work, listening to audiotapes of ourselves and watching videos of our classroom teaching, for example, our remembering becomes something that we can re-experience and re-see. These and other ways of re-experiencing help us to look for patterns and consistencies as we strive to make sense of our experiences as teachers. 'Thus our conscious awareness is constituted and influenced by our cognitions, by our ways of thinking (as well as feeling). So we attribute meanings to events and responsibility for actions' (Stevens 1996:19). Arguably, reflection-on-practice should have a positive consequence so that it can and should be seen as much more than private contemplation and 'navel-gazing'. A way of putting this is that reflection should help us to do things, to initiate new and better actions and events. This process is often referred to as 'agency'. Reflection can help us develop a sense of agency. One consequence of this is that we are more likely as teachers to hold ourselves and each other responsible for the actions we have or appear to have chosen to do. Reflection then encourages us to account for our actions (if only in our mind), and to give reasons for why we acted as we did.

Second, we are affected by *internal school and other organizational influences* – particularly the pressures and opportunities which coalesce to form visions for the future and ways of achieving them. For example, each school's brochure or prospectus both creates a picture of school life and contains a vision of what the school claims is worthwhile education. However these are constructed and communicated, they require us to locate or situate ourselves and our practice within them.

Third, we are influenced by *external agencies* – networks, associations, unions and governments – who formulate guidelines, frameworks and policies aimed at enhancing the quality of education through school improvements. So to the two questions raised earlier – namely, 'What kind of teacher am I?' and 'What kind of teacher do I want to be?' – we can add a third and more provocative one: 'What kind of teacher am I forced to be?'

The nature of professional values

'Values' is a contentious word in education. Some simply believe that it suggests that the worth of anything derives from someone or other choosing it. This is only a very partial view (Totterdell 1997). For us, an educational value is something which is socially constructed, consciously and critically reflected upon, and discussed and reflected in our feelings, thoughts and actions with our children and colleagues. In this sense, our view of values shares many of the attributes of what Carr (1992) calls 'principled preferences'. He argues that these are of 'quite considerable importance' and that 'unlike other sorts of preferences which are based merely on personal taste or natural disposition, values are standardly a consequence of something approaching intelligent deliberation and are thus, in principle, susceptible of rational appraisal and re-appraisal' (Carr 1992:244). Teachers have to make choices every minute of their working day. Every choice implies an underlying value, a 'because', an 'ought', and so on. This means teachers' actions are guided by their values, and makes education a value-laden enterprise.

Values are everywhere. Hardly anyone will say that values do not matter (Ashton 1997:2). But they do not float around in some kind of void. For example, in the latest version of the Primary National Curriculum in the UK, in the section called 'Assessment', the values that underpin the curriculum's assessment strategy are very clear. They are as follows:

1. The learner is at the heart of assessment
2. Assessment needs to provide a view of the whole child
3. Assessment is integral to teaching and learning
4. Assessment includes reliable judgements about how children are performing, related, where appropriate, to national standards.

(Qualifications and Curriculum Development Agency 2010:31)

'Values don't grow on trees or fall like manna from heaven, or just look after themselves. On the contrary, they are always vulnerable to the darker side of human nature such as selfishness, greed, self-deception, vanity, lust and cowardice' (Carey 1997:2). Values are located historically, socially, culturally and politically. They are in what we say or choose not to say, in what we do and do not do. When teachers insist on precision and accuracy in children's work, or praise their use of imagination, censure racist or sexist language, encourage them to show initiative, or respond with interest, patience or frustration to their ideas, children are being introduced to values and value-laden issues (Jackson *et al.* 1993). Values can be heard and read about in school documents, in those from OFSTED, the Qualifications and Curriculum Authority, from government ministers and so on. For example, when the then UK Prime Minister Tony Blair took up office in May 1997 for New Labour, he espoused a commitment to 'decent values' (*Runnymede Bulletin* 1997). In general, this commitment embraced notions of compassion, social justice, liberty, fighting poverty and inequality, and so on. With regard to education, the White Paper *Excellence in Schools* (Great Britain 1997) set out the way the government valued 'equality of opportunity', 'high standards for all' and the way society should 'value our teachers'. Further, values can bind people together and give them a sense of belonging, shared commitment and understandings that are central to a collective sense of the moral purposes of education and accountability. But they can also serve to disunite them and highlight differences between them.

> The expectations of interested parties are thus often in conflict, and schools sometimes become the battleground where groups with different value priorities vie for influence and domination ... The values of schools are apparent in their organisation, curriculum and discipline procedures as well as in the relationships between teachers and pupils.
>
> (Halstead and Taylor 1996:3)

Differences can lead to conflict, but this does not necessarily have to be destructive. Differences in values can be resolved in school, but this takes will, determination, an openness and receptiveness to other points of view, and perhaps compromise. However, 'the way in which we see our own values and the kind of significance they have for us will affect our attitude towards compromise' (Haydon 1997:53). It is important, though, to appreciate that we can feel threatened and vulnerable when our values clash with those of others. The resolution of conflicts that arise from teachers' different value stances is a fundamental task when, for example, groups are working to plan curriculum policy (Johnston 1988). Values can give us a shared language and yet can be used to illustrate how difficult it is at times to be heard and understood by others. For example, alongside the Labour Government values of the past 13 years since the first edition of this book run values couched in another discourse – namely, that of the marketplace. In this scenario it is the 'market', occupied by providers and consumers, which decides which values are important and should be upheld (Elliott 1994). In this scenario, the market forces of efficiency, effectiveness and economy 'rule OK'. A market culture within education suggests the centrality of three key values; namely, those to do with rights, choice and accountability.

> Parents' rights *vis-à-vis* the educational establishment are strengthened through membership of school governing bodies ... The language of rights is also promi-

nent in the way the State compels schools to provide parents with more information ... Education reform has also lifted restrictions on enrolment and opened up possibilities for parents to send their children to schools outside their catchment area ... parents are now supposed to be in a position to make informed choices on where to send their children. Finally ... the imperative of the market which forces schools to market themselves ... and the intimidating pressures of the inspection process, suggests that schools are much more accountable to parents.

(Wyness and Silcock 1997:3)

This 'values discourse' (or language of education) contains reference to inputs and outputs, audits, league tables, value addedness, target setting, performance indicators, metrics, delivery of curriculums and benchmarking. All this has amounted to what has been called the 'commodification of education'. It is a values discourse of corporate management. Using the commodity metaphor, new children at a school, for example, are 'raw materials'. 'Batch processing' generates efficiency and economies of scale. As the quality of the raw material cannot be guaranteed, then the 'factory', to extend the metaphor, has to invest in the processes of selection and standardization (Curran 1997). This is a powerful image and one that some teachers might object to quite strongly, particularly if they espouse other values. For example, Hill (1997) describes 'neo-conservative' values which are quite contrary to those above, with their wish to restore a culture of 'back to basics' and their emphasis on traditional values such as respect for authority. Values may also be relatively fixed and reasonably long-lasting, or much more transient and, like fashion and 'Top Ten' tracks, come and go according to the interests and attitudes of the moment.

Teaching is, however, a profession of values, and these values are fundamental to understanding ourselves as teachers, how we relate to others and discharge our role competently and ethically (Scott *et al.* 1993). I suggest it is important to reflect on our values in the light of growing cultural diversity, a widening gulf between the values of imposed educational reform, and teacher self-generated improvement. We need to see how the new Liberal Democrat–Conservative Coalition Government (post-May 2010) in the UK puts its values into action. If values in society in general are controversial, then it is not surprising that values in education are anything other than slippery and contestable things also. Halstead and Taylor (1996:4–5) encourage us to examine the links between values and education by asking ourselves questions such as:

1. Is there a distinction to be made between private and public values?
2. Do particular values (whether political, aesthetic, moral or religious) have validity only within particular cultures and traditions?
3. Are there overarching principles by which conflicts between values may be resolved?
4. Is there a sufficient basis of shared values in our society to support a common framework of education for all children, or should parents be free to choose between schools and different sets of values?
5. Do the values which are currently taught in schools necessarily reinforce (intentionally or otherwise) the privileged position of certain social classes or religious or cultural groups?

6. Are there any absolute values, or merely changing and relative ones?
7. Should schools reflect traditional values, or seek to transform these?
8. Should schools instil values in pupils, or teach them to explore and develop their own values?
9. Should teachers aim for a neutral (or value-free) approach to their subject matter?

In trying to take a firm hold on the nature of values, it is important to question three of the common assumptions that we make about them, namely that:

- values are something that come from within us;
- values are contested;
- there is a relationship between values and practice.

How far do values come from within us?

If, for example, you hold values that have something to do with encouraging children to be responsible for their own actions, to be truthful and considerate towards others, or with developing for your children a just, fair and democratic learning milieu, then you might usefully ask yourself the following questions. How far:

- did I choose values like these freely?
- were these values of mine chosen from a set of alternative values?
- am I able to articulate the consequences for myself and my children of holding these values?
- are these values that I care passionately about?
- are these values publically affirmed and supported in school by my colleagues, significant others and children?
- do I try to live out these values in my daily teaching?
- do I 'hang on in there' and not let these values go, or compromise on them when faced with difficulties living them out?

Our responses to questions such as these will generate certain kinds of knowledge. It might be practical knowledge grounded in our teaching realities, associated with our past experiences, professionally and politically appropriate or astute, linked to liberal or moral values, an ethical standpoint, associated with notions of lifelong learning or vocational preparation. But one of the most problematic areas in the field of improving teaching is linked to the question, 'So what kinds of knowledge are worth knowing if we wish to improve what we do?' (Lewis 1993). It was Polanyi (1962) who said that only by expressing our tacit knowledge can we ever hope to subject it to some analysis, and, through scrutiny, erect a justification for it. In line with this, we believe that one important kind of knowledge worth knowing is what we shall call 'values-based knowledge'. This is knowledge that is not just linked to teaching but also tied inextricably to, and derived from, that practice. Values-based knowledge has the power to inform and constantly transform practice. The problem is that often we do not know the values we have. Goldhammer (1966) expresses this well:

The vast majority ... of values and assumptions from which our ... professional behaviour is governed are implicit. They're inarticulate, they're nebulous, they're buried someplace in our guts and they're not always very accessible ... We can't always rationalise exactly what we're doing ... We can't always make explicit the justifications for the acts we perpetrate ... Only after these things have been made explicit, have been brought to the point where you can enunciate the damn things, can we begin to value those that seem to have some ... integrity and disregard those that seem to be inane.

(Goldhammer 1966:49)

What are your own values?

In the first edition (Ghaye and Ghaye 1998), I said that they felt it would be inappropriate in a book such as this and in a chapter that focuses on values if we, the authors, did not do what we were advocating. It seemed a contradiction. In other words, we said that expressing and justifying our values is a good thing to do, but we were not doing it ourselves. We felt this way because we were building an argument that is trying to persuade you, the reader, to set out and explain your values, and arguing that this is the bedrock upon which reflection-on-practice rests. We were also saying that the reflective process needs to explore the extent to which we are able to live out our values in our everyday teaching. We were suggesting that this process was the catalyst for improving practice.

Some excellent examples of how you might articulate your values are contained in the work of the Kingston Hill Action Research Group (Lomax and Selley 1996), and in an book edited by Lomax (1996) where, in Chapter 1, Lomax and colleagues set out their values in relation to the issue of what constitutes good quality educational research (Lomax et al. 1996). In the Lomax and Selley (1996) publication, a four-part 'enabling framework' is used. For example, Lomax uses it to show how she claims to have developed and supported the Kingston Hill Action Research Network. The Kingston Hill framework contains:

Explaining my values: e.g. 'I care that individuals have open access to higher education and that no one is left outside "to rub their noses against the window".'

Describing my actions: e.g. 'I have encouraged students and their tutors to present their action research at national and international conferences and this has had a practical impact on gaining acceptance for the idea that research should be the basis of teaching and managing in education.'

Explaining the steps I have taken to ensure the appropriateness of my actions: e.g. 'I reflect upon my actions in terms of my values which provide the main criteria against which I judge myself.'

Evidence of how my actions have led to the achievement of my purposes: e.g. 'My own writing which makes explicit my values and provides authentic accounts of my own learning that can be understood by others.'

(Lomax and Selley 1996:3–4)

In the first edition we set out an alternative way and one that we believed was highly appropriate also for beginning teachers. It really embraced the first two parts of the framework above. It was intended to encourage you to think carefully about both the content and the form of your value statement. Value statements, in my view, should be personally or collectively meaningful, understandable to others, and enable evidence to be gathered to help us to appreciate how far we live the value out in our teaching and general professional lives. My suggestion is that a value statement needs to be in two parts. It begins with the phrase 'I believe...'. This is followed by the use of the word, 'because...'. The first half of the statement is concerned with the 'what', while the second half focuses on 'why', or the rationale for the 'what'. There is no need to be a slave to this structure; it is simply provided to help you to express what you might consider to be your 'positive core values'. Remember, these are the things you really care for and are passionate about. They are the things you want to hold on to. They make you who you are. Some of the core values Ghaye and Ghaye (1998) believed in their work with teachers and student teachers were thus:

We believe:

- that it is important for us to try to enable others to think and talk about their values because values give teaching its shape, form and purpose
- that reflection is at the heart of the learning process because without reflecting systematically and rigorously on what we do, how can we ever learn from what we have just done?
- that we encourage others to represent what it is they claim to know in courageous, understandable and imaginative ways, because in this way their work might have a positive impact on practice and foster improvement
- that our teaching and writing should help to give others the means of critical understanding and access to new possibilities because without this we may be constrained and imprisoned by the values, diktats and whims of others
- in trying to promote educative research with others which is dialogical and which emphasizes the question-posing process that helps us to reveal the contradictions in our work and through dialogue, come to some mutual understanding about how practice might be moved forward.

Value statements are everywhere in education. Some of them do indeed come from within us, but some also come from elsewhere. For example, if we go back to the 1988 Education Reform Act in the UK, we find that schools were required to provide a broad and balanced curriculum. The value position was clear. Schools were to prepare young people for 'the opportunities, responsibilities and experiences of adult life' (Great Britain Statutes 1988). At that time, just exactly what these qualities and values might be were left undefined.

In setting out what makes a successful primary teacher, the Teacher Training Agency spoke in terms of 'an accomplished communicator and administrator', someone who is 'creative, energetic, enthusiastic, sensible' and with 'a good sense of humour' (TTA 1996/97). They made their values explicit when stressing that it is 'vital to create the correct climate for teaching and learning', and that successful primary teachers would 'need to strike the right balance to allow freedom of expression and creative thought, while maintaining the necessary discipline' (TTA 1996/97:5). These are the qualities they valued in primary teachers. But these qualities have to be nourished during our professional lives. This nourishment often comes in the form of in-service training. In the TTA paper (November 1997) called *Invitation to bid for TTA Inset Funds*, what was valued as an appropriate bid from institutions of Higher Education for future in-service teacher training was clearly stated. For example, the TTA valued INSET that would lead to 'the improvement of pupils' performance through the improvement of school teachers' or head teachers' professional knowledge, understanding and skills and their effectiveness in their teaching and/or leadership and management' (TTA 1997:3).

Another important source of values came from the School Curriculum and Assessment Authority (SCAA 1996). For example, in their paper on values in education and the community, these statements were to be found:

THE SELF: We value each person as a unique being of intrinsic worth, with potential for spiritual, moral, intellectual and physical development and change.

RELATIONSHIPS: We value others for themselves, not for what they have or what they can do for us, and we value these relationships as fundamental to our development and the good of the community.

SOCIETY: We value truth, human rights, the law, justice and collective endeavour for the common good of society. In particular we value families as sources of love and support for all their members, and as a basis of a society in which people care for others.

THE ENVIRONMENT: We value the natural world as a source of wonder and inspiration, and accept our duty to maintain a sustainable environment for the future.

(SCAA 1996:3–4)

Promise less but do it more often

In this second edition I wish to add some further personal thoughts about values. The first is a suggestion that it might be prudent to promise less but to do it more often. So what does this mean? First, I mean that if values are to guide what you do, it might be wise to promise (or espouse) less and put these values into practice more often, rather than the other way around – that is, promising (or espousing) more, but putting them into action less. We might enhance our professional credibility if we do the former. My suggestion is that as an educator, and as part of an educational institution, if you choose just a few values to talk about (to espouse) day in and day out, you stand a much better chance of actually putting those values into action and building those values within your work group. So how many is a few? What I have learned is that the more values you juggle, the harder it is to put them into action. It is easy to lose focus. Three values seems manageable and focused; six is less so. So articulating your values requires selection. Selection requires criteria for choice. My suggestion is that if you want students, colleagues and others to know what you stand for as an educator, keep the list short and the statements understandable. When organizational mission statements espouse too many values, they can become dead documents. Nobody can remember them, yet alone put them all into action. Too complex a set of values sets up a situation that is ripe for misunderstandings, as the complex list of values gets reinterpreted and distorted, as in the game of Chinese Whispers. There is the danger that each work group adds their own subtle nuance to the overall statement, until the original becomes unrecognizable. Values will, by their very nature, be open to different interpretations. But if the list is too narrow, it may be uninspiring. So one thing I have learned about values is to promise less, and put everything I have into making those values I espouse a reality. Take fewer values, then celebrate these values every waking moment. What do you think?

The language of living by your word

By this, I mean doing what you say you will do. If you feel that it is important for learners to take responsibility for their own learning and show initiative, perseverance and a commitment to self-improvement, then it is imperative that you do your best to create a context for such a value to be put into action. If you feel that one of your professional values is recognizing that achievement builds self-esteem, confidence and resilience, then how will you keep your promise to create opportunities for learners to achieve? These are not simple matters, of course. In the process of teaching and learning there are many uncertainties. There are limits to what we can do. Perhaps we should be more alive to the dangers of causal overpromising. Perhaps we should get better at discussing awkward truths – for example, the consequences of a change of plan, a colleagues' poor performance, or a tight deadline that can't be overshot. Arguably, professional integrity requires us to keep our promises and live by the values we profess. Both of these things boil down to living by our word, and colleagues believing that your word is your bond. But there is a difference between professional integrity that comes from keeping our promises, and a values integrity. Simons (2008:98) puts it like this:

> It is possible to always either keep your word or to come back and renegotiate it proactively. I do believe that's within our power. I don't believe we can live by our values 100%. One, because we're just human beings; we're not perfect. Two, because in the real world, there are competing values, and limited time and resources. And three, it's not always clear what the heck it means to live your values in a given situation.

How far are values contested?

Many educators have had to address a particularly pervasive value; namely, 'that which can be quantified and measured is what is deemed to be important and worthwhile to know'. If we reflect on this example, it usefully serves to raise a number of fundamental problems for us to address. These problems are some of the things which tend to make values contestable. First, there is the problem of which values. Second, there is the problem of which values have more legitimacy and authority. By this I mean which ones are more appropriate, and in what contexts. The first two problems point up the distinction we should make between 'what the values are' and 'what they should or might be'. These are different issues. Third, there is the problem of knowing how to reconcile differences between values. In the context of a school, it is the issue of knowing what to do when colleagues either do not appreciate, or wish to subscribe to, a particular value or values. It is important, I suggest, for teachers to reflect on the nature of their value disagreements. Finally, there is the problem of how we might most competently and ethically live out our values in our teaching and practitioner research.

How far do you subscribe to the view that values are social constructs created and evolving in relation to particular social conditions? Some have argued that:

> ... they are not inherently innate and homogeneous and do not necessarily reflect consensus in a given socio-historical situation. Values are only meaningful in the context of the political and social space from which they emerge. As societies change, so too do their values.
>
> (Ratuva 1997:1–2)

Some believe that common values may well be something of an aspiration rather than a reality in a culturally pluralistic world. An important point in this argument is that commonality is marred by the inequalities which exist in society, and in the domination or subordination of different groups (Morrison 1997). Some dominant individuals or groups in education also have the power to impose meanings and values on others. This kind of impositon of 'alien' values on teachers and their work can lead to conflict, or the reproduction of values that prop up and legitimize the dominant group (Gramsci 1971, Bourdieu 1994). Alternatively, others argue that common values need to be sought out and agreed, and that these shared values need not be bland, obvious or uninteresting. An important part of this argument is that individual and collective liberty requires and rests on a common set of moral values:

> Without values such as trust, honesty, consideration for other people, love of justice and peace, there can be no liberty, because there can be no orderly society within which individuals can grow and express themselves in interdependence with others.
>
> (Carey 1997:3)

The argument here about common values is one that does not support the view that they somehow have to be anaemic and bland. They need illustration and contextualizing to bring them to life, and need to be debated and defended with passion as well as reason.

When articulating our individual or whole-school values, Prilleltensky and Fox (1997) suggest three things. The first is that we try to advance our values in a 'balanced' manner. They say this because they believe that we are prone to over-emphasizing one value at the expense of others. In schools, we might be accused of over-emphasizing self-determination, autonomy and independence, which includes a focus on the individual child, while values such as collegiality and collaboration are under-emphasized. Second, they suggest that our particular collection, list or configuration of values needs to be fluid and responsive to change. Values should provide a vision of what is good, just and educational at school. They should not be a ball and chain around our feet, but need to be constantly reviewed in the light of changing circumstances. The remnants of old lists of values should not hinder the creation of new ones that form the basis of improved educational practices. Third, they suggest that certain values have more potential for transforming society than others. This is a very important point. For example, caring and compassion may be important values that give our teaching with young children its shape, form and purpose, but living these out in relation to individual pupils may not be enough to change the culture of a school which undermines these values by promoting competition.

Some more thoughts about the relationships between values and practice

Some professionals in education, teachers and schools argue that a certain set of core values gives them their sense of identity, purpose and integrity. This point is made by Thompson when she argues, 'A shared understanding and appreciation of a profession's values and ethical responsibilities are central to the profession of teaching as they are to other professions' (Thompson 1997:1). She goes on to say why a Code of Ethics, which she describes as 'a statement of fundamental values and broad ethical principles', is important for the teaching profession. The reasons she lists are these (Thompson 1997:2):

- It would serve to help society to judge the integrity of the relationship between the teaching profession and children.
- Without such a Code, teachers would work on influential but individual 'educational platforms'.
- It would demonstrate that teaching is fundamentally a moral enterprise.
- It would enable professional values to be reviewed and revised in the light of changes and developments in education and society.
- It would help to raise the profession's morale, raise its self-confidence, sense of purpose and commitment, and adjust its expectations, thus improving professional standards.

However, some would argue that it is unlikely that one single list of values suits everyone, particularly in a culturally plural society. This is why promising less but doing more was suggested earlier. This issue of common or core values is one central point of discussion in the values debate. Another focuses on the difficulties which arise when we try to implement them, or 'live our values out in our teaching'.

In working this through, teachers might be helped by Schein's three professional states, which describe different relationships between values and actions (Schein 1969). The states are:

1. *dynamic stability*, where there is felt to be a congruency between stated or espoused values and values in action;

2. *precarious stability*, in which we are aware that we are not able to live our values out fully in our practice – this is a state where we are trying to make some adjustments in values and/or practice;

3. *instability*, in which values and actions are clearly incongruent and where we are not bothering, or are unable and feel powerless, to take steps to try to live our values out, more fully, in our teaching.

You may feel that in the course of a working week you oscillate between all three states! A powerful and significant contribution to this debate, about the links between values and practice in the last two decades, has come from Whitehead (1985, 1989, 1992, 1993, 1996, 1997). The fulcrum of Whitehead's contribution to educational knowledge is the way he encourages us to account for our own educational development through the creation of our own 'living educational theories'. While not denying the value of alternative forms of understanding, he argues that educational theory should be in a living form containing descriptions and explanations of our own development and in so doing acknowledging the context in which the living theory is being produced. He argues that the explanations given by teachers in trying to make sense of their practice come about from addressing, in a serious and critically reflective manner, questions such as 'How do I improve my practice here?' Living theory, then, is educational theory based on educational practice as lived and experienced by teachers themselves. These theories are 'claims to know', which, like all kinds of theory, have to be able to respond to questions of validity. This means that we have to have some standards or criteria that we understand and can use in order to test the validity of a teacher's claim to know his or her own educational development. In its most straightforward form, the issue of validity is reflected in the question, 'How do I/we know that what the teacher says about their own educational development and practice is true?'

> A living theory is one that is continuously created and recreated through the validated explanations that individual managers offer of their own practices as they pursue their educational goals. These explanations are stimulated by intentional, committed action that stems from practical concerns about managing, and are reached through the analysis of careful descriptions that depend on rigorous methods of data collection and analysis.
>
> (Lomax *et al.* 1996:16)

At this point, I want to draw your attention to the way living theory helps us understand the links between values and action. *The Educational Journal of Living Theories* (*EJOLTS*) is a rich archive of papers on this topic. A foundational paper is that by Whitehead (2008) called 'Using a living theory methodology in improving practice and generating educational knowledge in living theories'.

Living educational theory coheres around notions:

- that teaching is a value-laden activity;
- of the living 'I';
- of the self existing as a living contradiction.

With regard to the first notion, Whitehead states, 'I think values are embodied in our practice and their meanings can be communicated in the course of their emergence in practice' (Whitehead 1992:193). He also argues that values offer explanations for our actions. The notion of the living 'I' is contained in the action-questions that character-ize enquiries that seek to develop this form of knowledge – questions such as 'How do I improve my teaching?', 'How do I improve this process of education here?', and 'How do I live my values more fully in my practice?' This living 'I' is such a potent idea, and relevant to the kinds of reflection-on-practice that I am advocating here. The living 'I' arises, in my view, in part from the way we act within and upon the world. It derives also from an awareness of the 'me'; namely, an image of the kind of teacher that I am. The living 'I' can be seen, then, as a fusion of what we might call 'personal' and 'social' identities. Our individuality as a teacher is expressed through the values we place on the different experiences and things that make up our professional world. The living 'I' is nourished by our ability to be reflective, to stand back and acknowledge the potential we have to improve how things are in our teaching. The living 'I' lives in the worlds of the actual, the possible and the desirable.

The final notion of 'I' existing as a living contradiction in the creation of living edu-cational theory is appealing and liberating. Whitehead puts it this way:

> [T]hink about how you have tried to overcome problems in your professional prac-tice. I think such a reflection will reveal that you have experienced a tension in holding certain values and experiencing their negation at the same time in your practice.
>
> (Whitehead 1992:6)

Put simply, this means as a teacher we often say we value something (for example, facilitating pupil discussion) and then do the opposite (we dominate the classroom dis-course). We talk too much! Here we exist as a living contradiction. When I say that I want to give all my children an equal amount of time and then I find myself concen-trating on those who demand more of my attention, I am denying my values in my practice. Again, I am a living contradiction. We can view the contradictions within our teaching as professional growth points: tensions that need to be reflected upon. Some-times we may feel a sense of powerlessness when appreciating the fact that we hold cer-tain values while at the same time experiencing their denial in our practice. Sometimes, through reflection, we develop new appreciations about what is possible and where improvements can most usefully be targeted. Sometimes we just have to say to our-selves, 'Well, that's how it is here right now and there isn't a great deal I can do about things for the time being.' It is too simplistic to think that practice moves smoothly and unproblematically from values being negated in practice to a position where we do live them out. Moving forward and developing our practice may involve some kind of cre-ative synthesis of previous contradictions. This view of practice, which has the notion of a contradiction at its heart, is a 'tensioned' one, and is called a 'dialectical' view. If we hold this view, we aim to develop our insights and understandings through a pro-cess of posing questions and trying to answer them.

Moving our thinking and practice forward is fundamentally about understanding the links between our values and our educational activities. The nature and educative potency of our values needs to be seen in relation to our practice: our values emerge through our practice. Our teaching reflects our values-in-action. As we accept responsibility for the education of our children and students, so we need to accept responsibility for making sincere, transparent, systematic and convincing efforts to try to live our values out as fully as possible in our teaching. What I have learned is to commit, mean it, and keep it up. I say to myself, 'If I am not willing to make that commitment (to this or that value), then there is a risk to my professional credibility and maybe, therefore, I should stop and reflect'. Some further ways we might do this, and the role of reflection in the process, is the subject of the next chapter.

6

Voicing Concerns and Asking Questions

In the last chapter I said that one of the best ways to characterize teaching was through the values that permeate it and give it its direction and purpose. Teaching children is the act through which values come alive. By watching the interactions between teachers and their children, we should be able to infer the teacher's values. Values help the teacher to make decisions on how to proceed. But there is something else which is central to this process of making wise, creative and professional decisions, and that is evidence. Confident and competent teaching requires teachers to reflect systematically and rigorously on evidence derived from practice. Evidence comes in many forms: it can be formal and publically available evidence, such as OFSTED reports, National Curriculum SAT scores, the school's performance in the form of league tables and school brochures. Then there is formal but relatively less available evidence, like minutes of school governors' meetings, school policy statements, and teachers' schemes of work. There is also evidence that teachers might gather regarding children's learning and their own teaching. All this evidence can be collected in different ways, by different people, at different times, with certain interests and audiences in mind. It can, for example, be gathered through observation, discussion and conversation, tape and video recording. Evidence can also be analysed in a variety of ways and presented to highlight issues, themes, trends, tensions, accomplishments, areas for concern and action. Reflective teaching and learning, then, needs to be evidence-based. To understand this more fully, we need to explore the links between teaching, evidence and reflection.

There are three important sources of influence that serve to illustrate the nature and importance of the links between teaching, evidence and reflection. These are the political, the professional and the personal. I will illustrate each one with reference to the induction of new teachers, the teacher-as-researcher movement, and a personal commitment to compiling a development profile.

The political: the induction of new teachers

In the government consultation document (DfEE 1998a) *Induction of New Teachers*, the links between teaching, evidence and reflection are set out. For example:

> We will establish a new national framework which will give every new teacher a clear statement of what is expected of them; a guarantee of the necessary support and guidance to meet those expectations; sufficient time and space to reflect on and

develop their performance; and opportunities to exchange experiences with other teachers, both others new to the profession and those already in schools, and, above all, the chance to learn from observing the best, experienced teachers at work.

(DfEE 1998a:3)

Reflection is explicitly mentioned. Without systematic reflection-on-practice, how are new teachers able to develop their performance? Evidence in the form of observations of practice will create the chance to learn if the new teacher reflects on this evidence in a creative and critically reflective manner. Later in the document, we find 'From May this year (1998), for the first time, all students completing teacher training courses will have a Career Entry Profile, which will summarize the new teacher's particular strengths and priorities for their further professional development' (DfEE 1998a:8). In the same paragraph (para. 10) the phrase 'record agreed targets and an action plan for their achievement' is used, and in the following paragraph we find that the new teacher should 'observe and learn from the best existing practice'. In Section 6, which is about an effective programme of support, the government sets out an impressive list of key elements. Pertinent to this discussion are Element 3 and 'regular observation of teaching and feedback', Element 4 and 'regular discussions ... to review professional practice ... and update the action plan', and Element 7, which states that new teachers will 'have their work observed and commented on by the Headteacher and access to the Headteacher to discuss any additional training needs or difficulties they may be experiencing' (DfEE 1998a:9–10).

In Section 8, on the standards required to be met by new teachers, we find another statement which links teaching with evidence and reflection. The final standard, Standard 13, states that teachers must, when assessed, demonstrate that they 'can take responsibility for their own future professional development and keep up to date with research and developments in pedagogy and in the subject(s) they teach' (para. 22). In assessing the new teacher against the standards, a wide range of evidence is relevant. Six forms of evidence are identified. These are:

- a written report from the line manager, drawing on formative assessment that has taken place throughout the year;
- where the line manager is not the Head, an interview between the new teacher and the Head to review progress;
- any reports from any mentor teachers or other external trainers or from schools who may have contributed to the new teacher's programme;
- evidence of achievement of pupils for whom the new teacher has particular responsibility;
- the Career Entry Profile; and
- any judgements of the new teacher's performance by OFSTED inspectors (para. 29).

The consultation document gives us much to think about. For example, for those involved in initial teacher training, emphasis will be need to be made on helping students with needs and wants analysis, and knowing the difference, in action learning (McGill and Beaty 1996) and action research. Target-setting that is realistic, appropriate and in harmony with the context in which the student or new teacher is working will also be important. Targets also have to be meaningful. Students as well as new teachers will need to be helped to distinguish between those targets that have some kind of personal meaning for them – meaning for their children and for others in the school. Targets are set for different reasons and serve different ends. Clarity will be needed to sort out targets, as ends, and the most appropriate means to achieve them. Not only this, but the purposes behind the setting of one target rather than another will need to be articulated.

Evidence in the form of observations of practice was also a prominent part of the consultation document. Making observations of practice has been a central feature of the teaching profession for many years, with the ORACLE project (Observation Research and Classroom Learning Evaluation) being the most extensive piece of classroom observation research in the UK to date. One of the aims of the project was to describe 'some of the richness and variety of what goes on in a modern Primary classroom', and 'to search for patterns from among those events in order to help explain why certain teachers do one thing while others do something else' (Galton *et al.* 1980:4). The lessons learnt from this major project and the critiques of it (Scarth and Hammersley 1993) seem very pertinent, given the exposure that observational evidence receives in the consultation paper. What is observed, how, when, in what ways and with what purposes in mind, are enduring questions. In the document a number of different 'observers' are identified, such as the new teacher's line manager, mentor, headteacher and OFSTED inspectors. All these people are likely to have different kinds of experience and abilities to observe. They are also likely to have their own agendas, and perhaps conflicting ones. Even if they are working to some kind of common goal, the settings in which the observations are undertaken – that is, teaching and non-teaching (DfEE 1998a: para. 30) – will make the formulation of assessment that follows a 'nationally agreed format' a challenging business.

Feedback was also 'talked-up' in the document, be it in relation to revising action plans, in the guise of 'discussions' with the new teacher's line manager, or through the 'interview' process with the headteacher. Feedback, like observation, is another conventional plank upon which professional development is traditionally facilitated. Important distinctions will need to be made between confirmatory and corrective feedback. The former is feedback where the new teacher gets to know that he or she is on course, that things are moving forwards in an acceptable manner – that is, with a shared understanding of achievements and agreement about where to exert action in order to enhance practice. Corrective feedback is what it suggests; it is the kind of feedback that focuses on and emphasizes changing things with a view to improving the current state of practice. This should not overwhelm the new teacher, otherwise it will defeat the purpose of the whole process: corrective does not mean punitive.

To stand a chance of helping to move the new teacher's practice forward, the teacher needs an opportunity to comment on the feedback, to expand upon it, and to be helped to discover real ways of doing things differently that are within his or her compass. Often, in reality, feedback to teachers on their performance contains a bit of both types. The bottom line is that feedback should be in the service of two intentions: first, that it should help teachers to manage their work effectively, competently and ethically by offering new perspectives on things and by opening up unnoticed possibi-

lities and alternatives; and second, that it should help teachers to become better at helping themselves to move their own thinking and practice forward. Providing quality
feedback is a skilful business. Those involved in the induction of new teachers will need
not only a repertoire of basic communication skills, such as empathy, attending, listening, understanding, probing and summarizing, but also some fairly sophisticated and
advanced communication skills, of which handling resistance and reluctance, helping
new teachers to challenge their own teaching and helping them to move from possibilities to making choices will be essential. Quality feedback is dependent upon making
sense of reflections-on-practice, the new teacher's practice. The skilfulness of the new
teacher's line manager in this regard is important.

In the final standard, Standard 13, new teachers are encouraged to demonstrate that
they are keeping up to date with research. This is placed in the context of taking
responsibility for their own professional development, and is another hugely complex
demand. Some of the central issues here involve the type of research, the new teacher's
access to it, and its usefulness in and impact on practice-in-context. For many new
teachers, research is still something rather abstract, 'out there', unrelated to everyday
practice and undertaken by 'others' rather than teachers themselves. Time constraints
and lack of skills are frequently cited reasons for others doing it rather than the teachers
themselves.

Research being done by others raises the issue of ownership. If teachers have no
stake in the knowledge generated through research, then how can they feel committed
to it and believe in it? Teachers also need research that helps them to explain aspects of
their everyday practice in their own particular school settings. If you think that research
is only about the search for generalizations, you may also believe that what is being said
applies to all contexts of practice. But what happens when you find that, having put
your confidence in this research, the research does not fit, does not work, does not help
to explain your practice with your own children? You might try to force-fit it, but it
still does not help! In this scenario, we might need to get access to a different type of
research. Some teachers have difficulty in understanding research because of the way
the research account is written. To benefit from research, teachers have to be able to
understand it. These suspicions, misgivings and stereotypes are still around (Ghaye *et al.*
1996b). However, just as there are different types of reflection and evidence that serve
different interests, so too are there different types of research, generated in different
ways to serve different needs.

In the context of the consultation document, it is likely to be 'educative research'
(Gitlin and Russell 1994) which new teachers might find useful. This research has a
number of relevant features – for example:

- It encourages the participants in the research to jointly negotiate the meaning of
  what is being studied.
- It acknowledges that what is discovered through the research is embedded in a particular historical and cultural context.
- It follows a responsive question-and-answer approach. Formulating an appropriate
  research question and using questions with which to confront practice is
  important.
- It questions the taken-for-grantedness of everyday practice.

113

- It gives a voice to practitioners themselves as they jointly construct new meanings about practice, and question the influences and structures that serve to reinforce and constrain the production of new meanings and alternative ways of doing things.
- It views research as a process and not just as a product. Research as a product gets teachers into thinking that research is not grounded in their practice, but rather obtained from elsewhere and applied to their practice. Educative research is primarily a process with turning points and critical incidents that redirect the inquiry, that has the power to alter the questions being asked and influence teaching as insights are progressively accumulated.
- It places the researcher (the teacher) within the research account. The teacher's views, biases, perspectives and subjectivities which serve to influence the research process and give the account its form and character make the research authentic.
- It changes the traditional view of the terms validity and reliability. Validity is about truthfulness, and how far the reader can trust the researcher's account. Reliability is about the extent to which different researchers, using the same procedures, might come to the same conclusions. In educative research, 'truthfulness' is arrived at through discussion and the mutual understandings that are derived from listening to and challenging all participant views and positions. The reader needs to have access to the processes that precipitate these constructed and negotiated understandings. Reliability is altered because of the commitment educative research has to develop the voice of the teacher in his or her own school setting. It is often both undesirable and inappropriate for procedures to remain unchanged from school setting to school setting. What is important is that the procedures are justified in relation to the research question, relevant to the school context, and reported in such a way that others can judge how far they have been deployed systematically and rigorously.

The final thing I suggest that it is important to be clear about is what is meant in Standard 13 when it is stated that new teachers need to take responsibility for their own future development. Again, we need to articulate some of the links between teaching, evidence and reflection that this poses. One restricted interpretation of this is to say that responsible action is when teachers ask themselves why they are doing what they are doing. Dewey (1933), however, had much to say about responsibility in the context of professional development through reflection; he extends our interpretation. Essentially, for him it was about the consequences of the act of teaching and school practices. He regarded responsibility as a characteristic of reflective teaching. Being responsible is being prepared to consider what is worthwhile in the educative relationships teachers have with their children. Responsible action is more than just considering 'what works' for me here, right now, and involves a reflection on both the means and ends of education. Issues such as in what ways my teaching benefits my children and its impact on them are addressed, as opposed to questions of the kind, 'How far have my learning objectives been achieved?' Broader issues such as these inevitably draw us into the realms of the politico-economic, socio-cultural, moral and ethical as we strive to act responsibly (Ashcroft and Griffiths 1989). It draws us into the world beyond the classroom and school, and invites the teacher to consider the structures that serve to constrain and curtail responsible action.

Dewey also talked about open-mindedness and wholeheartedness as essential attributes of reflective action. The first is about reflecting on what we do, confronting those things upon which our practice and that of others is predicated and being open to other possibilities. The latter concerns the fundamental mindset and approach of teachers to their work. Wholeheartedness for Dewey is about being energetic and enthusiastic, and about approaching teaching in a frame of mind that accepts that there is always something new to be learned from each lesson and working day. In the work of Zeichner and Liston (1996), this responsibility for professional development is clearly linked to reflective practice.

> When embracing the concept of reflective teaching, there is often a commitment by teachers to internalise the disposition and skills to study their teaching and become better at teaching over time, a commitment to take responsibility for their own professional development. This assumption of responsibility is a central feature of the idea of the reflective teacher.
>
> (Zeichner and Liston 1996:6)

There are many lists of the attributes of the reflective practitioner (Pollard 1996, 1997, Pollard and Triggs 1997), and much debate about their contents. One that provides a useful start and which is congruent with much of what we have said thus far is that advanced by Zeichner and Liston (1996:6). They argue that a reflective teacher:

- examines, frames and attempts to solve the dilemmas of classroom practice;
- is aware of and questions the assumptions and values he or she brings to teaching;
- is attentive to the institutional and cultural contexts in which he or she teaches;
- takes part in curriculum development and is involved in school change efforts;
- takes responsibility for his or her own professional development.

Some of the important things to note here are the focus on dilemmas in practice, values in a context, and the notions of development and change. Eraut (1994) helps to take us further by arguing that the teacher as a reflective practitioner is based upon the following set of assumptions:

- A teacher needs to have a repertoire of methods for teaching and promoting learning
- Both selection from this repertoire and adaptation of methods within that repertoire are necessary to best provide for particular pupils in particular circumstances
- Both the repertoire and this decision-making process within it are learned through experience
- Teachers continue to learn by reflecting on their experience and assessing the effects of their behaviour and their decisions
- Both intuitive information gathering and routinized action can be brought under critical control through this reflective process and modified accordingly
- Planning and pre-instructional decision-making is largely deliberative in nature; there is too little certainty for it to be a wholly logical process

- These processes are improved when small groups of teachers observe and discuss one another's work.

(Eraut 1994, in Eraut 1995b:231–2)

Eraut's assumptions intersect with a number of the principles for reflection set out in Chapter 3 – for example, with Principle 1 and reflective practice being understood as a discourse, and Principle 2 with reflection being energized by experience. When there is talk about new teachers being responsible for their own future development this hits home, as it is centrally about what it is to be a professional. Eraut (1995b:232) argues that what makes a reflective practitioner also a professional practitioner is:

- a moral commitment to serve the interests of students by reflecting on their well-being and their progress and deciding how best it can be fostered or promoted;
- a professional obligation to review periodically the nature and effectiveness of one's practice in order to improve the quality of one's management, pedagogy and decision-making;
- a professional obligation to continue to develop one's practical knowledge both by personal reflection and through interaction with others.

Taking responsibility for one's own future development is dependent upon the new teacher's ability to reflect on his or her own practice and that of others. Reflective practice is responsible action. But teacher development through reflection can be undermined. Gore and Zeichner (1995) suggest that this can be done in a number of ways – for example, by devaluing the practical wisdom and theories of teachers and celebrating the knowledge held and generated only by those in the 'academy', and by restricting reflection-on-practice to a consideration of utilitarian and technical issues rather than the moral purposes of education, questions of equity, and social justice. In other words, by focusing on the 'what' and 'how' of teaching rather than on the reasons and purposes of it – for example, by focusing on the classroom and neglecting to understand that, although immediate, concrete and well-known to the teacher, the classroom is part of a bigger social, political, cultural, economic and historical context. Finally, development through reflection is undermined if teachers see reflection as a solitary and introspective activity only, and one where they refer only to their own work. I have argued that reflection can also be collaborative, collegial, discursive and public. Through this process they can 'position' their work and understandings in relation to others. Reflection-on-practice as responsible action in this sense is therefore about collaborative learning, and self and collective re-evaluation of practice.

To bring this section on teacher induction up to date, in September 1999 the DfES in England introduced a compulsory period of induction for newly qualified teachers (NQTs). The induction period follows initial teacher training and the award of Qualified Teacher Status (QTS), and must be undertaken by NQTs who wish to continue teaching in maintained schools and non-maintained special schools. The induction period may also be taken while working in city technology colleges, some independent schools, sixth-form colleges, city academies and, since September 2008, some further education colleges. During the induction period, NQTs have to demonstrate that they have continued to meet the standards for the award of QTS, and that they meet the core standards. NQTs have an individualized programme of support during their induction year from a designated induction tutor. This includes observation of the teacher's teaching, watching more experienced teachers in different settings, and a professional review of progress at least every half term.

Reflections on success and failure

Learning from failure

As I have stated earlier, failure, or fear of it, can be a powerful force for changing what you do. You may be inclined to more readily reflect on past problems and failures. You may feel these are the things you need to prioritize and 'fix'. Your 'failings' may require urgent attention. This may be perfectly justified. Sometimes failure stimulates a greater willingness, or readiness, to consider alternatives. Failures can encourage you to be more critical of the way you currently do things. Sometimes failures are linked with personal issues like denial, avoiding risk, self-protection and defensiveness. These are tricky things that need sorting out.

Learning from success

Failures are only one source of motivation for changing your practice. In this second edition I have been trying to suggest a new kind of reflective practice; one that seeks to amplify and develop strengths. So it follows that another source of motivation is to learn from your successes and those things you feel you do best. What do you do really well? Like failures, successes should not be left unexamined; they need to be reflected upon. This is because your success might be limited to a particular task or activity, or to an individual or group. By reflecting on significant incidents or encounters, you can learn to notice and appreciate the successful aspects of your work, no matter how small. These can often go unnoticed. If recorded, these successes can create positive memories for you. These can balance personal feelings of frustration that you may experience when trying to develop your competence.

Matters of judgement

Success and failure are extremes. Often, in your daily work, 'being good enough' or 'doing the best you can' is all you can hope for. These expressions and others, like 'I did what I could' and 'this is all I could manage', fall between these two extremes. Success and failure are matters of judgement. To make such judgements, I suggest that you need to reflect on three fundamental questions:

1. What am I trying to achieve? This helps you focus on the change (if any) you wish to make, on how you would like things to be better and what would be regarded as a success. Having a clear and agreed view of how you plan to improve your current practice is vital.
2. What action can you take that might lead to improving your practice? This is about being realistic and practical. You might like to ask yourself, 'What do I feel I can do myself, and what do I need help with?'

3. How will I know that something is a success? This can be a bit tricky. Clearly not all change is a success. Also, things can change and your practice can get worse! So not all change improves the existing situation. Sometimes things get worse before they get better. Much depends on the evidence used to make such judgements (like relative success or failure) and how the evidence is interpreted. These things can be discussed in your after-action 'reflective conversations' with someone more experienced than you.

The teacher-as-researcher

One of the purposes of reflection is to play its part in the complex process of improving individual and collective action. It is about helping to move thinking and practice forward. There are many ways to realize these intentions. A fundamental part of the process of improving the quality of action in classrooms and schools is teachers researching their own practice. Personal and collective knowledge about improving teaching and learning develops in and through practice. It develops when teachers study or research their own practices themselves. Reflections on the role of self and the research process as it unfurls in real-world settings such as classrooms is an explicit and integral characteristic of certain styles of research, such as action research (Ghaye and Wakefield 1993).

The idea of teachers viewing themselves as researchers in their own teaching situation emanates principally from the pioneering work of Lawrence Stenhouse in the late 1960s (Stenhouse 1968, 1975) and the Schools Council Humanities Curriculum Project (1967–1972), which he directed. There are many excellent accounts of the profound and lasting impact his work has had on the notions of school-based curriculum development and teachers' professional development (Stenhouse 1980, 1983, Elliott 1997, Noffke 1997). Of particular relevance to this book are his ideas that teachers:

- should regard themselves as researchers and 'best judges of their own practice' (McNiff 1991);
- need to reflect critically and systematically on their practice;
- should have a commitment to question their practice, and that this should be the basis for teacher development;
- should have the commitment and the skills to study their own teaching and in so doing develop the art of self-study;
- might benefit from their teaching being observed by others and discussing it with them in an open and honest manner;
- should have a concern to question and to test theory in practice (Stenhouse 1975:143–4).

In discussing the relationship between theory and practice, Carr (1995) refers to Stenhouse thus: 'The relationship between theory and practice ... must be understood in terms of the public sphere rather than the private' (Carr 1995:15). The Stenhouse view of research as a public activity, as systematic and sustained enquiry, planned and self-critical, which is made public, is an extremely important idea (Stenhouse 1981:113). He argued that if teachers were to develop their practice and their understandings of theory, they would have to place their research in the public domain where it would be critiqued and perhaps utilized. The process of teacher development was not a private act of private reflections on practice, but a public process of one kind or another.

The thrust, then, of Stenhouse's work is that:

- all teaching ought to be based on research;
- the idea of teachers as researchers supports, nourishes and extends the professionalism of the teacher;
- that research is an important element in the professionalization of teaching; and
- research can reinforce the teacher's sense of professional autonomy and responsibility.

For Stenhouse,

> curriculum development was synonymous with professional development, and professional development was itself construed as a research process in which teachers systematically reflect on their practice and use the results of this reflection in such a way as to improve their own teaching. By relating this idea of 'teacher as researcher' to an analysis of professionalism, Stenhouse was able to argue that professional development required teachers to be provided with opportunities and resources to study their own practice through systematic reflection and research.
>
> (Carr 1989:7)

This was being advocated nearly 30 years ago. It is interesting to note that in the DfEE consultation document (DfEE 1998a), the same issues, identified by Stenhouse, of appropriate 'opportunities and resources' were being advocated for the proper induction of new teachers into the profession.

Just as action research was an important part of the theory of development which emanated from the Humanities Curriculum Project, so too was the recognition that the quality of the teacher's reflective framework was a decisive factor in teacher development (Day 1987). Action research involved the conscious act of reflection-on-practice. There have been many excellent texts that describe the nature, purposes, processes and impact of action research on teachers' thinking and practice, and the context in which teaching and learning takes place (Carr and Kemmis 1986, Kemmis and McTaggart 1988, Henry 1991, Zuber-Skerritt 1996, O'Hanlon 1996, McNiff et al. 1996, McKernan 1996, Goodson 1997, Hollingsworth 1997). There have also been numerous action research projects undertaken by individuals and groups which have been written up and disseminated through, for example, the Classroom (and more recently) Collaborative Action Research Network's (CARN) Bulletins and the international Journal of Educational Action Research. The experiences of some of the major British-funded action research projects have also been well reviewed (Sarland 1995). In summary, Sarland found that a number of themes and issues emerged from his analysis. These were that action research might usefully be seen to be about:

- the worthwhileness and authenticity of practitioner knowledge;
- practitioners taking control of the ways teaching and learning is understood, and of the production of this knowledge;

- the generation of theory in the classroom;
- cycles of action and reflection;
- collaborative ways of working;
- outsiders as facilitators;
- the contribution action research studies make to educational knowledge;
- the process of writing to promote the action researcher's own understanding;
- a belief that action research is best suited to professional and curriculum development.

In a complementary view, McNiff *et al.* (1992) argue that action research may be characterized as a way of working that:

- is practitioner generated;
- is workplace oriented;
- seeks to improve something;
- starts from a particular situation;
- adopts a flexible trial and error approach;
- accepts that there are no final answers;
- aims to validate any claims it makes by rigorous justification processes.

Whitehead (1993) suggests that the improvement process might most usefully begin with a reflection on the negation of values in practice thus:

- I experience a concern when some of my values are denied in my practice.
- I imagine a solution to the concern.
- I act in the direction of the solution.
- I evaluate the solution.
- I modify my practice in the light of the solution.

Action, reflection and resolving teaching concerns

Elements of Sarland, McNiff and Whitehead in particular can be found in the following extract of the work of a First School (5–9 years) teacher called Kay, who is researching her own practice. In appreciating this example, we should remember that action research is not monolithic. There is not just one type, and there is much debate about its aims and methods. For example, you will find that people write about participatory and collaborative forms of action research. Additionally, Carr and Kemmis (1986) distinguished between technical, practical and emancipatory types of it; these are summarized in Zuber-Skerritt (1996). What follows is an example of action research which is both collaborative and practical. Kay has sought and gained the support and participation of her children, school staff, governors and parents. By 'practical', I mean that it shows how the teacher is trying to become more effective in her work and also how she is endeavouring to understand her practice more fully and richly. Kay is engaging in a transformatory process which has the potential to enable her to make wiser, more competent and ethical decisions. She used Whitehead's framework as the basis for an action plan. Her research question was:

How can I use the principles and procedures of action research to improve my teaching of health education and link this to the development of a whole school health education programme?

She posed the following questions and offered a personal response.

Question 1: What is my concern?

'Health education is not coordinated well within my school. There is no policy or even guidelines. Teachers depend upon their own, often limited, knowledge and rarely seek guidance from myself. This suggests to me that a rather complacent attitude exists. Most staff, I think, feel that health education is being taught adequately. From what I see and hear, I strongly believe that this is not the case. My concern is that health education at school should be a relevant and meaningful learning experience for all children. This means that staff have to be informed, confident and enthusiastic about it.'

Question 2: Why am I concerned?

'Health education is an important area for children of this age, and one which is not given the attention it deserves. Many aspects of health education are being neglected simply because staff are not aware of them. The National Curriculum Council (1991) suggested nine "topic" areas which should be developed. Similarly, various authorities have produced guidelines aimed at improving general public awareness. My belief is that the message is still not being received by staff and children.'

Question 3: What do I think I can do about it?

'My principal aim is to motivate members of staff to recognize the value of health education and to encourage them to incorporate it more frequently into their practice. I also intend to emphasize cross–curricular links and to reassure colleagues that this "additional" subject need not be regarded as "yet another extra in an already over-crowded curriculum"; I want them to see it as an extension of aspects of their current good practice.'

Question 4: What kind of 'evidence' can I collect to help me make some judgements about what is happening?

'I believe there to be four crucial steps:

1. Assessment of my own classroom practice and the extent to which I incorporate health education in my teaching. At present I know that I do not fully practice what I preach! I do not live out my own educational values and I want to change this, but this is not as easy as it seems.
2. Requesting help from colleagues in assessing their own health education values. Although I realize that this could be problematic, I believe it to be very significant to determine how important staff members consider health education to be,

bearing in mind individual priorities and the politics within the school. They have got to want to change things. It's then my job to try to give them the skills and courage to do this.

3. Begin looking at the accessibility of resources within the school, paying particular attention to how frequently colleagues request information. This will involve the compilation of a resource guide/list for ease of reference. Resources at the health education centre would also need to be included.

4. Determine how parents and governors regard health education. I will need to involve parents in the study by requesting their views on health education − their fears or concerns. This necessarily involves collaboration with the headteacher and, from experience, I believe that she will be only too willing to assist.'

Question 5: How do I plan to collect such evidence?

'My intention is to work through the following steps (corresponding to those issues identified in Question 4):

1. Careful monitoring of my own teaching to include field notes on the amount of time spent on health education and a record of the nature of that teaching.

2. Staff curriculum meetings. These will be both formal and informal, the headteacher having already agreed to give directed time for meetings concerned with curriculum development. This will enable me to tape meetings, supplement my field notes and reflect upon the staff's opinions to plan the next step. It will also mean exposing my own teaching practices and results of my personal investigation, which I believe to be a necessary part of the process. I will also prepare guidelines for colleagues based on a simple questionnaire style − yet to be devised. Informal comments will be logged as soon as possible after the event. The importance of this is evident in McNiff's (1991:71) statement, "Immediate recording of events as they happen will avoid inevitable skewing of the data and give a truer picture of the action and how we interpreted the action."

3. Liaison with the health education department will help me to assess the relevance of resources in school at present. It will involve visits to the health education centre and discussions with the staff there. I have arranged with both my headteacher and the health education department to take time to do this. This will enable me to keep up to date not only with current trends, but with political initiatives also. A resource library can then be established within the school.

4. Requests for parents and governors to air their views will be carried out in the form of a questionnaire. I appreciate the limitations of a questionnaire, insofar as it is notoriously difficult to get the information desired, but feel that it is a pragmatic response to gain an insight into the *general* feelings of our parents and governors.'

Question 6: How shall I check that my judgement about what has happened is reasonably fair and accurate?

'When first introduced to the notion of a "critical friend", I spoke to a member of staff concerning the possibility of using her honest opinions and advice. She happily agreed to act as a critical friend and would, she said, be prepared to make constructive comments regarding matters of curriculum development.

Similarly, I have already heeded the advice of a college critical friend regarding the focus of my research. We met to discuss each other's proposals and I was able to use his suggestions to re-direct my thinking and to define my plans more clearly. Through discussion with him, I realized that I was being too ambitious and needed to "scale down" the project to concentrate more deeply on the *process* of developing a health education policy, rather than the hurried implementation and evaluation of one. In this way, I can be more thorough in my research and hopefully produce an informed workable document for the school.

I am also fortunate enough to have a supportive headteacher who is prepared to assist me wherever possible during each stage of development. I would hope that all three critical friends will help validate my findings by commenting on my procedures and results.

As I progress from analysing my own classroom practice to involving other members of staff in the policy-making process, I shall use their comments and criticisms to help structure future plans. This will enable me to validate my findings as I progress, and hopefully reduce the risk of any misunderstanding. I appreciate the fact that colleagues need to be kept informed of developments throughout the research, and have received assurance from them that they will support me during this project. I think my colleagues will judge the worthwhileness of the whole very soon after I expose them to it. I intend to do my best to keep in touch with their thoughts and feelings so as to produce an effective shared policy.

I would also hope to use the children as a source of validation. Since my own classroom practices will be re-structured to a certain extent, the children will be encouraged to make comments regarding the changes. I believe that, at nine years of age, many are capable of making constructive suggestions and of reflecting upon the work covered. I anticipate that this will be in the form of tape recordings during discussion times and, perhaps, through the use of diaries. I shall, of course, use my own field notes as a source of information and validation.

Finally, I hope to use tutorials at the college where I am studying part-time for a Masters degree to discuss what I am doing and how I am progressing. While I can collaborate with colleagues and children within my workplace, I think it is necessary to liaise with an "outsider" who is involved less directly with the research and who may see matters from a different perspective.

I can but do my best!'

This action plan gave Kay the structure and direction for carrying out her health education improvement agenda. Carr and Kemmis (1986) define much of the character of action research when they say that it is:

> ... a form of self-reflective enquiry undertaken by participants in social situations in order to improve the rationality and justice of their own practices, their understanding of these practices, and the situations in which the practices are carried out ... In terms of method, a self-reflective spiral of cycles of planning, acting, observing and reflecting is central to the action research approach.
>
> (Carr and Kemmis 1986:162)

The work of Kemmis and McTaggart (1988), which evolved from Lewin's earlier work (1946), refers to the spiral of action-and-reflection as the four 'moments' of action research. The same terms are used:

1. *Plan:* Develop a plan of action to improve what is already happening.
2. *Act:* Act to implement the plan.
3. *Observe:* Observe the effects of the action in the context in which it occurs.
4. *Reflect:* Reflect on these as a catalyst for further planning and subsequent action.

Reflection-on-action involves trying to determine, individually and collectively, what has been learnt from the enquiry process, the consequences of the intervention, and the need to re-formulate the teaching concern if necessary.

> Action research thus has an individual aspect, action researchers change themselves; and a collective aspect, action researchers work with others to achieve change and to understand what it means to change. That is, action research is concerned simultaneously with changing individuals, on the one hand, and, on the other, the culture of the groups, institutions and communities to which they belong. It is important to emphasise that these changes are not impositions: individuals and groups agree to work together to change themselves, individually and collectively, and to document the nature of, and changes in their work.
>
> (Henry 1993:60)

Just as there is much debate about the nature and aims of action research, so too there is debate about how teachers conduct their enquiries and work to resolve their teaching concerns. For example, the 'Teachers as Researchers in the Context of Award Bearing

Reflection	Inward	Outward
	Personal reflection	Reflections about problem situations and solutions
Involvement in change (agency)	Close	Distant
Focus of change	Pedagogy, pupil learning, curriculum, assessment, staff development, parent–teacher relations, school governors, etc.	
Locus of change	Local, e.g. personal	Broader, e.g. school, public perceptions
Knowledge base addressed	Practitioner	Expert/disciplinary

FIGURE 6.1 Teachers as researchers

Courses and Research Degrees' project in the UK, funded by the Economic and Social Research Council, explored the claims made for action research and the criticisms levelled against it (Elliott *et al.* 1996). One of its major findings was that 'a great diversity of approaches [were] exemplified in the dissertations' (p. 14). The main kinds of variation found are summarized in Figure 6.1.

Common to all these conceptions of research is the question, who decides which form of research is appropriate? Additionally,

- who participates and who is left out?
- whose problem, question or success is it?
- from whose perspective, and which perspectives are left out?
- who decides what's important to reflect upon and to action?
- whose reality is expressed, in what ways and why, and whose is left out?
- who can access and use what is learnt and who cannot?
- who benefits and in what ways and who does not?

Educational action research and the role of reflection

Diversity of purpose and approach is also a feature of the reflective part of the action–reflection cycle. Reflection is an integral part of action research, but there is a lack of clarity about it. Reflection needs to be built into each part of the action research process. In particular, in four parts of this process reflection is crucial. They are:

- problematizing teaching and learning;
- observing and creating a 'text' about our work;
- confronting ourselves and the teaching context;
- refocusing and creative action.

What follows is a pervasive view of action research – one that begins by addressing problems and concerns, not explicitly achievements, strengths, and successes.

Problematizing teaching and learning

- This can involve an element of discomfort, even threat, as we look at ourselves and our working environment. It is far easier to accept our current circumstances and adopt the line of least resistance!
- There is a need to reflect on what you perceive to be the inadequacies of your teaching, and also on your strengths and how to nourish and sustain existing good practice.
- It is not mandatory to introduce new and different perspectives from 'outside', but, through collective action, to reflect upon the basis (values) on which practice is taking place and to examine the real possibilities which practice, on this occasion, chooses to ignore or cannot enact.
- Problematizing teaching and learning means we reflect upon what is happening and why, what our educational intentions are and why we hold them. So in this sense problematizing can apply equally to 'problems' as it can to successes.

'Text' creation

- The process of reflection should generate a 'text'. This is a record and evidential-base derived from practice. One important 'text' is the reflective conversation. Another could be evidence in the form of a learning journal, or evidence in a personal positive portfolio or Career Entry Profile.
- The 'text' then needs to be 'read'. That is to say, through a reflective dialogue, it is opened up (deconstructed), the different messages are made sense of, and a new text is constructed with richer insights and meaning. The emphasis should be on learning from experience, and on moving thinking and practice forward in the light of this.
- Conferral and dialogue are essential in this process.

Confronting ourselves and the teaching context

Some key reflective questions that individual teachers might ask themselves are:

- What is my practice like?
- Why is it like this?
- How has it come to be this way?
- What would I like to improve and why?

Additionally, through peer observations and collaborative action it is important that the following questions are confronted:

- How far do I live my educational values out in my work?
- How far does the 'culture' of my workplace help or hinder this?

Refocusing and creative action

Reflection needs to have a consequence. One consequence is to strive to improve the quality of education. Becoming involved in 'improvement' is not only about becoming 'better', but also to do with becoming 'different' through questioning the taken-for-grantedness, the habits, the comfort blankets that we wrap around ourselves from time to time and by adopting a more problem-posing teaching posture. Fundamentally, this is about having a certain reflective disposition. It is about questioning practice with confidence so as to open up new possibilities and new directions for action.

Critical reflection re-framed

In developing a more strengths-based reflective practice, I have been criticized for being overly optimistic – almost Utopian. I have also been criticized for a lack of 'critical edge'. I would argue that being creative and critical are not oppositional. They are not naturally antagonistic towards each other. Critical reflection has become something of a buzzword recently. I set out my views on this, with others, in Ghaye *et al.* (2008). I suggest that creative and critical thinking (if indeed you wish to take reflection as a kind of thinking!) are different, but they can (and indeed should) coexist and help each other. One way of looking at things is to see creative thinking as the ability to generate new ideas and to see things with fresh eyes. Critical thinking is the ability to judge the worthiness of these ideas and fresh ways of seeing. It is very difficult to generate and judge at the same time. If we are overly critical, we can judge our ideas out of existence! The longer we can defer judgement, the more ideas we may come up with. So creative thinking is generative, non-judgemental and expansive. Arguably, then, critical thinking is the *yang* to creative thinking's *yin*. An important role for critical thinking (or critical reflection, as we have come to know it) is to be analytical. By this I mean it serves the important function of probing, questioning and putting ideas under pressure. Second, it has a role in helping us to come to decisions and to make judgements. In other words, it helps us determine which ideas are worth pursuing. Finally, critical thinking helps us be selective, it helps us narrow down long lists of ideas, possibilities and options, it helps us make choices. In this second edition I am suggesting that there is a place and role for both creative and critical thinking to flourish.

> Imagine a kayak paddle. One side stands for creative thinking, the other for critical thinking. If you always used the creative paddle, you'd go around in circles. If you always used the critical paddle, you'd go around in circles the other way. The key is to alternate between the two, that way you develop enormous forward momentum.
>
> (Hurson 2008:46–7)

A more strengths-based reflective practice is not insensitive to the perspective of critical theory and the way history, identity construction, power, politics and different discourses, for example, affect the way we feel, think and can act in certain organizational contexts. This 'interest' is the one that explicitly manifests itself in 'critical reflection'. What I am centrally concerned about with some expressions of 'critical reflection' is the way they seem to neglect, or downplay, the role of emotion, achievement and creativity in enabling individuals, groups and whole organizations to move forward. I am becoming increasingly anxious that some practices of reflection are becoming so analytical and rational that the intuitive, aesthetic, creative, appreciative and affective are being crowded out. Much of the way reflection is assessed in the context of award-bearing modules/courses seems to bear this out. In short, I would suggest that some reflective practices, which are more strengths-based and more sensitive to the feelings of others, are getting lost. I would wish to argue that we need to find an appropriate role for emotion in reflective practices – one that enhances and deepens understanding and improves action; a role that does not detract from building collective wisdom and acting with values in mind.

Reflective practices of one kind or another can, and have, drawn upon critical theory in a number of ways – for example, with regard to the nature and impact of 'critical thinking', 'critical action' and 'critical reflection upon action'. The first is about the need to be able to adopt a critical frame of mind when appropriate. We may also call this a critical disposition. Arguably, critical action is a collective capacity and capability to see ourselves and our actions in new and better ways, and to do different things. However, I believe that a central concern of a new strengths-based reflective practice is to exercise a critical spirit that enables us, at the same time, to be optimistic and hopeful (Freire 1994, Brookfield 2000). The view of the importance of the critical self and collective reflection can be traced to the work of Schön (1991). He argued that critical reflection was essentially about the way we 'see' or 'frame' problems and challenges in the first place. It also involves questioning what might routinely be taken for granted and those actions which are perceived to be oppressive.

McCormack and Titchen (2007) in particular, and Higgs *et al.* (2007) in general, suggested that the critical paradigm alone does not provide sufficient ontological and epistemological support for work that is concerned with fostering creative and transformational cultures of effectiveness and innovative organizing. Strengths-based reflective practices are aligned with this view. They also involve praxis, defined generally as reflection followed by action. Within a strengths-based reflective practice, praxis includes thinking and action that is not only about critical dialogue and contestation, but also appreciative and creative. Explicitly, this involves creative thinking, creative discourses and the making and taking of creative action. By implication, then, a strengths-based reflective practice not only has an interest in the active role that people play in their own subordination, self-creation and self-fashioning, but in their emancipation and collective abilities to build a better future from aspects of the positive present. It is therefore concerned with contemporary conditions and possibilities for developing a kind of communicative freedom that opens up fresh possibilities for working in the contested terrains that combat oppressive and limiting systems of thought. It is these that inhibit our capacity to imagine other possible ways of working and organizing.

A commonplace view of critical reflection is that it can lead to improved action because it tackles the context, or the 'system', in which teaching is embedded. It does this by asking challenging questions such as:

- Whose interests are served and denied by my/our practice?
- What conditions nourish and constrain my/our practice?
- What organizational and other influences prevent me/us working in alternative ways?
- What alternatives are available to me/us?

The central concern I have about the use of more critical forms of reflective practice is this. How can I/we be both critical and safe here?

Reflective moments

The reflective moments in the kind of action research described above are usually given relatively scant attention. It is often caricatured as a private, solitary, introspective activity, with the main cognitive process of 'replay and rehearsal' helping the practitioner to make sense of practice. I often hear teachers say, 'We just mull things over'. There is no definitive and correct way of doing action research. The same can be said of reflecting-on-practice. To maximize its potency, however, reflection needs to be both structured and supported, and the interests it serves sorted out.

In a recent review of approaches to reflection, Ghaye and Lillyman (2006a) identified four interests that reflection might serve. This links us back to Principle 6 in Chapter 3, and reflection being 'interest serving'. They are as follows.

1. *A personal interest*: reflection on personal successes, personal agendas, emotionality, self-study and enhancing feelings of self-worth, esteem, efficacy and identity.
2. *A learning through experience interest*: reflection on past actions and encounters; an active exploration of teachers' own and others' experiences. This requires practitioners to value their own experience, and have an openness that enables them to learn from the experiences of others (Kolb 1984).
3. *A competency-based interest:* reflection focused on skill development, problem-solving, and improvements in the technical and practical domains of educational work.
4. *A transformatory interest:* reflection that challenges the status quo, challenges the oppressive and disempowering influences on practice and tackles the barriers to improvement.

The reflective moments in the ongoing action research process are so very important. Reflection is like the glue that holds the research process together. It is misleading to think that it is 'fourth-in-line' in the cycle of events, and 'done at the end' before formulating a new, improved action plan.

Reflection-on-action is a complex business. It is wise for action researchers to appreciate that there are a number of conceptualizations of reflection, some of which may be more appropriate and supportive of their intention to improve practice and the context in which it takes place than others. For example, some conceptualizations of reflection are:

1. *As a dichotomy* of reflection-in-action and reflection-on-action (Schön 1983, 1987). The latter is a retrospective interrogation of practice to come to know the knowledge used and the feelings that accompanied action within a particular situation. The process of *reframing* lies at the heart of this conceptualization. It is a process where data drawn from our practice are seen differently.
2. *As intentional activity* (Ghaye 1996a) in that we reflect on purpose and with a purpose in mind. It is no accident that we reflect. Something usually triggers it.
3. *As for knowledge and skill development* (Steinmaker and Bell 1979, Benner 1984), where reflection is claimed to develop and enhance particular cognitive, affective, and psychomotor skills.
4. *As creating practitioner-derived knowledge* (Smyth 1991) that is worthy, valid, and relevant to particular educational situations.
5. *As resolving problematic situations* and the basis for problem-based learning (Dewey 1933, Schön 1991, Woods 1994) where systematic reflections enable us to think through and resolve educational situations that we perceive as being characterized by uncertainty, disorder and indeterminacy.
6. *As a process of becoming different* (Giroux 1987) in which reflection helps to equip us with lenses to read the world critically in order to improve it.

Having thought this through, the action researcher might then be well advised to clarify which function(s) reflection is to serve. For example, the function of reflection might be:

1. *to act as a bridge* (Silcock 1994) from tacit knowledge to considered action, and from the practice world of educational settings to the process of theory generation;

2. *to enhance the quality of action* (Olsen 1992), in that it enables us to talk about our practice (critically reflective conversations with self and others) and to practise different things. Reflection without action is just wishful thinking (Freire 1972);

3. *to increase accountability* (Diamond 1991), because the principles of technocratic efficiency emphasize hierarchically structured, top-down models of accountability with an increasing burden for professional accountability residing with the individual practitioner;

4. *as a much-needed counter discourse* (Smyth 1991) to challenge the ensconced and pervasive technicist views of educational practice that marginalize and de-legitimize the teaching experiences, histories and practical wisdom that practitioners use in mediating their lives. This counter discourse is no less important for student teachers. The point Whitty *et al.* (1987) made over two decades ago is still pertinent:

> It is still possible to foster a spirit of critical reflection amongst student teachers. Indeed, their experience on teaching practice of declining material conditions and teacher morale generates a positive demand for critical reflection not only on their own practice but upon the ways in which state policy impinges upon it.
>
> (Whitty *et al.* 1987:174)

Action research for improving thinking, practice and working context takes as its starting point the socially-constructed, value-laden nature of practice. Action for improvement can be usefully conceived as a dialogical and reflective process. Action research is not only about learning – it is about knowledge production and about a commitment to improve practice. The principles and practices of action research can play a significant part in helping us all to establish, sustain and nourish new and more meaningful work environments. If action research cannot promise to be empowering, liberating and emancipatory, if it cannot promise to develop 'enchanted' workplaces, what is the least that it could claim? Perhaps the most humble claim is that it could give us a greater sense of control over our own work and free us somewhat to increase our avenues for alternative action. Perhaps for these reasons alone we should give action research, and the part reflection-on-practice plays in this process, serious consideration.

Developing a strengths-based reflective competence

Reflective competence is a term that refers to our ability to be fully aware of ourselves, our feelings and thoughts in a given situation. It is also;

> Seeing the dynamics as they are played out in the full context of the situation ... at the same time you are in the movie and watching the movie run before your very own eyes. In the organisational context, we have moved beyond simple data collectors, information users and knowledge managers to co-creators of new knowledge.
>
> (Stratton-Berkessel 2010:15)

As I have tried to explain earlier, the old reflective competence paradigm was largely about focusing first on problems or weaknesses. It was these things, and the feelings and behaviours that defined them, which we attended to. Competence was associated with our ability to fix that which we felt needed fixing. Because of this, all those things that brought us joy, satisfaction, happiness, a sense of pride and accomplishment didn't grab our attention. There was a feeling that if we devoted our time to sorting out our problems, the good things were able, simply, to look after themselves. Therefore, a measure of competence was the amount of time, money, energy, intellect and emotional labour that we invested into those things that didn't work for us. So why has this been such a dominant paradigm for so long? If you were a gambler and placed a bet on a racehorse or greyhound to win, you wouldn't bet on the weakest but on the best and the strongest! You'd focus on trying to find out the strengths of each individual animal. You'd focus on their strengths, not their weaknesses. And if you were an animal trainer, you'd try to nurture and further develop a natural strength in each horse or greyhound. I would be surprised if you'd do it the other way around – focus on the animal's weaknesses at the cost of nurturing their natural talents and strengths. So when it comes to learning through reflection, why do we do it the other way around? Why is there this pervasive belief that we need to eliminate weaknesses to achieve optimal performance and job satisfaction? How far do you see a role for a practice of reflection that builds individual, team and organizational strengths, so that weaknesses become irrelevant? Is this a pipe dream? Is it unworthy? Is it unsound? It seems that we may be genetically programmed to tackle weaknesses first. What if you work in an organization that uses 360-degree performance reviews. What do you do when you get your Report? Do you go straight to the page about weaknesses and what your line manager wants you to work on? How many of you have done this? How long does it take for you to get to the page where it says what you do best in your role?

I suggest that strengths-based reflective competences are those where we demonstrate that we can:

1. Create teaching and learning environments that strengthen existing talents and gifts.
2. Build positive emotions in all those involved.
3. Use the power of positive questions, because we tend to grow in the direction in which we ask questions. The very first question we ask starts the change process. If we ask the question 'how was it at work today?', we will get one kind of response. Usually a short one! If we ask 'what was the best thing that happened at work today?, we will get another. The second question is likely to take the conversation off in a totally different direction. If we ask 'what are your weaknesses that you need to work on?, we will grow in that direction. If we ask 'what are your strengths that you can develop further in your current role?', we grow in a very different direction. We live in the world our questions create.
4. Use flip-it strategies to turn negatives into something more positive and hopeful. In other words we don't focus on what our students don't like doing or can't do, but instead we focus on what will energize, motivate, enthuse and even delight them!
5. Address problems from a position of renewed strength, confidence and appetite which comes from a strengths-first reflective practice. What we focus on grows. Focus on problems and they will grow. The same happens when we focus on

strengths. This competence also helps us identify what we need to change or stop doing.

6. Be better at what we do in the future, through identifying and amplifying aspects of the positive present.

7. Take practical action to develop, and constantly hold under review, that which constitutes our '*positive core*'. This is the sum total of our positive attributes and strengths. Your positive core comprises 'what you want and are proud of', not what you don't want and are ashamed of.

7

Evidence-based Reflective Practice

Student teachers are often asked, on school experience, 'How might your lesson have been improved?' This can be received in a number of ways. Sometimes it is decoded and felt to imply that the lesson was not very good, things went wrong, the supervising tutor and class teacher are unhappy. It is interpreted to mean, 'Please do not do it like that again', and 'Let's think seriously about changing things'. Another interpretation is that the lesson was far from being a 'disaster', and that the tutor and/or class teacher are trying to help pinpoint certain aspects of the lesson which might be further strengthened. There is another view, too, which is that this is the kind of question that conscientious and reflective teachers ask themselves all the time. When the word 'improvement' is used, it brings with it a range of thoughts and emotions. Some are rather more negative, and relate to teacher deficits. Others are embedded in conceptions of what it means to be a professional, of teacher development as a lifelong learning process and associated with nourishing strengths as well as working at relatively weaker areas of practice.

If, as I have argued, the fundamental purpose of reflective practice is to improve the quality of education, then we must ask the question, 'So, what does improvement mean?' Improvements in individual and collective workplace competence are inextricably linked to changes in the quality of human interactions. Just as we need to question the notion and processes of change, so too do we need to question the slippery concept of improvement. Not all change may be considered to be improvement. Similarly, what is thought to be an improvement for a particular work environment – say, in one particular class – is not inevitably and always seen to be supportive of the interests of all those who work in other classrooms.

Ghaye (1995) argued that workplace improvement needs to be considered in relation to five questions. Each question needs to be reflected on and talked about in school.

1.   *The question of time*

   ■   When are the most appropriate times for our improvement efforts to take place?
   ■   When are the consequences of these improvements likely to be felt and noticed?

2.   *The question of scale*

   ■   What is the scope of the improvement?
   ■   How many people are involved, and what resources will it consume?

- What are the nature, magnitude, and educative potency of the consequences of the envisioned improvement?

3. *The question of uncertainty*

   - For example, how far can we be sure that the new conditions, action, motivations and orientations are indeed an improvement?
   - What does valid evidence of improvement look like?
   - How far do we understand the links between perceived improvements and concrete and visible improvements in the quality of educational interactions in the workplace?
   - Are these improvements real or imagined?

4. *The question of micro-politics*

   Institutional politics provoke questions that are central to any improvement effort. Improvement is a value-laden concept and process. It is therefore not surprising that people in a particular work environment think differently and want to act differently in order to influence and shape their future and the futures of others. Understanding the politics of teacher improvement efforts is a recognition that, in school, there is inevitably an interplay between competing interests. Reflective practice will raise political questions, because improvement is concerned with 'interests', 'power', and the resolution of 'conflict'. Improvement can be seen as who gets what, where, how, when and why.

5. *The question of penetration*

   Sometimes, because of weak or misguided improvement efforts and external pressures, we pay too much attention to the impressionistic and the facade that decorates the surface of our work environments. This is at the expense of working at those things that are more fundamental and that give rise to and tend to sustain these 'surface' attributes. Perhaps teachers have grown accustomed to improving things without paying sufficient attention to the culture of schools on which their improvement efforts are predicated. School improvement is one thing. However, school transformation is different, because it penetrates deeply and improves the quality of the educational relationships of all those in the organization. This deep kind of penetration involves the careful management of both the external and internal school structures and influences. Too much emphasis on internal development will not lead to school transformation. The connection with the wider environment is vital for this (Fullan 1994).

Improvement cannot take place unless we learn from experience. Failure to do this is resigning ourselves to being prisoners of our past. Reflection-on-practice is intentional action; the intention is to improve the quality of educational experiences through a rigorous reflection of the learning that has accrued as a consequence of engaging reflective practices of one kind or another. In a reflective account, the learning from experience needs to be transparent. The reader should be able to *see* the professional landscape in which the writer is working. The reader should *hear* the way the reflective dialogues have moved thinking and practice forward. The writer should also attend to the way his or her account helps the reader to *feel* and empathize with the teacher's workplace achievements and ongoing struggles.

Reflections on learning from experience are predicated on three things: first, that experience must be had, it cannot be taught (Munby and Russell 1995:173); second, that we can make some sense of what is happening around us; and third, that we are able to communicate this in some understandable manner. We can call a product of reflection a 'text' or 'account'. Making sense of teaching is always a learning process. Reflection helps us to become more aware of the potency of our experience and what we can take from it to move our thinking and practice forward. Miller and Boud (1996:9–10) offer some important views in relation to this. They are that:

- experience is the foundation of, and stimulus for, learning;
- learners actively construct their own experience;
- learning is holistic;
- learning is socially and culturally constructed;
- learning is influenced by the socio-emotional context in which it occurs.

Central to this chapter are Miller and Boud's ideas that, first, what teachers (and children) experience is influenced by their own unique past, the current learning milieu and future expectations. Second, while teachers and children construct their own learning, they do so in the context of a particular social setting, namely that of the school with its own values and things that it regards as worthwhile. Third, learning from experience is a social, cognitive and affective activity. I have argued earlier (see Chapter 1) that reflection-on-practice has an important emotional component.

> Emotions and feelings are key pointers both to possibilities for, and barriers to, learning. Denial of feelings is a denial of learning. It is through emotions that some of the tensions and contradictions between our own interests and those of the external context manifest themselves.
>
> (Miller and Boud 1996:10)

Using positive questions to create a text

So what kinds of positive questions might we use in order to create a text? Here are some suggestions. All the following might help you develop your positive core.

1. What were you doing recently, in managing your time, that enabled you to use your strengths?
2. What actions were you taking when you were successful at prioritizing those things that you are really good at doing?
3. What was happening when you found yourself thinking, 'that really worked well?
4. What did someone say, or do, to make you feel that your professional experience was greatly appreciated?
5. What strengths do you feel you have to 'fight fires' at work? (Fire-fighting is about constantly fixing problems and dealing with what's urgent rather than what might be important.)
6. What did you do that prompted a colleague to say, 'thank you, that was very helpful?'

7. What were you doing that prompted a colleague to say, 'It's great working with you?'

8. What did you say to a colleague that enabled them to say, 'thanks for understanding my situation?'

All of these eight questions might be followed up with, 'What do your answers tell you about those things you really value (your values) and the positive actions you can take to put them into action?'

A positive question is one that invites us to reflect upon and then to give voice to those aspects of our lived experience (van Manen 1997) that give us a sense of joy, fulfilment and satisfaction in our work and workplace. By asking positive questions, we give ourselves a chance to create powerful vocabularies of possibility – in particular, thinking about the possibility of positively re-experiencing past successes and doing more of what satisfies and achieves agreed goals. Through *an ethical and appreciative reflection process*, the asking of positive questions can become habitual. This habit embraces two fundamental conceptions of reflection; namely, the acts of looking back and of looking forward – looking back and rediscovering joys, excellence and innovation, then looking forward and asking the positive question: 'What single thing, were it to happen again, *and more frequently*, would make a significant and positive difference to my work here?' When I invite individuals and groups to reflect upon this question, there is usually much discussion around the inclusion of 'and more frequently' and how omitting it from the sentence changes it substantially. The phrase 'significant and positive' is also a cause of much debate.

How far can reflection be both ethical and appreciative?

If we make the processes of reflective practice *ethical* and *appreciative*, we have a chance to:

1. *Release new positive vocabularies*

   Positive questions refocus our attention away from problems and toward possibilities. By asking positive questions, we invite participants to use words, phrases, sentences and ideas that typically remain uncelebrated or under-used in much of what constitutes normal organizational conversation. This has two consequences.

   > First, it begins to loosen the hammerlock that patterns of deficit discourse have on the organisation ... Second, because the restrictive grip of deficit vocabularies is loosened, the positive questions immediately boost energy for action within the organisation. People begin to feel a sense of their own authorship within the organisation. They recognize the strengths and resources that they and others bring to their jobs and this enhances their sense of esteem and efficacy for getting things done. It also generates new ideas for action.
   >
   > (Cooperrider 2001:28)

2. *Affirm variety of experience and encourage full voice*

   If a significant part of improving our practice is about the co-creation of (better) meaning and understanding, we are, by implication, adopting a social constructionist view. So it follows that language provides the means through which we communicate the sense we make of our worlds. The language we have available to us, to an extent, determines our possibilities for action. Positive vocabularies give us a chance of acting in the world, positively.

3. *Help ourselves value others even more*

Asking positive questions enables us to appreciate what others value and cherish in their work – and so, understandably, what they want more, not less, of.

4. *Foster relational connections*

Asking a positive question invites those participating in learning through reflection a chance to think about their practice and to think of something significant to them. These are essential things that connect us with others.

5. *Help build a sense of community*

'By inviting participants to inquire deeply into the best and most valued aspects of one another's life and work, it immediately creates a context of empathy, care and mutual affirmation' (Cooperrider 2001:31).

6. *Generate innovation*

Finally, I suggest that a reflective practice which is both ethical and appreciative enables those involved to grow and evolve in the direction of their most positive guiding images of the future. When we use the practices of reflection only as an opportunity to explore our misgivings, weaknesses and deficiencies, we gain expert knowledge of what is 'wrong' (or less than desirable) with our own practice, the work of others and our workplace. If reflection is only about this, we may become (even) more proficient problem-solvers. By doing this, we lose an opportunity to strengthen our collective capacity to imagine and to build better educational experiences. We miss out on seeing reflection as a process where we create and sustain a culture of possibility and innovation within teaching and learning.

I have argued elsewhere (Ghaye 2005) of the importance of trust for both personal and team improvement. Although a complex process to establish and sustain, trust is usually assumed to be a prerequisite for building shared values, meanings and positive action. Trust is not always easy to achieve, especially where the weight of past betrayals and hostility hangs heavy (Rothstein 2000).

Without trust, reflective conversations of positive regard, and then the creation of positive texts, are non-starters. Reina and Reina (2006) help us with two things: to appreciate how important trust (and betrayal) are in the workplace, and how to build trusting relationships. At the heart of their book is the notion of transactional trust. This is a process of mutual exchange, reciprocity and something created incrementally over time. In other words, we have to give trust in order to increase the likelihood that we will receive it! They set out three types of transactional trust:

1. *Contractual trust*. This is essentially a trust of character. Put another way, it's about people actually doing what they say they will do; doing what they promise. It is about keeping agreements, honoring intentions and behaving consistently.

2. *Communication trust*. This is essentially a trust of disclosure. Put another way, it's about people's willingness to share information, to tell the truth, admit mistakes, celebrate achievements and successes, maintain confidentiality, give and receive constructive feedback. Trust influences the quality of our conversations, and vice versa.

3. *Competence trust.* This is essentially a trust of capability. How far do you trust the people you work with? Or trust your line manager? Do you trust them to do a good job? How capable do you feel your colleagues are in giving you constructive feedback? How capable are they in providing you with what you think you want and need to know, in order to continue to improve your practice?

I suggest that the benefits of learning through reflection are heightened when we think deeply about two fundamental questions: '*What do I believe about others?*' and '*What can I learn from others?*'

Experienced-based improvement through open listening

Kahane (2004) gives us a sharp reminder of how not to conduct ourselves when we have the opportunity to have improvement-focused reflective conversations. He says:

> The root of not listening is knowing. If I already know the truth, why do I need to listen to you? Perhaps out of politeness or guile I should pretend to listen, but what I really need to do is to tell you what I know, and if you don't listen, to tell you again, more forcefully. All authoritarian systems rest on the assumption that the boss can and does know the one right answer.
>
> (Kahane 2004:47)

Communication trust means talking openly and honestly. It brings with it a willingness and ability on our part to disclose *to* others what's in our head and heart. Listening openly, on the other hand, means being willing and able to positively embrace something different and new *from* others. This isn't as easy as it may sound, because it involves issues about interpersonal relations, power, value alignment, and so on.

> My team worked hard to learn how to listen, without judging, to what another person was trying to say – really to be there. If we listen in the normal closed way, for what is right and what is wrong, then we won't be able to hear what is possible.... We won't be able to create anything new.
>
> (Kahane 2004:77)

Listening sounds so simple, doesn't it? So I ask, when was the last time you felt you were listened to, openly? How far can you think of a positive experience, between you and a colleague, when you felt you were listening openly to them? How do you know this? What made you feel this way? What were the circumstances that led up to this? What was the root cause of such a positive experience?

So what kinds of behaviours support the way we might listen openly to, and learn from, colleagues? How might this help us build a conversation and then a text between us of positive regard? Wheatley (2002) offers us some useful thoughts in what she eloquently describes as 'seeing how wise we can be together' (p. 28). What we can learn from her work is that we have to learn not only to *listen openly*, but also to *listen reflectively*. Some of her thoughts are as follows.

- *We need to learn how to acknowledge one another as equals.* A language of positive regard requires us to acknowledge that we are equal as human beings (unequal when in role) and that we need each other. We can't always improve our own practice by trying to figure things out on our own.

- *We should try to stay curious about each other.* We need to be genuinely interested in what our colleagues have to say, not fearful. We need to test out our commitment to a value of the kind, 'I believe that I can learn something significant from every colleague I meet, each day' (Ghaye and Lillyman 2000). This weaves openness together with reflection.

- *We need to help each other listen openly and then act appropriately.* It can be hard work to listen – especially when we are busy, feeling certain of ourselves, or stressed. Try to think of a positive experience with your colleagues when you know you listened to their views and then acted appropriately on them. What made this a positive experience?

- *We need to slow down to make time to listen reflectively.* If listening is an important part in developing a language of positive regard, so too is slowing down. Often we need to make time to listen to each other's views and to reflect on them. So a reflective conversation should not be experienced as a rush through to the end of a list of things!

- *We should expect conversations to be messy at times.* Usually conversations don't move in a straight line. When learning through a reflective conversation, it is probable that some things don't appear to connect with our experiences and perceptions. Experiences can be diverse. Listening openly and reflectively means that we resist the impulse to tidy things up and put experiences in little boxes. We need to learn the benefits of being 'disturbed'. By this, I mean having our ideas and practices challenged by others. How can we be creative in improving our own practice and improving the quality of teaching and learning, if we are not willing to be disturbed?

> To create new realities, we have to listen reflectively. It is not enough to be able to hear clearly the chorus of other voices; we must also hear the contribution of our own voice. It is not enough to be able to see others in the picture of what is going on; we must also see what we ourselves are doing. It is not enough to be observers of the problem situation; we must also recognize ourselves as actors who influence the outcome.
>
> (Kahane 2004:83)

Creating a reflective text

Here are some practical ways to begin to create texts of different kinds. The first is called a PMI. You can learn more about this technique at www.holstgroup.co.uk. Try to complete Table 7.1 and the PMI framework with a particular experience or encounter in mind.

Another way to create a text is by using the PAP framework. Try to complete Table 7.2 and the PAP framework.

TABLE 7.1 The PMI framework

EXPLANATION	TEXT
P = PLUS POINTS Things I felt were particularly good and worthy about what I saw, heard and/or did	
M = MINUS POINTS Things I felt didn't quite work and could be a source of further reflection and possible improvement	
I = INTERESTING POINTS Things which particularly interested me, surprised, intrigued, puzzled me	

TABLE 7.2 The PAP framework

EXPLANATION	TEXT
P = POSITIVE What were the things that you did that enabled you to use your strengths at this particular moment?	
A = ACTION What single thing, if it were to happen more frequently, would make a significant difference to your work right now?	
P = POSSIBILITIES What thing(s) need(s) to change so that you can use your strengths, more often, in the future?	

Here is a third way to create a very different kind of text. It's called a 'draw a house task'. The aim of this is to heighten your awareness, sensitivity and understanding of how you relate to others. Sometimes we think we are working *with* someone when we are in fact controlling the whole situation!

1. Choose a partner.
2. Hold a jumbo marker pen together in such a way that you are able to both write and draw with it.
3. On your blank paper, draw a house and write a title for your drawing.
4. Keep silent during the drawing and writing process.

Now reflect on the following questions and write down your responses:

- What were your feelings during the task?
- What feelings helped or got in the way of you doing this task?
- What strength(s) were you able to use in drawing the house?

A fourth way to create a text of another kind, is called a 'life pie task'. Why not have a go at this? It is best done with others.

1. On a piece of blank paper, draw a pie. Make each slice represent the various, but important, parts of your life.

2. When done, place your pie face down in the middle of a table. No need to sign it unless you wish to.

3. Mix up the pies. Choose one (hopefully not your own at this stage), and offer an interpretation of it to others in the group.

4. What are you learning?

5. Now re-claim your own pie. Share, with others, the significance of the different pieces of your pie.

6. On the reverse side of your pie, re-draw it in such a way that it reflects a better and more preferred way of valuing your time (not managing you time!).

7. Now share this with others in the group.

8. What is the most important thing you feel you have to change, in your current situation, to bring this preferred pie into existence?

The reflective journal as a text

Journal writing is an important aid to making sense of teaching and learning (Ghaye and Lillyman 2006a). It is also popular, so it is discussed it in some detail here. Journals form a part of many initial teacher training and continuing professional development courses. They are a popular aid to reflection, and they are also about the construction and interpretation of meaning. What follows are some responses to the questions that are most frequently asked when introducing the idea of reflective journals.

What is a learning journal?

This can be answered by looking at its contents and how they are communicated. A learning journal should contain the educator's practical knowledge and wisdom. *What* is written about is the content. When written down, a 'text' is created which enables educators to re-examine fundamental issues associated with teaching and learning, and the contexts which mould it. The text can comprise a range of evidence and be written in a creative and interpretative manner so that the meanings, which reveal themselves from the re-examination of journal entries at a later date, can inform future practice. Choosing what to write about is a question of selection, which I have discussed earlier, and is often difficult, for everything seems relevant at times. The bottom line is that the content can be justified as being professionally significant, at that moment in time. Learning journals serve many purposes which in turn influence what teachers write in them. For example, they can be a repository for evidence about children's learning, for examining changes in your self-image, as an evaluation mechanism for aspects of your practice, to facilitate critical and creative thinking, to release feelings and frustrations, and to see different 'truths'.

How the chosen and significant encounter or experience is written about, the mediums and genres used, is the writing process. Learning accrues from this process, and is facilitated by responses to questions such as, 'What kind of teacher am I?', 'How have I come to teach this way?' and 'How can I amplify my strengths and improve my practice?' Teachers know their practical worlds in general, social and shared ways, and also in unique and personal ways. In constructing accounts of practice the past is not irrelevant but provides a context for present thinking, action and future intentions.

When do I write my learning journal?

Entries should be made regularly and perhaps at least once each week. Learning has to be given a chance to emerge, so educators need to make a series of entries and then re-read them to search for patterns, themes, issues, conflicts and so on. It is often useful to keep a small notebook to jot down the essence of interesting, satisfying, worrying and/ or puzzling encounters and conversations as you go through the week. These can then be elaborated upon in the learning journal later. The longer the writing is left, the more you have to trust your memory. This can be tricky!

What interests do learning journals serve?

The work of Thomas (1992, 1995) is helpful to develop a number of 'portraits' to illuminate the interests learning journals might serve.

Portrait 1: The learning journal as 'A collection of anecdotes'

Personal anecdotes are experiences, and so have a value. A collection of anecdotal evidence may reveal something worthwhile about a teacher's thinking, feelings and practice. To be more useful, the anecdotes need to be placed in a context and need to be re-visited, re-read and evaluated over time. If anecdotes tell you nothing about how to improve what you do, then you need to change the content and process.

Portrait 2: The learning journal as 'An interpreted story'

Just as stories have structures, entries in a journal can also be structured. An entry might usefully have a clear beginning and a middle. It might not have an end, just a range of 'messy bits' and unresolved issues. As with story-making, the content needs to be carefully selected and certain aspects of the entry given more emphasis than others. Journal entries of this kind, just like stories, have to be interpreted. Out of this comes the learning.

Portrait 3: The learning journal as 'A fulcrum for professional development'

Some of the characteristics of learning-enriched work environments are collegiality, open communication, trust, support and help. Having the time to talk through the problems of practice is also a vital ingredient of both personal and collective professional development. For some, the learning journal fulfils a need to tell, to enter into dialogues and to expose and explore various interpretations of 'This is what I did, for these reasons. This is what it felt like, so what do you think?'

Portrait 4: The learning journal as 'A means of asserting that teaching is evidence-based'

This can be done if entries are guided by the following ideas:

- you are trying to live out the things you believe in;
- you wish to account for your actions;
- you are actively seeking to improve your practice;
- you acknowledge that claims for moving practice forward have to be supported with evidence.

Portrait 5: The learning journal as 'A means of bringing order to turbulent educational environments'

In trying to make sense of our educational worlds we need to hold the turbulence still for a moment. A single journal entry is a piece of frozen text waiting to be reflected upon. For a moment, it brings a kind of order to things. Teachers are not confronted with issues, challenges, dilemmas and problems that are independent of each other, but rather with dynamic, turbulent and often chaotic situations which interact simultaneously. Ackoff (1979) calls such situations 'messes'. Journal writing has the potential to help us make sense of such 'messes'.

Portrait 6: The learning journal as 'A means of searching for the truth'

Each journal entry should not be viewed as some absolute, fixed and verifiable truth – i.e., the last and final word on the matter under consideration. Teaching is value-laden, so truths are often partial, contested, inter-subjective and elusive. Learning through reflection on journal entries is a continuous process of redefinition and reconstruction. It is a creative enterprise.

Portrait 7: The learning journal as 'A basis for building a better world'

Journals should have a prospective quality. Constructive, creative and critical reflections on past events should constitute a new beginning or an action plan to improve what is already being experienced and in existence.

What are the ethical implications of keeping a learning journal?

Moving thinking and practice forward requires not only expertise and commitment, but also honesty and integrity. Some of the more obvious ethical issues (which I expand upon later in this chapter) associated with journal writing in particular are set out below, under three headings. These are rights, risks and benefits, and consent.

The issue of rights

When teachers reflect on their practice through their journal, they have certain rights. These are related to self-respect, self-esteem and dignity. Whether or not teachers keep their journal entries to themselves or share them in some way, they have the right to self-determination. No teacher should be coerced into making public what is written in his or her journal; the teacher has the right to privacy. The owner of the journal should be the one who determines the time, extent and context under which his or her journal entries are disclosed. Teachers have the right to decide what to withhold and what they share. If teachers share the contents of their journal with others, it is important that this issue of rights is sorted out early on.

The issue of risks and benefits

In keeping a learning journal, feelings of discomfort and vulnerability may arise because teachers are asking questions such as, 'Why is my teaching like this?', 'How did it come to be this way?' and 'How can I improve it?' A commitment to learn from journal writing is a commitment to a great deal of introspection, honesty with self, and a frame of mind that will be able to handle what you come to know in a constructive way. Sharing your journal entries with others may also put at risk such things as your level of self-confidence, call into question aspects of your practice, and challenge your much cherished professional values. There are also risks for those who support or facilitate reflection through journal writing, such as teacher educators and school mentors. What should or must they do, for example, if they hear an account of malpractice or teaching which they would consider to be unprofessional? What happens to notions of trust and confidentiality between people in such circumstances? Who becomes vulnerable, perhaps marginalized or peripheralized? Questions such as 'How far is the account true?', 'How far are we sure of it?' and 'What are the risks associated with not being sure?' need to be asked and responded to.

The issue of consent

It is important to think through this issue if, in the contents of the journal, teachers are drawing upon the experiences of colleagues as a means to further their own ends. If journal entries are made public and shared, for example, with peers, issues about who is telling what, to whom, and why, need to be clarified. Additionally, the general dialogical environment needs to be supportive of this activity, and requires some warmth and collective engagement. In listening to another's account, we are given an entrée into someone else's educational world. In disclosing what is in a learning journal, 'tellers' needs to be sure that they can trust others with what may be a sensitive but certainly a professionally significant issue.

What are some of the tensions that need to be resolved in keeping a learning journal?

The contents and processes of keeping a journal are held in a 'tensioned' relationship. Some of the most important tensions that need resolving are discussed here.

Tension 1: Between writing personal and safe responses

Developing teacher professionality through journal writing requires the development of an ability to write what you feel needs writing in a fair, accurate and honest manner, and often to say things in a critical yet constructive way. Sometimes safe responses are written in a context of fear, disempowerment and blame. Sometimes they are written up so as not to offend if they were to enter the public domain in some way.

Tension 2: Between teacher-centric and 'significant other' perspectives

The journal is a medium through which teachers can present their view of things. No account is free from bias and a certain amount of distortion (wilful or unconscious). No account is neutral and impartial. The journal can be used to represent alternative perspectives that allow the teacher to see the same teaching incident in different ways. It can serve to illuminate the subjective connections of self with significant others (e.g., teacher colleagues, parents, governors).

Tension 3: Between privacy and the right to know

This is a complex and very 'contested' issue. We have said that teachers have the right to keep the contents of a learning journal private if they so wish. But this raises the moral problem concerning the rights others have to know the content of the journal. Some of these rights are to do with journal writing in a context of professional and organizational accountability. Other rights are more legalistic in kind, and relate to the way evidence from a journal might be used in a process of litigation. Then there is the right that some might exercise in terms of 'I have the right to know what it is you are writing about me!' This is about the right to know, and the right to intervene in the light of that information. Rights are problematic because they often contain appeals to different political, professional and moral values (Pring 1988).

Tension 4: Between structure and freedom

Sometimes, if keeping a learning journal is an initial teacher training or in-service course requirement, expectations are raised about how far there is a predetermined structure or format for each entry. Keeping a learning journal offers teachers the freedom to express themselves in whatever style they choose, unfettered by 'academic' conventions and traditions.

Tension 5: Between the particular and the general

One journal entry is an account of a particular instance of practice, an encounter, a dialogue, a feeling, an achievement, and so on. It is dangerous to read too much into one entry. Journals that contain numerous entries over time provide the potential for generalization. This might be a generalization about a personally-preferred value position in relation to effective learning, about a general strategy for managing a full and busy classroom, and so on. In this sense, 'general' means what a teacher tends generally to do, think and feel. It may or may not be generally true for others. It is important to appreciate the difference between what is generally the case for one teacher and what is not. In reflecting on journal entries it is also important to try to tease out what is particular and different in certain teaching situations, and what are the more patterned, regular, and therefore more general things. If teachers make these general things known to others, they give them the opportunity to generalize from it to their own teaching situation. This is called naturalistic generalization (Stake 1995).

Tension 6: Between moving forward and disillusionment

The learning that accrues from reflective 'text' construction has to be known and valued by the teacher who is keeping the journal. The benefits have to be articulated in such a way that the teacher feels that he or she is moving forward. This sense of moving forward will often be defined in very personal ways. Without this sense, journal-keeping can quickly lead to disillusionment, and to feelings that the process was a 'waste of time'.

What are some of the common problems in keeping a learning journal?

Four of the most common are:

1. *The problem of procrastination.* This is a particular problem if it is felt that keeping a learning journal is unworthy of the attention that initial teacher training or in-service coursework assignments/exams appear to warrant.
2. *The problem of superficial and unreflective entries.* There is no virtue in trying to describe and faithfully regurgitate what has happened. The idea is to set out the significant encounter or teaching incident and then to interrogate it through the processes of writing and critical reflection (in some cases), and through peer or collegial discussion.
3. *The problem of waning enthusiasm.* To make learning happen it needs to have a chance to take hold and be apprehended. It may help to view the learning journals as a companion, to be committed to make regular entries and re-read them over time.
4. *Unwillingness or inability to reflect.* Reflection-on-practice is not just a cognitive activity, but a moral, affective and ethical art form. Teachers need to be encouraged to read about keeping a learning journal, about reflection being a complex activity, and about the benefits that arise from structured and supported reflection-on-practice.

Examples of journal writing

There are many ways to create a reflective 'text'. Above all other things, each entry must be concerned with something professionally significant and written in the journal in such a way that it makes sense to you, who have written it.

There is no real virtue in trying to follow some notion of 'academic convention' each time you write in your journal. You need to create the kind of 'text' described earlier. A 'text' is something that you can learn from; there are no 'writing rules'. You might usefully let go of any notions that you have of trying to 'get it right first time'. The personal relevance and meaning of the entries are important qualities. In keeping a journal you should not get bogged down with issues of 'better' or 'worse', about writing better, tighter, more economically, more perfectly! More important is trying to create entries which allow you to search for new angles on developing your strengths, on your professional concerns, biases, fragmented and woolly thinking, new juxtapositions and important associations that perhaps had remained unknown and uncelebrated. It is also important to avoid the 'paralysis by analysis syndrome'. Try to be patient and realistic with what you want to get out of your journal writing. It is unrealistic to think that new, wonderful insights about teaching and learning will emerge, as if by magic, from one or two short entries!

In this chapter I illustrate six of the more common types of journal entry. Each type represents a different way of representing what the teacher wanted to record in his or her journal. Sometimes a series of entries in a journal might be in the same form. But there is no reason why you should not change the form of your entry, in the same way that you might change the focus of it. One entry might also embrace more than one form. I have labelled some types of journal entry thus:

- faithful regurgitation
- off-load
- extend and revise
- concept-mapping
- knotty and messy
- living contradiction.

There is a natural blurring of the edges between types. In reality, each 'text' is often part of a 'tangle-of-texts' (Sumara and Luce-Kapler 1993) which convey a sense of the complexities of teaching and learning. In all of them the writer is clearly positioned within the text.

Example 1: The faithful regurgitation type

The emphasis in entries of this kind is upon 'what I've done'. They tend to be mainly descriptive reflections-on-practice, and can be written up in a vivid manner. They are personal views on things.

> I prepared everything so carefully today, or so I thought. We were due to have our PE lesson, practising our catching and throwing skills, and we were going to develop this into a game towards the end of the lesson, introducing large bats. I'd arranged the groups so that each group had at least two children who could hit the ball and one who could catch relatively easily. The children were excited, and I had spent ten minutes in the classroom organizing the children and explaining what they were going to do. Each group had a team leader, and each person in the group had a job to do and a piece of equipment to collect from the PE store. They had all remembered to bring their kit, and were bubbling with excitement. I sent Katy to fetch the key to the PE store. She came back with the message that Mr Johns had the key. So she went to his classroom to be told that Mrs Dickens had the key, or at least she did have it first thing in the morning! And so it went on. Each time Katy returned, the children groaned.

In the end, I decided that we may as well go out onto the field and warm up. For ten minutes we jogged and chased and skipped and jumped, until a triumphant Katy appeared waving the elusive key on the end of a string! The children cheered. We all trooped to the PE store and took out the equipment. Five minutes later it was all set up. Children threw their first ball. A crack of lightning streaked across the sky. Screams went up from all sides. Thunder followed. More screams. We raced to pick up equipment and charged to the hall. Rows of faces greeted us. A parents' meeting, which I had completely forgotten about, had just started, and an embarrassed head teacher gave me one of her looks! I turned quickly, motioned to the children to retreat, and fumbled my way back to the classroom with 29 deflated children in tow. A complete disaster.

(Class Teacher, Year 2)

Example 2: The off-load type

Entries of this kind tend to be high on emotionality, with the teacher often claiming that the entry is 'personal and pertinent'. They often focus upon a significant encounter with others, often colleagues, and can contain disagreements over educational practice and/or policy. The entry is 'significant' in that it might make us joyful, proud, or cross. What is written about might not go away, might not have been resolved. The content may question your professionality. Some entries of this type can be quite judgemental. The writing process can also be cathartic. Through it, we can purge ourselves of pent up emotions (Holly 1989).

If I have another lesson like today, I think I'll pack the job in altogether! I'm persevering with the group story because I want the children to learn that they have to listen to each other and to write collaboratively. There are too many individuals in this class who think that they know best and everyone else should be doing as they say! It makes me so angry when I spend hours encouraging them to be thoughtful and to respect each other and then they just argue and fight and get on each other's nerves. It makes me feel a failure. I can't see why they have to behave in this way when I try to make the lessons enjoyable and different.

(Student Teacher, Year 5 class)

Example 3: The extend and revise type

This type can only be found in journals where the teacher has made a number of previous entries. It comes into being through revisiting, reviewing and re-appreciating earlier entries. It is evidence of a systematic and committed approach to reflection-on-practice. With entries of this kind there is an opportunity to do a number of things, such as:

- celebrate the good and rewarding aspects of practice;
- re-relieve yourself of any feelings of frustration;
- remind you of the things that you had forgotten about the incident;
- re-appraise earlier responses to significant incidents;

- look again for values, prejudices and blind spots that get in the way of moving practice forward;
- separate out those things that you have some control over and can influence from those that you presently cannot control;
- take stock of 'where you are at';
- clarify action plans.

In adopting this style it is important to date each entry. In this way you will be able to place altered or confirmed thoughts, feelings and actions on a time line. This temporal dimension to your journal entries might give you a way into understanding, more richly, notions of professional 'development'.

16th September

I think I am going to find it extremely difficult to work with the other Year 3 teacher, Mrs Jenkins. She has a completely different way of handling the children and managing her classroom, and she expects me, as the new teacher, to follow her example. We've almost had two confrontations so far, but each time I have bitten my tongue because she clearly thinks that she knows best. Perhaps I am not as tolerant as I thought I was, but the thought of having to work in the classroom next to her for a whole year is depressing me. I can hear her shout at the children and humiliate them when they have done something wrong, and she obviously feels that this is the best way to sort out difficult behaviour. I wonder if she realizes what she sounds like.

21st October

Four weeks since I wrote about my arrival as a new teacher to the school. It feels like four years! I am pleased that I have formed a really good relationship with Mrs Jenkins, despite the fact that we are still poles apart in the way we respond to children's behaviour. On reflection, I now know that she is actually very insecure and her attitude is defensive because she cannot find another way to deal with difficult situations other than by shouting. She has even commented on the way I have calmed down some of the 'difficult' children in my class and how she thought I wouldn't stand a chance with my 'softly, softly', approach. A back-handed compliment, I think! I'm trying to teach by example and prove that there are other ways, but it's hard to imagine that I can make that much of an impact on such an experienced teacher.

(Newly Qualified Teacher, Year 4)

Example 4: The concept-mapping type

Entries of this type are more pictorial or 'graphical' than literary (see Figure 7.1).

A concept map contains teacher knowledge which is represented in the form of a labelled-line graph structure in which the three fundamental elements are nodes, links and relations. These can be defined thus:

- *nodes* – key ideas or concepts;
- *links* – lines drawn between the nodes;
- *relations* – the meaning given to the nodes by the nature of the links between them.

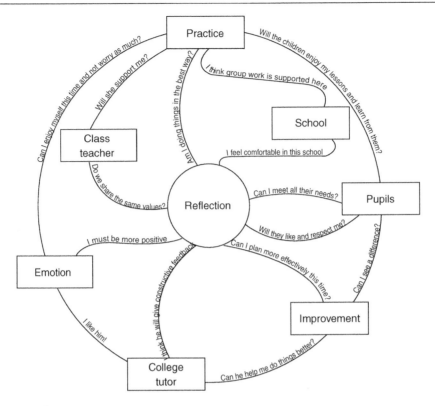

FIGURE 7.1 A concept map

In essence, concept maps, like journal entries, are personal reality maps, constructed by you, either alone or with others. They express the sense or meaning you currently have of a particular facet of your work. They are your subjective construction of an aspect of your world. If a journal contains a number of maps which focus on the same area or issue, significant learning can arise because reflection on them can reveal:

1. how you might fine-tune your 'know that', 'know how' and 'know why' knowledge;
2. how far ideas remain isolated or become more integrated and structured in your mind;
3. how you may have changed your views of aspects of your practice over time.

Sometimes you might think of your own key ideas that you wish to put on your 'map'. Sometimes you may wish to negotiate common ones with a colleague or work team. Its sometimes helpful if you try to limit the number of key ideas to six or seven, and to put these onto sticky (coloured) labels so that you can place down on the page in a creative and meaningful way. Figure 7.2 shows this in practice. Once the 'map' is complete, try to share it with others. What do they say? What are you learning?

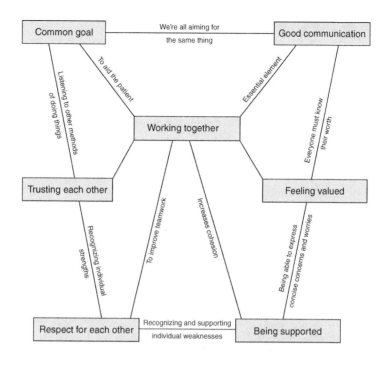

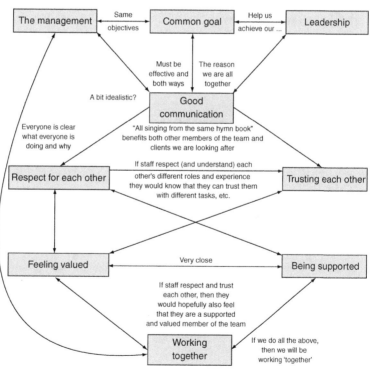

FIGURE 7.2 Two concept maps

Example 5: The knotty and messy type

'Knots' have been described by Wagner (1987) as the interrelationship between cognitive and affective processes which lead to conflict and professional dilemmas. Drawing upon theories in cognitive and clinical psychology and psychotherapy, she identifies six types of conflicts or 'knots', some of which might be short lived, others lasting for years. What each type of 'knot' has in common is that they arise due to a discrepancy or dilemma between 'what is' and 'what must or should be'. Knots can affect the quality of teaching. Sometimes we react to knots by complaining. Untying the knots is a learning process. Messy texts (Denzin 1997), as we might describe these entries, are always unfinished, open-ended, and can move back and forth between description and interpretation.

> I was so pleased when I got this promotion to deputy head. I fought off some real competition from other candidates and I know I'm right for the post. But I'm already sensing conflict between still being 'one of the crowd' and working alongside my colleagues and helping them, while also being expected to support the policies of the headteacher and governors, even speaking on their behalf when I'm not sure that I agree with them. It's very difficult to please everyone, especially when I have to say 'no' to invites from staff because I'm working on a policy that needed completing by yesterday! Also, I'm not sure that I like being privy to information that staff confided in me before I got this post. Like Mr Sladen saying that he has no respect for the head and can't wait to get out of the school. He's only keeping in the head's good books to make sure that he gets a decent reference for the job that he wants in January! It's a strange feeling to be pulled in so many different directions, and I'm not sure how I will cope with it.
>
> (Deputy Head and Class Teacher, Reception/Year 1)

Example 6: The living contradiction type

Seeing ourselves as living contradictions is a situation where we don't do what we say! (see Chapter 5). Entries of this kind can focus upon how far teachers are able to live out their values in their practice.

> When I'm standing in front of my student teachers and we are talking about classroom practice, I can hear myself saying the same things, 'Be positive with the children, find things which they are good at, take the time to listen to them and talk to them about what they enjoy'. The students busily take notes, write up their lesson plans and deliver some interesting and stimulating lessons.
>
> And what of my role? Having imparted my words of wisdom and feeling really good about the impact of my teaching on the students, I visit them in schools, observe lessons and give feedback. We talk, I write copious notes for them to look through, and I leave the school ready to visit the next student teacher. I pride myself on being a good tutor. When, therefore, I overhear a comment from one of my students saying, 'I wish she wouldn't focus on what I do wrong rather than what I do right', it sets me back with a jolt. It suddenly dawns on me that I am

doing the complete opposite of what I tell my students to do. I probably do comment on the more negative aspects of their teaching. I'm not sure that I give that much positive feedback, or really look for the things that they do particularly well. I think I do spend more time talking than listening to what my students have to say at the end of the lesson, and I think, if asked, that I would justify my lack of listening to the fact that I always feel in a rush to get to another school or to get back to College in time to teach.

Being confronted with such a contradiction in my own practice has concerned me, and made me realize that I need to be very careful about the way I relate to students in future.

(Higher Education Lecturer/Supervising Tutor)

These examples of 'texts' emphasize the importance of reflecting on particularity and the minutiae of everyday teaching and learning in the search for new knowledge, understandings and sensitivities that serve to improve practice. In turning to chaos theory, we find ample support for this belief:

The modern study of chaos began with the creeping realisation in the 1960s that quite simple mathematical equations could model systems every bit as violent as a waterfall. Tiny differences in input could quickly become overwhelming differences in output ... In weather, for example, this translates into what is only half jokingly known as a butterfly effect − the notion that a butterfly stirring the air today in Peking can transform storm systems next month in New York.

(Gleick 1988:8)

Reflection on the entries in our learning journals is an attempt to make sense of particular aspects of practice. In the stirrings of these butterfly wings, we have the starting point for transforming our understanding about the nature of our professionalism and for improving the quality of education.

Ethical issues concerning reflective portfolios

In this book I have tried to suggest a number of things that might go into something that you may wish to call a reflective portfolio. In a paper I wrote (Ghaye 2007), I posed the question 'Is reflective practice ethical? (The case of the reflective portfolio)'. The whole area of reflection and ethical practice is a relatively silent one. This is surprising, given the emotive and personal nature of many kinds of reflective practice.

So how far can we confidently say that the practices of reflection, however they are conceived, are practised ethically? That the what, how and why of reflective practices can be adequately described, explained and justified, ethically? A suggestion is that we take another look at writing a reflective journal and explicitly ask ourselves the question, 'How far is this particular kind of reflective practice ethical?' And, if we do this, see what learning emerges. The example that follows comes from the world of the award-bearing course, where university staff require students to keep and present, for assessment, a reflective portfolio. So you might say I am focusing on 'applied ethics'. Every piece of reflective writing has the potential to contain a plethora of ethical issues

– for example, about rights-to-autonomy, confidentiality, anonymity, privacy and dignity, scarce resource distribution, professional competence, interpersonal conflicts, fairness, conflicting loyalties, discipline, and encroachments on personal liberty.

In Ghaye (2007), I drew on an example from a third-year female nursing student studying in the UK. I wonder what feelings and thoughts it triggers in your mind? How far do you feel it is an example of ethical practice?

> As students, we are expected to fill our portfolios with reflections on our nursing experiences; this includes writing about things that upset us, reflecting upon possible triggers and how we felt afterwards. I remember leaning against the door of the sluice with my fingers in my ears to drown out the sound of an elderly patient calling again and again for her dead mother, who she swore had just gone to the corner shop. I remember becoming nauseated when entering the room of a dying patient and being transported back to the age of 11 when I had experienced the same smell in my father's room at the hospice.... My husband and best friend are the only two people I wish to confide in. My feelings are private – yet I am expected to frame them in prose and submit them to my university.
>
> I don't know my lecturers or personal tutor intimately. What right has anyone to ask for such personal information, let alone ask that it be graded by a faceless lecturer? As nurses, we respect patient's rights not to disclose their personal feelings. Yet no such right is afforded to students. I have had reflections returned with requests for more details about my feelings. I comply, but deeply resent being asked to do so.
>
> (Sinclair-Penwarden 2006:12)

This student's experience is a very uncomfortable one. So what issues does it raise, and what lessons can be learnt from it? For me, the issue is centrally an ethical one. How far can we claim that practices such as this are ethical practices? What does it mean to be ethical or unethical, and who says so? One answer is because being ethical is about how we treat our fellow human beings (in this case a student) and, in the context of an award-bearing programme, how we best meet their learning needs. Another answer has to do with thinking through the consequences that our actions (in this case, requiring a student to complete a reflective portfolio) have on her. The student has to complete her portfolio (or it could be any kind of reflective account) and hand it in for assessment. She needs to receive a 'pass' grade in order to successfully complete her nurse education programme. So the result matters to her. Completing the portfolio demands a kind of cost–benefit analysis from the student. This is a weighing up of personal 'hurt' against professional gain. And there are other things going on here. The completion of a reflective portfolio is a course requirement. It is mandatory. Another way to put this is that it's a 'rule'. The student has to act in accordance with this rule, or she will not qualify as a nurse. No matter how flawed, inappropriate and uncomfortable this is ('I have had reflections returned with requests for more details about my feelings'), she has to comply, or fail. What are the university lecturers thinking when they ask their students to give more details about their feelings? They would, no doubt, be able to justify this request. However, as it stands, this is a rule. But what about the consequences? One more thing. What about 'only do unto others what you would like them to do to you'? For many people, this is the only ethical principal they know, even if they don't describe it in this way. Here, the student says, 'I am expected to frame them [her feelings] in prose and submit them to my university.' Some educators have said to me that they would never ask their pupils or students to do anything that they themselves would not be prepared to do. The case here raises this question. If we require students to complete a reflective account, how far can we, as teachers, mentors or lecturers, put ourselves in the student's place and imagine how it would feel if we were asked to do the same thing by a 'faceless' but significant other (in this case a university lecturer)? How does an 'ethics of care' manifest itself in this case? In Tronto's (1993) sense, where is the practice of care? Who is caring about what? Who is taking care of whom? Who is giving and receiving care of some kind?

Do you think this student is being over-emotional in reacting like this? Irrational in her thinking? Is she over-reacting to her lecturer's (reasonable) request? Hollway (1991) argues that we are culturally coded as over-emotional. We are sentimental workers. Given this, it is perhaps surprising to note that the links between feeling, thinking, and creating reflective accounts of one kind or another have generally been under-represented in publications and under-theorized in practice. There may be many reasons for this. I'll cluster some together. One may be the (still) pervasive notion that reflective practice is essentially a cognitive activity. Another may be the enduring Deweyian belief that reflection is essentially a problem-solving process that begins with something that is perplexing and worrying. Another might be the view that 'cognition and rationality are usually seen as outside of, or superior to, emotions' (Swan and Bailey 2004:106). And another might be associated with the positivist preference for separating reason from emotion, values and subjectivities from situated action. This kind of thinking is based upon dichotomy and binary opposition. We see it everywhere in Western societies. 'We talk about right and wrong, nature and nurture, public or private, heart or head, quality or quantity; and of course, rational or emotional' (Carr 2001:421). When we use language like this, we elevate one term whilst simultaneously inferring a denigration of the other.

Emotionality in the reflective texts we create

I don't think we should underestimate the emotionality involved in the practice of reflection; its nature, intensity and role in learning. For example, a common kind of practice, which Schön (1983) called reflection-on-action, requires us to re-experience something of past significance. Something significant might be a wonderful experience. It might be the recollection of when we felt proud of what we had achieved – or it might be something much less positive. In both cases, and with everything in between, there is an emotional content. Raelin (2001) suggests that emotions can act as catalysts for reflection. If we feel an aspect of our work, or a particular workplace encounter, made us feel jubilant and uplifted, we might reflect on the reasons why we felt that way, if only to try to create conditions, or develop behaviours, so that we can feel this way again. Reflective practices can generate emotions. If we reflect on an aspect of our work, a painful truth might emerge about it. Maybe it is a sense of powerlessness (Parry 2003), or that we are not coping well with the pressures of work. Brookfield (1994) talks in some detail about the way certain kinds of reflective practice can generate feelings of anxiety, insecurity, sadness and loss. So reflective practices must come with a health warning!

The construction of meaning

In making sense of practice through journal writing, we are essentially talking about reality construction and interpretation. This process allows teachers to see and understand particular lessons, objects, utterances or situations in distinctive ways. We are always trying to make sense of our professional lives, and using language is how we do it (Harre and Gillett 1994:127). Reflective practitioners are meaning-makers who appreciate that;

> ... problems do not exist 'out there', readymade, well defined and waiting to be solved. Instead, a problem is seen as a human construct which arises out of a particular perception or interpretation formed about a unique educational context with its values and ends; the values, interests and actions of its inhabitants; and crucially, the particular relation of these features to a theoretical perspective which describes and explains them and their interrelations.
>
> (Parker 1997, 40)

A helpful theoretical perspective is social constructionism (Richardson 1997). This acknowledges that reality is socially constructed, and that writing texts is a way of 'framing' reality. It asserts that our way of seeing and interpreting the world is influenced by something other than 'the way the world really is', and 'by our emotions, intentions and purposes – our attitude to existence' (Young 1992:29). Making sense of teaching and learning is construed as a building or construction process by teachers (and children) interacting with the physical and social world. The challenge it creates for teachers is the problem of multiple perspectives. Simply put, we do not all see the world in the same way; reality is not fixed or given. Teachers (and children) partake in its co-creation (Ravn 1991:97).

Burr (1995) lists 'the things you would absolutely have to believe, in order to be a social constructionist'. They are:

- a critical stance towards taken-for-granted knowledge;
- historical and cultural specificity (understanding depends upon where and when in the world one lives);
- that knowledge is sustained by social processes (people construct and negotiate understandings of the world between them);
- that knowledge and social action go together (that there are numerous possible constructions of the world, and each construction brings with it or invites a different kind of action).

Classroom realities: Richard's reflections on his practice

Richard is a fourth-year primary student teacher who is keeping a reflective learning journal during his final school experience. He has completed a scheme of work on farming in the local environment and carried out a comparative study of farming in a Kenyan village as part of his National Curriculum (Historical, Geographical and Social Understanding) work with his Year 5 children (9–10 years old). He has been particularly concerned with offering the children appropriately differentiated tasks. He talks a lot to them during and after his lessons, monitoring their progress and giving feedback. He reflects on these conversations, which then become the content for his journal. By extending and revising his journal entries, a number of insights have emerged. The knowledge he has personally constructed has a profound effect on his teaching. He comes to understand that his children 'typify' his lessons in certain ways. The most commonly occurring typifications were the extent to which the children perceived his lessons as 'hard/easy', as a desire or otherwise for the lesson to continue, and the way the present lesson was or was not perceived as a continuation of the previous lessons.

With regard to the hard/easy typfication, Richard writes:

> It seems that most of the children talk about the lesson as being hard or easy, or in-between. I've been concentrating on trying to present tasks well-matched to the abilities of each child, so I've been interested in their comments. One thing I've really learnt is that an apparently straightforward phrase used by Helen, such as, 'I thought the lesson was quite easy', meant one thing to her and could mean something very different for Alex or Rob. For example, Helen always seems to link this to the kinds of activities I set her. Alex seems to link it to the time he has to do things. Rob to the clarity of my explanations. He hates it when he doesn't think he understands what he's got to do. He can get very dependent on me, and demands a lot of my time. Angus seems to make sense of what I ask him to do when he can relate things back to what he already knows, like our earlier work on local farming. When he can do this he's happy and talks about the lesson being 'easy'. And this reminds me of another thing. When Anna, Jenny and Sanjay talk about the lesson being hard or easy for them, they usually link it to their level of enjoyment.
>
> Then there are more subtle things I've begun to appreciate, like when two or three children all talk about the same bits of the lesson. It's different for different children. For example, we did some work where I wanted the children to empathize with the daily routine of Kenyan villagers having to use hand tools to dig the ground and then to bring the water to the crops in buckets from a long way away. Chris had difficulty with the whole business of empathizing, whereas Ranjit said the bit about measuring the distance they had to walk to fetch water, by using the map, was hard. Amir just said he couldn't get into it.
>
> So what am I learning? The children don't all make sense of the lesson in the same way. So what's new! Then, when they use the same words to describe it, the words can mean different things to each child. I have learnt to stop guessing what they mean and ask them what they mean by it. It's made me much more aware that I shouldn't get complacent. Not all the children will enjoy and get something out of the lessons; some will, some won't. Even when I think it was a really good lesson, there will always be some who will think differently. They interpret things in their own way.

Teachers literally co-create professional knowledge. Clandinin and Connelly (1995) use a landscape metaphor to describe this. They argue that teachers create and inhabit a professional knowledge landscape 'composed of at least two kinds of places: the in-classroom place where teachers work with students and the out-of-classroom communal, professional place' (Clandinin 1995:28). The landscape metaphor is particularly appropriate; like professional knowledge, landscapes evolve and change with time. They are made up of many things that are positioned and interrelated in particular ways. We can get lost in a landscape and need maps to find our way and give our journeying a sense of purpose and direction. Reflections-on-practice in the form of interpreted texts can function as important way-finding maps. As teachers oscillate from one part of the landscape to another, from the one behind the classroom door to those professional places with others, reflection-on-practice becomes crucial in order to make sense of the 'dilemma-laden quality of being in both' (Clandinin and Connelly 1995:5).

Social construction is a theory about how we learn. Based upon the work of Fosnot (1996), we can tentatively establish some principles of learning derived from constructionism.

1. Learning requires skilful self-organization on the part of the teacher.
2. Disequilibrium facilitates learning, and contradictions in particular need to be illuminated, explored and discussed.
3. Reflection-on-practice is the driving force for learning.
4. Reflective conversations within a 'community of teachers' engenders further learning. Dialogue, for example, through learning journals and face-to-face with peers, is crucial. In this way 'reality' and 'truth' are accepted insofar as they make sense to the community. Interpretations of teaching and learning thus become regarded as 'taken-as-shared'.
5. Practice moves forward as teachers build cognitive structures and critical thinking frameworks, and develop 'big ideas' which help to bring aspects of teaching and learning into an integrated whole. The enabling model upon which this book coheres is an example of such a 'construction'.

The validation of practice

At the heart of making sense of reflections-on-practice are three assumptions. They are that developing our professionality means being able to:

- justify what it is we claim we know from reflecting-on-practice;
- justify how far this knowing, which we have co-constructed, is worthwhile;
- demonstrate the links between improvements in our thinking and our teaching.

When you present a claim that, through reflection, your practice has moved forward, I suggest that you will need to be selective, convincing and criterial. Being selective means that you should carefully choose one aspect of teaching, and learning that might be regarded as a good example of improvement. You then have to present your claim in such a way that others might find it convincing, understandable and authentic. Finally, you need to specify the criteria that you wish others to use if they are to make valid judgements about the worthiness of your claims or assertions. You should exercise your right to establish the criteria you believe are appropriate, based on your practice-based knowledge. But I suggest you should be prepared to justify them. People who might judge the worthiness of your claims and assertions may not share, understand or value your criteria. They may employ criteria of their own. Differences of this kind often lead to misunderstanding and a different perception of the nature and validity of the claims being made. The issue of the nature of the criteria, and who owns them, is contentious and contested. Who makes the judgement, and who has the competency and right to judge the validity of the claim, can also be highly problematic.

There are three main types of validation. They are *self-validation*, *peer-group validation*, and *public validation*, which involves having work accepted for publication. Self-validation has been something of a golden thread throughout this book. In this process, teachers must be prepared to look for and accept evidence which is supportive, appropriate and confirmatory of their feelings and sense of developing self. They also need to avoid turning a blind eye to evidence which challenges and confronts their currently held values and practices. Teachers' inability to be open to this kind of threat will affect, and perhaps distort, their understanding of their practice and the context in which it is situated.

Peer-group validation is a complex process with three important differences to self-validation. It is a public not a private act. It is enacted in a group rather than done alone. An understanding of the purposes of the process, group dynamics, of roles and responsibilities is therefore essential. It uses communication with others to bind the process together. Peer-group validation depends for its richness on a group who are willing to share and constructively critique claims that practice has indeed moved forward, if indeed this is the claim being made. Peer groups can usefully be regarded as a community of 'critical friends'. The principle function of such friends is to generate a constructive, helpful and yet critical dialogue about the trustworthiness of the claims being made. Critical friends are often hard to find, so it is important that you think through the attributes of such people.

When acting as a critical friend, it is worth considering adopting the disposition of 'reflective scepticism' (McPeck 1990). This means that we suspend (or temporarily reject) the available evidence as sufficient for establishing the truth or 'worthwhileness' of the claim being made. The notion of 'good reasons' is important here. Claims should be based on good reasons. Critical friends need to look out for them as teachers present their claims to know. This requires them to be astute, open-minded, and good listeners. Paul (1990) recommends that the process of 'intellectual give-and-take' be used when teachers test out, in a public forum, their claims that 'things are different now'. Dialogical and dialectical thinking are ingredients of this give-and-take. Dialogical thinking refers to 'thinking that involves dialogue or extended exchange between different points of view' (p. 339). Dialectical thinking refers to 'dialogical thinking conducted in order to test the strengths and weaknesses of opposing points of view' (p. 340).

An illustration: Fragments of teacher talk from peer validation meetings

- I found it difficult to be precise. My claim was huge. A silly claim really, that I had improved communication in school. I didn't really specify where, in what ways and how I know what I know. I didn't back things up with evidence. I don't think I was very convincing, so it was no wonder that I felt they took me to the cleaners!

- We wrestled, as a group, with this word 'evidence' and how it could best be used to support my claim that I had developed my classroom questioning skills.

- My claim is that I am better at delegation now than I was this time last year and that this has made me more effective in my job as head teacher. Well, I soon appreciated that I was making two claims and not one, and that I needed evidence about delegation and effectiveness.

- It's now obvious to me that I can get some evidence to support my claim more easily than other types.

- If I'm claiming that I have improved my listening skills, then why shouldn't anyone believe it?

- The really big problems are communicating what I am claiming to be true, clearly and convincingly. The message and the medium are important. From the reactions I got, I obviously failed. Maybe they were never going to accept what I said. If so, then we should have agreed to differ. I've learnt that I could have done more, gathered more evidence, done more analysis, more and more. But this isn't the point as I see it. All I wanted from them is some acknowledgement that what I was claiming was indeed reasonable, given the evidence and the constraints I was working under.

- The peer group were wonderful. They listened, but not for too long. They asked questions, but not in a confrontational manner. They allowed me time to think and to reflect on the way the thing was going. They challenged me, but did so in a professionally empowering manner. I definitely got a lot from it, and I hope they did also. I think there was trust, tolerance and fairness between us. It is these things that I believe are fundamental to any significant educational enterprise.

A reflective writing strategy

By creating a text, I mean making a reflective account that helps you to learn and move forward positively. An account can include conventional 'writing' as a pattern of words. It can also include the use of photos, diagrams, storyboarding, painting, mind maps, and so on. Each kind of account makes different demands on you. When you've decided what kind of account you want to create, you need a strategy.

Let's take the act of writing in the form of some kind of reflective journal. Writing can be both easy and difficult. There are many ways of doing it (Bolton 2004). Sometimes is hard to know how to begin. Wyllie (1999) asked students and staff about the strategies they used when writing. Five were identified, and were described as the watercolourist, architect, bricklayer, sketcher and oil painter.

1. *Which is your preferred strategy?*
2. *Which strategy is best for creating what kind of account?*
3. *How far would you describe your writing strategy in another way?*

THE WATERCOLOURIST You tend to make mental plans. You write in one go, from beginning to end, with few pauses or revisions. You don't make plans on paper. You just write. If you use a computer, you tend to review the text on the screen, rather than printing out drafts.

THE ARCHITECT You tend to make detailed notes, plans and headings to guide your later writing. You may not write in a sequence, but instead begin with the easiest bit. If using the computer, you tend to print out drafts, correct then revise on-screen.

THE BRICKLAYER You tend to write by building an account sentence-by-sentence. You revise as you go. You tend to polish up one sentence before moving onto the next. You revise frequently, trying to get your account 'right'. You work bit by bit and sometimes get preoccupied with detail.

THE SKETCHER You tend to produce rough drafts of everything you think you might write about. You organize your text under broad headings. You may stray or even abandon these once you begin to write. You feel this wastage is an important and necessary part of the writing process. You jump about in your writing.

THE OIL PAINTER You tend to have a very rough plan in your mind and jot down ideas as they occur to you. You then go back and organize them later. Your writing is rarely sequential. You like 'filling out' broad headings. You have the 'broad shape' of what you want to write about in your head, the general ideas, then you 'colour' them up with some detail.

8

Reflection-on-context: Partnership in Practice

Reflection-on-partnership

Ask most student teachers what makes a 'good' school experience, and they will name four key things:

1. their relationship with the class teacher;
2. their relationship with the children;
3. the general school environment and culture;
4. the links between the school and the higher education institution (e.g., a university).

Put another way, the *context* in which students find themselves is critical and affects how they approach their school experiences, how they make sense of what it means to be an effective teacher, and what they learn from the experience. The class teacher, children and the school's culture can 'make or break' many student teachers. Coming to terms with managing the context in which they are teaching is part of the repertoire of skills that inexperienced teachers need to develop. Contexts often range from the very supportive, collegial environments, where the student teacher and class teacher work alongside one another and learn from one another, to less supportive, even hostile environments, where student teachers feel uncomfortable in the class teacher's presence and unwelcome in the school.

Few providers of initial teacher training would wish for their students to find themselves in the latter situation. Indeed, there is a requirement on all providers to ensure that schools work 'in partnership' with them. The lynchpins of these partnerships are the co-operating teachers, acting as mentors, guiding the 'seeing' of student teachers (Dunne and Bennett 1997:225). Since 1993, UK government intervention has made partnership more formalized and systematic (Nicholls 1997). There is now a requirement that 'schools are fully and actively involved in the planning and delivery of initial teacher training, as well as in the selection and final assessment of trainees' (DfEE 1998b). The notion of partnership carries with it a resource implication, which generally involves the exchange of professional expertise, training of mentors for school experience, funding for school placements, in-service training related to initiatives such as the Literacy and Numeracy Hours, and developing a support network involving teachers, mentors and tutors. One of the most important resource issues is that of the cost of school-based training (Cunnah *et al.* 1997). This is notoriously difficult to determine in an educational context. At its simplest, partnership involves a transfer of funds away from traditional providers of initial teacher training, such as universities and colleges of higher education, to schools. This financial remuneration is designed to cover the cost of such things as time spent mentoring student teachers (Mardle 1995). But all schools have to weigh up the actual costs of training against any other 'profits' or benefits that such an involvement with traditional providers might bring. In OFSTED (1995b) language, these were called 'difficulties' and 'benefits'.

The more informal, non-prescriptive partnership between schools and providers of initial teacher training, which has existed for decades, was replaced with explicit terms and agreements which, it might be argued, changes the whole nature of partnership. Some have argued that partnership has had a 'transformative cultural effect' as schools embrace the work of the training of student teachers and make it part of their professional life (Cunnah *et al.* 1997). But Fowler (1997) reminds us of the difference between the espoused benefits and the reality of implementation.

> The understanding of true partnership as essentially functionalist, implying the greater good for all, the sharing of expertise and an altruistic commitment to a common objective can sometimes become blurred by the pressures associated with resources.
>
> (Fowler 1997:11)

Some of the fundamental questions with regard to the partnership between schools and traditional providers of initial teacher training are raised by McIntyre and Hagger (1996:6–7). The questions are:

1. How clear are the conditions of the partnership – what is expected of the partners in terms of what will be done when, and how, and in relation to what criteria of quality?
2. What division of labour is seen as being appropriate between universities and schools, and as being realistic in terms of each institution's capacity to make effective provision for different kinds of learning experiences?
3. To what extent, and in what ways, is student teachers' work in the two contexts integrated, so that what is done in the university is effectively used in school-based learning, and what is done in each context is effectively questioned in the other?
4. What kinds of constraints limit the realization in practice of theoretical conceptions of the kinds of partnership which should be operating between schools and universities?

Clearly defined selection criteria now have to be agreed, which address issues related to the quality of experience to which student teachers are entitled while working in schools. Roles and responsibilities of both schools and providers are explicitly stated, and in many instances a partnership contract is drawn up between provider and school. There is an expectation that schools will demonstrate a whole-school commitment to initial teacher training, and welcome student teachers into the full life of the school. Periods of time have to be set aside for observation, discussion, and reflection on the student's progress. Mentors must be identified who will undertake training and be responsible for the general welfare and supervision of student teachers while in the school. Formal assessment procedures need to be followed which are both formative (for example, using a profiling system) and summative (for example, writing final, summary reports). Each provider of initial teacher training is at liberty to set its own school selection criteria to suit particular needs and goals. This is generally agreed in partnership with schools through committee structures and meetings. Having once established the selection criteria, providers are required to ensure that all schools meet them. The DfEE clearly stated in 1998 that 'where partnership schools fall short of the selection criteria set, providers must demonstrate that extra support will be provided to ensure that the training provided is of a high standard' (DfEE 1998b:137).

There was an agreement between traditional providers and schools that student experiences will be monitored carefully and that steps will be taken to ensure that partnership incorporates a common understanding of the needs and entitlement of all student teachers. The rhetoric was clear on this (DfE 1992, 1993b). The government's official rationale for the establishment of partnerships was couched in the language of improving the quality of provision. In the Statutory Guidance on Induction for Newly Qualified Teachers in England, (Department for Children, Schools and Families 2008), it says this about monitoring and support (Regulation 13). The headteacher/principal and induction tutor should ensure that a suitable monitoring and support programme is put in place. A suitable programme must include the following components:

- support and guidance from a designated induction tutor who has the time and experience to carry out the role effectively;
- observation of the NQT's teaching and follow-up discussion;
- regular professional reviews of progress;
- regarding NQTs' observation of experienced teachers, NQTs should be given opportunities to observe experienced teachers to help develop good practice in specific areas of teaching. This could be in the NQT's own institution, or in another institution where effective practice has been identified. The focus for the observation should relate to the requirements for satisfactory completion of the induction programme and the NQT's objectives for development;
- other personalized professional development activities, based on the NQT's priorities for professional development, new areas of need due to the particular post, and the core standards; and
- in planning the activities that are needed to help the NQT meet his or her objectives, the NQT and the induction tutor will want to draw on the NQT's thinking at the end of initial teacher training, updating plans over the period.

In this document it also states that it is important that the NQT is fully engaged in this process and takes responsibility for his or her professional development as the induction programme progresses. It goes on to state that the school's leadership team will have a critical role to play in this, and in ensuring effective communication and handover between the NQT's induction tutor and any subsequent performance reviewer.

So why, in reality, and despite government legislation, do some student teachers find themselves in a teaching context which is unsupportive and one that appears not to facilitate their learning? Could it be that the benefits of partnership do not really exist in practice (Glover and Mardle 1996)? Certainly in the mid-1990s concerns were being raised. Some reports framed these as 'barriers to the successful evolution of partnership' (McIntyre and Hagger 1996). Barriers included, for example;

> ... schools' perceptions that they were not treated as equals, that they were not adequately funded, and that they were neglected by the HEI (Higher Education Institution) especially in coping with marginal students. Schools wanted both to be consulted and to have the freedom for College guidelines ... to be interpreted in the light of school needs.
>
> (McIntyre and Hagger 1996:152)

Concerns such as these raise questions about the (un)equal nature of the partnership arrangements. McIntyre and Hagger (1996:153) caricature an unequal partnership thus:

> [W]hat seems generally to be happening is that HEI's, preferably taking account of the views of schools, specify requirements and provide some financial resources and whatever limited support they feel they can promise. The schools get on as best they can with the more or less clearly specified task of teacher training ... From this perspective, then, the partnership looks basically to be one of the universities paying schools to train teachers.

On reflection, the principle and process of partnership was becoming understood and experienced, in the mid-1990s, in very different ways. Some of these were 'uneasy partnerships' (Taylor 1997). Those involved had to think through their commitment to the concept of school-based training, to what might constitute effective communication between all the parties involved, and the likely costs that would be incurred, and address the sincerely felt need for quality time to do the job properly (Campbell and Kane 1996). Responsibilities for teacher training were being shifted across to schools. One of the unresolved issues concerned the location of the real power base, and whether or not there was an equivalent transfer of power from higher education to schools. As Tsui *et al.* (2009) state, power relations can facilitate and constrain, support and participate in partnership arrangements. There are asymmetrical power relations between universities and schools.

Some models of partnership

Given this scenario, it is not surprising that different 'models' of partnership began to emerge in the 1990s which were a blend of responses to central government in the UK, directives, and accommodation to local conditions. Furlong *et al.* (1996) identified three 'ideal typical' models of partnership that had started to emerge by 1995, calling them 'collaborative', 'HEI-led' and 'separatist' partnership models. Although in reality local provision blurred the edges between the models, evidence for them as distinctive types was available. They argue that the models occupied the 'middle ground' between the traditional HEI-based schemes of 1992 on the one hand, and the School Centred Initial Teacher Training Schemes (SCITTs) on the other. The latter was provision where consortia of schools, rather than higher education institutions, received an income and provided some, or all, of the training. The differences between the models are shown in Table 8.1.

In the collaborative model, staff from higher education institutions and teachers work and plan together on a regular basis. The student experience is one where they are exposed to different forms of knowledge that come from the school and from higher education.

> Students are expected and encouraged to use what they learn in school to critique what they learn within the HEI and vice versa. It is through this dialectic that they are expected to build up their own body of professional knowledge
>
> (Furlong et al. 1996:44)

The HEI-led model is very different. Here, partnership is conceived as schools providing appropriate learning opportunities for students as defined and monitored by HEI staff. In the separatist model, schools and HEIs are viewed as having

> separate and complementary responsibilities but where there is no systematic attempt to bring these two dimensions into dialogue. In other words there is partnership but not necessarily integration in the course; integration is something that the students themselves have to achieve.
>
> (Furlong et al. 1996:47)

This model is a pragmatic response to limited resources. With financial pressures on HEIs leading to reduced numbers of school visits by tutors, a separatist model, with teachers taking greater responsibility for student development in agreed areas, was seen as a cheaper alternative to the other models of partnership. However in the majority of courses reviewed by Furlong and colleagues, the HEI-led model of partnership dominated. One of the fundamental reasons for this was the feeling that this model was a way of managing school-based student teacher experience so that it achieved what those in higher education regarded as effective training. HEI leadership in this was seen to be essential.

This raises a host of issues principally, and again, about power relationships, what constitutes quality provision, the nature of professional development and pragmatics. Lee and Wilkes (1996:110) try to be positive about partnership when they state that 'what is important is to have a vision of change which will improve the quality of students' experience, and encourage professional development of both tutors and teachers involved in new partnerships.'

TABLE 8.1 Ideal models of partnership

KEY CHARACTERISTICS	COLLABORATIVE PARTNERSHIP MODEL	HEI-LED PARTNERSHIP MODEL	SEPARATIST PARTNERSHIP MODEL
Planning	Emphasis on giving all tutors and teachers opportunities to work together in small groups	HEI-led with at most some consultation of small group of teachers	Broad planning of structure with agreed areas of responsibility
HEI visits to school	Collaborative to discuss professional issues together	Strong emphasis on quality control, monitoring that school is delivering agreed learning opportunities	Very few or none
Documentation	Codifies emerging collaborative practice	Strongly emphasized, defining tasks for schools	Strongly emphasized, defining areas of responsibility.
Content	Schools and HEI recognize legitimacy and differences of each other's contribution to an ongoing dialogue	HEI defines what students should learn in school	Separate knowledge domains, no opportunities for dialogue
Mentoring	Defined as giving students access to teachers' professional knowledge – mentor 'training' as professional development, learning to articulate embedded knowledge	Mentors trained to deliver what course defines as necessary	Mentoring comes from knowledge base of school
Assessment	Collaborative, based on triangulation	HEI-led and defined	School responsible for teaching assessment
Contractual relationship	Negotiated, personal	Directive with lists of tasks and responsibilities	Legalistic, finance-led with discrete areas of responsibility
Legitimation	Commitment to value of collaboration in initial teacher education	Acceptance of HEI-defined principles of initial teacher education	Either principled commitment to role of school or pragmatic due to limited resources

Source: Furlong *et al.* 1996.

'Why do you offer student teachers a placement in your school?'

Generally speaking, there is both a principled and a pragmatic response given by many teachers and headteachers to this question. The principled response is related to the nurturing of the next generation of teachers, to providing positive and experienced role models, and to the school being an integral part of the training of teachers. The pragmatic response is related to the notion that student teachers are 'another pair of hands', and that their presence in school 'releases' the class teacher to deal with other school and/or curriculum matters. This, in practice, means that those teachers who have year-group, whole-school or curriculum responsibilities and who are deemed to require 'time off' to focus on these aspects of their role are frequently given students to take over the teaching and management of the class. For this reason, final-year students are always popular with schools, and there is often an assumption that they will be independent and require little or no support and feedback.

Another (rarely acknowledged) reason given for placing students in particular classes and with particular teachers has a somewhat spurious professional justification. This relates to the use of student teachers as role models for weaker teachers who may be functioning in a less competent way than headteachers would like. In this instance the children's welfare and education are clearly at the heart of the decision-making process, but the student teacher's needs will almost certainly be neglected, leaving him or her often feeling isolated and unsupported. There is also a political link here: schools need to know that there is a return on their investment. Time is precious, teachers have full and busy working lives, classes are often large and stress levels high. Changes to the National Curriculum, impending OFSTED inspections and reports, the administering of Standard Assessment Tasks (SATs) and the publication of league tables, among other things, mean that student teachers are part of a much wider, complex educational context. Headteachers see opportunities to save on tightly squeezed budgets by using student teachers as supply cover when other members of staff are absent through illness, or are attending courses. Additionally, few teachers want to be faced with a 'weak' student or with a student who is known to require higher levels of support than others.

There is therefore a political assumption that all schools appreciate the purpose and value of having student teachers in school. 'High status, high standards' (DfEE 1998b) now trips off the tongue, and there is often a complacent attitude that the political definition of 'partnership' as stated in Circular 4/98 is mutually supported and understood by providers and schools alike. In reality, there is a danger that schools will resist the imposition of roles and responsibilities by providers, and argue that the very gesture of offering a placement to student teachers should be gratefully accepted. Few providers are in the enviable position of being offered so many placements that they can 'pick and choose'. This therefore means that schools, in practice, hold the trump card. Whatever model of partnership emerges locally, the bottom line is that partnership depends upon the recruitment of a sufficient number of good schools willing to take on the role of student supervision, and within a reasonable travelling distance from the HEI. Until the government makes it a requirement that all schools must form a partnership with a provider of initial teacher training (and this by its very nature would signify compliance rather than collaboration), there will always be students who find themselves in schools where pragmatic reasons have justified their presence rather than principled ones.

This is the nightmare scenario for all school-experience placement coordinators within higher education. Partnership agreements and quality assurance procedures dominate much of their workload, and negative reports relating to student experiences in schools can lead to feelings of frustration. The situation is further exacerbated by the government's requirement that providers of initial teacher training 'de-select' schools which do not meet selection criteria and where providers cannot guarantee extra support. However understandable this may be, in reality providers are then faced with a dilemma. Professionally speaking, only schools able to offer high-quality experiences should be considered for the placement of students. Pragmatically, there are often too many student teachers to place in schools and not enough schools in which to place them! Since providers guarantee students a suitable placement as part of their course, this leaves many institutions in a Catch-22 situation. Add to this inspection visits to HEIs from OFSTED, keen to assess quality assurance procedures and to discuss student experiences in partnership schools, and the situation becomes more problematic. Yet, despite all these issues, it might be argued that no amount of careful monitoring and selection can guarantee that schools will adopt an appropriately professional stance when accepting students. So, in reality, perhaps student teachers should be prepared for a diversity of contexts where both professional and pragmatic influences affect the quality of their experience while in school.

It is not surprising therefore that, given the above, student teachers can feel either liberated or constrained by the school context in which they find themselves. From the outset, students often have a *feeling* about a school. After just one visit, many are able to offer vivid descriptions of the school's atmosphere, the relationships between staff, the ethos, the response from the children, attitudes, expectations, and so forth. These things are part of the school's culture. The descriptions may be highly idiosyncratic and perhaps skewed, but they nevertheless impact on the student's feelings of self-worth, capability, and enthusiasm. One of the most pervasive influences on the quality of teachers' work is the school's culture. Reflection-on-practice means more than simply reflecting on individual work in the classroom; it also means reflecting on practice in a context. The context is the school, which is part of a wider socio-cultural and politico-economic 'system'. We should not only reflect on practice, but also reflect on the context in which practice is embedded. Two key questions here are:

1. What particular school cultures provide the most appropriate learning experience for student teachers?
2. What are the characteristics of a learning-enriched school placement?

Reflections-on-context: Jo's first morning in school

The following extract is taken from a journal of a final-year primary student named Jo, who reflects on the difference between her third- and fourth-year school experiences. She writes an insightful account of the impact School A's culture had upon her experience, and how this affected her ability to reflect positively on her developing professionality. She begins with her recollections of her first morning in a primary school during her third year of teacher training.

From the moment I entered the school, I felt uneasy. No one welcomed me as I arrived, and I was left wondering whether I was even expected. When I eventually found someone to speak to, I was greeted with the words, 'Oh, so you're the student? I think you're with Mrs S in Year 4'. This was not reassuring and, to make matters worse, on entering the classroom, I was met by a very frustrated, rather impatient teacher who announced, in no uncertain terms, that she was too busy to deal with me at the moment and could I make myself useful by taking the children's chairs off the tables because the cleaner had left them there overnight! Needless to say this was not the introduction that I had anticipated, but I wanted to remain positive and so waited for the opportunity to speak with her at another time. The bell rang. Children rushed into the classroom, seemingly oblivious to my presence, and pushed past each other to their seats. The noise level was high. I tried smiling at a group of children, but they just stared at me and then became convulsed in giggles. Things would be fine when the class teacher introduced me, I thought. After all, these children would be my responsibility for the next seven weeks. The teacher shouted, very loudly. I jumped. The children hardly seemed to notice. She shouted again, and then proceeded to call the register. Some children listened, but others continued to chat. They were instructed to take out their spelling books and then to copy lists of words off the board. Still no introduction. I was standing towards the back of the classroom feeling rather lost.

I decided to move around the room and see if any of the children needed help. One child asked who I was, and so I quietly explained that I was going to be their teacher for a few weeks and that I was really looking forward to working in their class. At this point another child, some distance away from me, asked in a loud voice, 'Who are you?' Feeling embarrassed at the sea of faces that turned to stare, I looked to the class teacher for support. 'Oh, yes, children', she started, 'this is the student who's joining us for a while. Say hello everyone'. My heart sank. I was announced as 'the student'. I had no name and little status. Any chance of respect from the children or of feeling on equal terms with the class teacher quickly disappeared. I felt dejected and disillusioned, and this was just 30 minutes into the school experience!

Jo must have wondered at this point why she had been accepted into the school, and why she had been placed in this particular class. Her personal reaction was to feel rejected and unwanted, but her professional reaction was to look for reasons why today may be stressful for the teacher, and why she ought to give things time before passing judgement. She continues with her account, describing the structured class routines and the way she tried to 'make herself useful and unobtrusive' until the point of playtime when the bell rings. She continues,

On hearing the bell there was a resounding, 'Yes!' from the whole class, a rummaging in desks for crisps and snacks and then a charge for the door. The class teacher sighed and then grabbed her coat, announcing, 'Monday's playground duty. Make yourself a coffee. It's Maths after play.' With that she disappeared. I was left wondering what to do. A child, who was searching ardently for something in a pile of coats that were strewn around the floor, asked politely if I knew where the staffroom was. I did not. As if recognizing my hopelessness, he offered to escort me there and then proceeded to tell me that Mrs S was the deputy head and a very busy lady who didn't usually have time to talk to visitors. I think this was meant to reassure me that I was not an exception to the rule! At least I felt that I had found a perceptive child who sensed a need to talk to me and help me find a way to another part of the school. This in itself comforted me. I was shown to a staffroom where teachers were busily making cups of coffee, engaging in conversation and thumbing through green sheets. I walked in and looked rather apprehensively around. No one seemed to notice me. I tried to catch someone's eye, but they all seemed rather elusive! Should I help myself to a coffee, sit down, start a conversation or what? I searched for a face to relate to and then, when I had almost given up hope, a young woman smiled at me and walked over. 'You're looking a little lost', she said. 'Are you a student?' It must be written all over my face, I thought.

I introduced myself and she explained that she was a classroom assistant and general dogsbody! She showed me the cupboard where mugs were kept and made me a coffee. A light in the darkness, I thought, albeit a flicker. Then, just as I felt that I was getting somewhere, two windswept little faces arrived at the staffroom door and announced that it had started raining and so Mrs S was going to blow the whistle! A groan went up from the assembled staff, mugs, still half-full, were deposited beside the sink, and everyone made a move back to their classroom. My one opportunity to make some sense of what was happening had gone.

Jo's perception of the school's culture is worsening. She has only received a positive response to her presence in school from two people; one a child, one a non-teaching member of staff. She has no idea who the headteacher is, or whether there is a student mentor in the school. The situation is not looking promising, yet she has to reassure herself that this is only a few hours into the practice and perhaps not an ideal time to assess what her prospects are in terms of a rewarding and valuable school experience. After eventually finding her way back to the classroom, her account continues.

Some children were finishing packets of crisps, others were sprawled across tables. The noise level was high, but fortunately no children appeared to be arguing or looking for trouble. There was no sign of Mrs S. I wished I hadn't returned so early. The children ignored me and continued their conversations. I felt as though I should be telling them to sit down and to get on with some work, but I didn't think that this was appropriate at the present time. I fumbled in my bag as though looking for a file or something. Perhaps, at wet playtime, the children always amused themselves. Perhaps Mrs S needed a comfort break. I started to write notes, any notes, just to look busy! One child fell off his chair. I moved towards him but he leapt up and pretended that he really wasn't hurt at all. Obviously he did not want me interfering.

Another child approached me and said that I had nice hair and what was my name and did I like her new shoes? I smiled and said that I thought her shoes were lovely and asked her her name. At this point she settled very comfortably on a chair next to me and proceeded to tell me everything about herself, her family, her friends (who were sometimes mean to her but usually nice), her pet dog called 'Wolf' and her favourite singer. A group formed around me and quickly fought for my attention as more and more personal information was thrust at me. Children seemed to be swarming from all directions and pushing to get closer. Hot breath, still sweetly scented with pickled onion crisps, began to stifle me, and so I awkwardly surfaced from amidst the group and suggested that I have a look at their work on the walls. Bad move. As I glanced around there was an obvious lack of attention paid to displaying the children's work, and those displays that did exist looked highly dated, with faded backing paper and work peeling at the edges where shoulders had been systematically rubbed against it. The children looked nonplussed and quickly changed the conversation back to far more important issues, such as the character assassination of Jamie who, to his credit, stood his ground defiantly beside me and denied all accusations made against him. Then, just as I was wondering what my next move was, an ear-piercing shout of 'Sit down now!' reverberated around the room. To my surprise, the children actually moved back to their seats and looked almost ready to do some work. The Maths lesson began.

A lively class without a doubt. Jo might describe them as interesting and challenging in one context, or overbearing and bewildering in another. Faced with the prospect of teaching in the school for seven weeks, she has to find a way to adjust to and manage her situation to the best of her ability. The current state of affairs suggests that she has received little or no recognition, and that everyone is too busy to pay her any attention. The tightly structured lessons which she goes on to describe, with children sitting in rows and working from textbooks, bear no resemblance to lessons that she has previously witnessed or taught, where children have been actively engaged in group tasks, working towards common goals, sharing ideas, respecting one another's opinion and generally being responsive to the learning environment.

Jo believes there is a conflict in her values. The conflict is between her perception of what school and classroom life should be about, and what she has actually experienced in School A. She feels the school's culture is not an empowering one because, although the children eventually warm to her and she works hard to build a relationship with them, there is no support given by members of the teaching staff. The headteacher has no involvement in her progress. The named mentor rarely observes lessons, and the class teacher, eventually recognizing Jo's ability to teach, leaves her to manage the class alone while she pursues her duties as deputy head. This is a very difficult culture in which to be a student teacher and, not surprisingly, affects the way Jo feels about herself and about the value placed on her contribution to teaching within the school.

A visiting university tutor would probably be alarmed at the situation, take steps to try to support the student, and address the sensitive issues. How tutors see their role when supervising students in school is crucial here (Lee and Wilkes 1996). Quality support is clearly what Jo needs at this time. For teachers, this means knowing how they might best help the student; intuitive and 'gut' reactions may not be an appropriate response from them (Hagger *et al.* 1995). It is not hard to imagine how difficult it would have been for Jo to engage in a reflective conversation about her teaching when she was experiencing such negative feelings. In her journal she describes how she became 'defensive, sensitive to criticism', and believed that any pupil misbehaviour was due to her 'inept performance'. She writes of feeling 'used' within the school, and receiving 'no encouragement or positive feedback'.

The fact that the teacher feels able to leave her class in Jo's hands does not alleviate her diminishing self-confidence. Her previous relatively high self-esteem is threatened, and any reflective conversation with a visiting tutor or other school staff member would need to be handled with great care to avoid making matters worse. An empowering reflective conversation would help Jo to work with her negativities and feelings of low self-esteem. Some appropriate kinds of support would help restore Jo's confidence, help her think more positively and enable her to reappraise or reaffirm the validity of her own values. This does not happen overnight, and the work of Borko and Mayfield (1995) does not give us grounds for a great deal of optimism. In their work on the influences of 'cooperating' teachers and university staff on student-teacher learning, they concluded that interactions with supervisors were too rushed and based upon insufficient data about the student's teaching. One consequence of this is that students come to have low expectations about what they might get out of reflective conversations with their supervisors.

Those who work with students, I suggest, need to address how far there is a 'shared desire to maximize comfort and minimize risks during teaching practices' (Dunne and Bennett 1997:226). Challenge with support is one of the hallmarks of learning from reflection-on-practice presented in this book. Challenge without support can be destructive. Support without challenge is about comfort, and always being comfortable can lead to blindness – a professional state in which teachers miss and dismiss opportunities to improve their practice and the quality of the learning experiences of their pupils.

Reflection-on-context: Jo's experience in another school

Jo is given the opportunity to restore her confidence, put things in perspective and develop her skills in a different school ten months later, when she embarks on her fourth and final school experience. Once again, her journal writing provides us with a vivid portrait of School B. Her initial thoughts about her forthcoming practice are thus. Jo writes:

As I nervously approached the reception desk, a friendly face looked up from a computer screen and greeted me with a smile. 'You must be Jo', she said, 'I'm Janet, the school secretary. Mr Peters asked me to take care of you while he sees a parent. Would you like a coffee?' I was taken to the staffroom and offered a seat. As the secretary made me a cup of coffee she chatted away and made me feel extremely comfortable. Several members of staff passed through the staffroom on their way to the classroom, and each time I was introduced by Janet and engaged in a short conversation. People seemed genuinely keen to speak and to make me feel welcome. After five minutes the door opened again and a bustling gentleman appeared with his hand outstretched. 'Jo', he beamed, 'Pleased to meet you. Come on through to my office. Mrs Willliams will join us just as soon as she has set the hall up for assembly.'

He took me into a warmly furnished room with children's pictures on the walls. One caught my eye. A very round, red-faced little man with spectacles and bushy eyebrows had been carefully drawn and painted in bright colours. Underneath were the words, 'To Mr Peters. I think you are very nice. Love Emma.' For an instant I recalled the fact that I had not even seen the inside of the headteacher's room in School A. This experience was so overwhelmingly different that it was almost unnerving. As I was invited to sit down, Mr Peters handed me a package with a school brochure and 'student information pack' inside. He asked me to find time to read through it and to see him at any time if I needed clarification on the contents.

At this point, Mrs Williams knocked on the door and came in. She was immediately invited to sit down and to join in the conversation. This was my class teacher who would be responsible for me whilst I was in school. Mr Peters continued, 'Mrs Williams is our deputy head...' The words went through me like a knife. Not again. Not another deputy head, I thought. Never any time to talk, overworked, and always stressed out! It was a dreadful image to have, but unfortunately that had always been my experience. Was the bubble about to burst?

He continued. 'She is our school mentor and takes care of all students in school. Mrs Williams will work out a programme with you that gives you time to get to know the children before taking over the class. She'll check your planning and observe your teaching every week so that we make sure all the curriculum subjects are covered.' Things looked more promising and, as I followed a chatty Mrs Williams to the classroom a few minutes later, I felt an immense wave of relief wash over me. Perhaps this was my lucky day.

Jo's account reflects a very positive and welcoming first impression, which suggests that the school is well prepared for students and appreciates the need to make them feel valued. She finds herself in a context that is understanding and supportive of her needs. The fact that senior members of staff had taken time to talk to her and explain the situation to her made her feel appreciated. The procedures that were in place for monitoring and assessing her progress were structured and formalized, which meant that she was likely to receive feedback on a regular basis and have the opportunity to reflect on key issues with her class teacher. Her planning would be checked and her lessons observed so that she could identify areas that needed improving and take steps to move her practice forward. The fact that her teacher was also the deputy head concerned her, but she was reassured by knowing that set periods of time were allocated to her for discussing her progress.

As Jo entered the Year 3 classroom, she recalls her perceptions.

The classroom was bright and colourful. Every inch of wall space seemed to boast children's work, display tables were full of interesting objects, and the children's desks were neatly arranged in groups. There was space to move around comfortably, a book corner with soft cushions on the floor and an achievements chart on the wall. I picked out some of the names. 'Ben, for being kind to Jodie', 'Sophie, for working sensibly with Darren', 'Paul, for helping Mrs Murray', 'Lucy, for trying extra hard'. I felt comfortable in the room. Mrs Williams had placed a seat next to her desk ready for me, and a file with her medium-term planning in it for me to look through while she prepared for the children to come in. As she busied herself around the room, she continued to chat about the children, the way she had grouped them and her general expectations. She was obviously a highly committed teacher who took pride in her classroom and who spoke very warmly about her pupils.

When the bell rang I almost expected little angels to walk serenely through the door, but in fact it was a boisterous, noisy bunch who scrambled in and made for their desks. As they passed me, several children said 'hello' and asked if I was their new teacher, Miss Harris. I smiled and said that I was, and that I would be working with Mrs Williams until the Easter holidays. They seemed happy with that. Mrs Williams raised one hand in the air and, as if by magic, a hush fell over the classroom. All the children listened as she introduced me and explained how much the children had been looking forward to meeting me. Then, as she marked the register, the children each said their name and told me one thing about themselves. It was a planned and rehearsed introduction, with giggles from some of the class and nudges from others as children took their turn. A cheeky comment alerted me to the class clown, and an almost inaudible whisper to the shy child by my side.

The impression that it made on me was lasting. The children's individual characters started to shine through, and I found myself warming to them immediately. There had been an obvious effort on the part of Mrs Williams to prepare my path and to help the children accept me. She had organized my work for the morning and managed things so that I would meet each group before the end of my first day. During breaks, she encouraged me to accompany her to the staffroom and to meet other members of staff. As the day progressed I was able to make reflective notes, collect together copies of planning sheets, and become familiar with her routines. It was the start of a promising eight weeks.

Jo's frame of mind was changing. The negative experiences that she associated with her previous school placement were gradually being challenged and the possibility of an improvement in her self-esteem and practice now seemed likely. In subsequent discussions with her it became evident that she learned a great deal from reflecting on her experiences in both schools, apart from the obvious, 'all schools are different'.

Returning to the issues of principle and pragmatism mentioned earlier, it could be said that School A had a very different agenda for offering student placements than School B. In School A, it could be argued that Jo was not seen as an 'emerging' teacher, who needed support and encouragement, but as an experienced professional who should know what to do and who would have to get on with it. Having clearly specified standards to attain (DfEE 1998b) did little to help her reflect in a reasoned way, and she became convinced that she was achieving none of her targets.

In direct contrast was her experience in a highly supportive environment, School B, where her status as a student teacher (rather than a fully qualified, experienced teacher) was understood and accepted, and where a professional stance was adopted from the outset. This gradually improved her low self-esteem and began to help her adopt a new reflective posture based on looking for what was positive and rewarding in her practice and nourishing this, rather than focusing only on that which was 'going wrong' and demoralizing her. In this context she was able to put mistakes into perspective and to identify where aspects of her practice could be improved. She could engage in meaningful discussions with her teacher that were non-threatening and constructive. This example illustrates not only the need for a shared understanding about the process of learning as a student teacher, but also the significance of acknowledging that we do not all hold the same professional values and that even if we did we might try to live them out in different ways. Where a teacher's values conflict with a student's own espoused values and values-in-action, tensions can emerge. Given this scenario, student teachers generally opt for one of the following:

1. *A rejection of their own values.* Where this is the case, the student may 'adopt' the values of the class teacher for the duration of the school experience. Many students take this option 'for a quiet life', to try to ensure that the teacher will approve of their approach to teaching and to give themselves a chance of passing the practice.
2. *A rejection of the teacher's values.* This normally occurs where students feel unable to use the teacher as a role model and dislike the way that the children are treated. It requires considerable confidence, maturity and strength, and brings with it the possibility of disapproval, rejection and a failed school experience.
3. *A compromise on values.* Students who compromise have usually reflected on the notion that rarely do two individuals share all the same values and that, from a professional point of view, an acceptance of a diversity of values is often a necessity and reality when working in school. These students respect some of the teacher's values while maintaining some of their own values. They aim to achieve a working synthesis for the time that they are in school. Each option carries with it certain implications, and these need to be fully appreciated by the student.

The articulation of individual and collective values and the culture of a school are inextricably linked. When student teachers 'take over' a class they inevitably convey certain intended and unintended values to the children and thereby influence the learning culture within the classroom. Experienced teachers, when observing the impact of a student's presence on the culture of their classroom, can, for example, feel threatened or reassured. Where the developing culture is conducive to effective learning, there is often little or no need to challenge the student teacher's practice. However, where a teacher feels that the 'new approach' inhibits learning and perhaps begins to undermine the teacher's good work, there is an increased possibility that the student's practice will be questioned. This may be perceived by students as a direct attack on their values, and as such brings with it the likelihood of disillusionment or disappointment. At worst this might lead to confrontation, but at best it could provide an opportunity to engage in a dialogue about the reasons for adopting certain approaches to teaching and managing the class in particular ways. In the ideal partnership, student teachers are encouraged to put their values into practice, to justify them, and to reflect on the appropriateness of matching means to educational ends. So if, for example, a student teacher values the notion of cooperation and collaboration, which in practice implies group work with shared goals, it would be professionally rewarding for the student to have the opportunity to try this out. But if it means that this move might change the learning culture in the classroom because, for example, the class teacher does not see the value of group work and prefers whole-class teaching with children sitting in rows, it might be professionally prudent for the student to maintain the existing system.

Taken one step further, it becomes evident how each of these two scenarios may impact on the student teacher's experiences and on their perceptions of self. Working within a culture where the student's and teacher's values are clearly very different can lead to tension and frustration. Student teachers need to reflect on this situation, to understand the constraints that face them, and learn to work within them or to sensitively and constructively question and challenge them. Where these are not seen by the student as viable options, students may feel pressure to demonstrate that they can reproduce and sustain the existing culture, to conform or withdraw from the situation altogether. Students are sometimes in an unenviable situation, caught between the pressures to conform to the culture of the host school while at the same time being encouraged to critically reflect on their school experiences by their HEI tutors. Campbell and Kane (1996) summarize many of the pertinent issues thus:

> If the culture in school does not engender critical appraisal and reflection, and if, as we believe, teachers themselves find reflection difficult, how can mentors stimulate reflection amongst students? There are many aspects of primary school culture which work against the development of critical reflection on practice: time and space in which to actually reflect ... the value of reflection is often diminished by the need to conform to the latest DfE initiative ... the pressure by inhabitants to socialise new recruits into existing culture and norms (despite an awareness of the dangers of cloning, mentors still referred to students as 'fitting in' at school); the collaborative ethos set up in many schools that encourages conformity rather than conflict.
>
> (Campbell and Kane, 1996:28)

In some cases students can indeed live out values associated with a different learning culture to the one that exists within the class. It is not unknown for teachers to change their own practice as a consequence of seeing student teachers put their different values into action. Indeed, in the true spirit of partnership, the relationship between student and class teacher might usefully be seen as one of mutual growth and learning, where both parties reflect on their values and their reasons for doing things in particular ways, and resolve to make improvements for the benefit of the children.

Reflections on the influence of school culture

As I have stated elsewhere in this book, our values make us the kind of educators that we are. I have argued that teachers should make sincere and deliberate attempts to live them out in their teaching – to do what they say. I have also made the point that this is not always possible. One of the major influences here is the school's culture. We should reflect not only on our teaching but also on the particular culture within which it is embedded. School culture serves to liberate and constrain us. It provides opportunities for achieving satisfaction, personal renewal and collective regeneration. The school's culture can also stifle, suffocate, marginalize and silence us. Critical kinds of reflective question can help to challenges those things that disempower and demoralize us.

School culture (and organizational cultures generally) is a vast field of inquiry and a complex phenomenon, but an understanding of it is important if we are committed to improving teaching and learning through reflection. It impacts greatly on what we think, feel and do in school. It affects our competence and confidence (Wu 1998). It is an appropriate focus for reflection. Chittenden (1993) sets the scene:

A central feature of school culture is the interpersonal sharing of special experiences and values. Schools have an important contribution to make and a responsibility to clarify and coordinate the various cultural elements because they espouse, either directly or indirectly, a composite of values, philosophy and ideologies which should educate a student intellectually and socially. As an organisation, the various groups in the school try to operationalize the group's values. This means that they are turned into tangible outcomes which attempt to develop coherence and identity.

(Chittenden 1993:30)

This idea that a school's culture is a 'composite of values' is examined in the work of Wu (1998), who researched the impact of school cultures on the competence of newly qualified teachers. As part of his work with 21 British secondary schools, he invited a number of teachers to reflect on and articulate their understandings of the term 'school culture'. The following examples help to place Jo's experiences in Schools A and B in a broader context.

1. A deputy head:

We believe that everyone in the school has the right to be treated as an individual and with respect. We value achievements of every kind, academic and non-academic. We believe that everyone in this school should have an equal opportunity to achieve their potential ... We expect everyone to set a good example, work hard and give of their best.

(Wu 1998:226)

2. An experienced class teacher:

What I like about this school's culture is that staff very much care for the children. Above all else, we try to look after every child individually and try to see if we can make every child's life better either academically or from the problems they have got.

(Wu 1998:230)

3. A deputy head:

I think the role of the senior management is probably the most significant thing. Whatever we do concerning education and management in the school will affect all the teaching and learning activities, and affect the culture. The senior management at the school are all in the public arena. We are the people who generally monitor educational quality, who work with the community on the school's behalf, who meet the parents ... who stand on the stage and talk to large groups of people. So what we stand for is particularly important for the culture.

(Wu 1998:231)

4. A deputy head:

I think it is a very valuable point that you want your newly qualified teachers (NQTs) to quickly imbibe your culture and subscribe to it. It is not enough for them just to know it. They have got to be part of it and be developing it, because school culture is made up of the people at the school. It is not a piece of paper that you read and throw away. School culture is the sum total of all the people that are there, hopefully with the common vision pulling in the same direction. What you want of an NQT is somebody who comes along, subscribes to that culture and makes some input into it, actually contributes to its development, not just simply receives it.

(Wu 1998:243)

Each of these reflections illustrates, in part, different aspects of the complex whole that makes up the phenomenon called school culture. Within one school, there may be groups who represent particular subcultures. Sometimes these are given names, such as the 'management', the 'workers', the 'old guard', the 'young turks', the 'liberals', 'trendies', 'reactionaries', 'subversives', 'resistors' 'saboteurs', and the like. In example (1) above, the teacher's reflections begin to say something about an 'achievement culture' (Pheysey 1993). Teachers are committed to their work; they are motivated professionals and want their pupils to achieve. In cultures such as this, work pressures are always great. In example (2), the teacher's reflections begin to describe the characteristics of a 'support culture' where mutual support, teamwork, collegiality and caring for each other are important features. In example (3), the teacher alludes to some of the attributes of what Pheysey (1993) calls a 'power culture'. The senior management group is a clear driving force and one which monitors standards. A strong sense of power, managerial control and responsibility begins to emerge from this transcript. Finally, in example (4), the teacher's reflections contain elements of 'role culture'. The deputy head sketches out her perceived role for NQTs in the school. Expectations are articulated, together with roles and responsibilities.

Re-seeing Jo's accounts

Reflection-on-context requires us to be skilful at 'noticing'. This is the precursor to making sense of all those things that impinge upon the nature and quality of teaching and learning in the classroom. We need to notice what is going on in school before reflection can take place. Notice the major events, the trends, the joys, successes, dilemmas, extremes, unusual things, the disruptions, routines, subtleties and interdependencies. If these are noticed, we have a chance to understand them. Jo's noticing skills were good: she was beginning to describe each school's 'personality' and 'spirit'. These are words often linked with school culture. Tye (1974) explains:

When an individual visits a school for the first time, he develops, almost immediately, a feeling about the school. This feeling is shaped by what he views. The hallways are empty, or they are bubbling with noise. Students sit quietly at desks, or they move about in various informal arrangements. Expressions are solemn, or they are soft, supporting and questioning. Room and hallway environments are stark, or there is a profusion of children's work, exhibits and plant and animal life. These factors and many more give each school a personality, a spirit, a culture.

(Tye 1974:20)

When we reflect on practice, we should appreciate that there is a dynamic relationship between teacher(s) and school culture. Reflecting on the interplay between the two helps teachers to clarify their feelings about and attitudes towards the school as a workplace. It also helps them realize the reciprocal nature of the impact that the culture of the school exerts on them, and they on it. Jo's reflective commentaries begin to illustrate the first part of this; Brown's work (1995) takes us further. He describes nine aspects of organizational culture. Teachers play a part in forming and transforming each one. In turn, each aspect influences what we think, feel and do, and determines our individual professional identities. They are:

- *Artefacts.* These adorn the built environment. They are the most visible and superficial manifestations of a school's culture. For example, displays and notices in the school's entrance can reflect how open and welcoming a school is perceived to be.
- *Language in the form of jokes, metaphors, stories, myths and legends.* What teachers say and how they say it tells us a lot about the culture of the school. For example, the use of 'we' instead of 'I' conveys messages about teamwork, collegiality and the way staff support each other.
- *Behaviour patterns in the form of rites, rituals, ceremonies and celebrations.* These include school fêtes, religious festivities, reunions, parent–teacher outings, fundraising activities, and so on. These behaviours serve to reinforce school values and bond people together.
- *Norms of behaviour.* These are the school's rules which make a statement about where it stands in relation to valuing individuals and the provision of quality educational experiences.
- *Heroes.* This refers to the school's characters. They can be relied upon to deliver and 'come up trumps' when the going gets tough. They are motivators, are popular, and serve the school in a number of supportive ways.
- *Values, beliefs and attitudes.* These are often evident in the school's brochure or prospectus, in the actions of staff and the behaviour of children. For example, if a school values honesty, integrity, hard work and equal opportunity, these aspects of culture should be evident in the daily life of the school.
- *Ethical codes.* When teachers have to make difficult decisions – for example, about pedagogy, differentiation, resource allocation, pupil exclusion, referral, staff welfare, redundancy and early retirement – an ethical code of conduct is needed. Here, culture is related to how far the school is seen to act in a fair, just, principled and democratic manner.
- *Basic assumptions.* These incorporate the school's response to such fundamental questions as 'What is this school about?', 'What makes it distinctive?', 'What are the givens and the things we take for granted?' Sometimes these assumptions are tacit and need digging out.
- *History.* A school's culture is not a static thing but changes over time. This can be influenced by both internal and external forces. A new headteacher, a rapid changeover of staff, a fall in the school's roll, a poor OFSTED inspection report, a new Board of Governors, a successful netball team at a national event, the decision to get together as a cluster of small rural schools, being given some extra computers, and so on, can all change the culture of the school over time.

Reflection and empowerment

It is possible for you to be reflective but thoroughly uncritical? Teaching experiences can be distorted, self-fulfilling, unchallenged and constraining. For these reasons alone they need to be questioned systematically and critically. Being a critically reflective practitioner is taking up a questioning disposition towards what teachers and schools actually do and want to do. It is questioning the way individual and collective teacher actions are liberated and constrained by 'local' structures and the wider 'system' within which teachers work. Critical reflection helps teachers to appreciate the nature and power of the forces that constrain them in working towards principled and valued educational outcomes. When undertaken in a collegial spirit of improvement, there is a chance that we can work at trying to change these conditions. Greene (1986) captures the essence of this when she uses the phrase 'teachers as challengers'.

The kind of educator we are is not simply a consequence of personal character, temperament, preference and individual will, important though these things are. The 'discourses, practices and structure of the school' (Hursh 1992:5) make some things possible because they serve certain interests. They also deny other forms of school organization and teaching action. Put another way, a school's culture can, for example, be enabling and supportive, can make judgements about what is more or less appropriate action or worthy of attention, can devalue your voice as a practitioner and your contribution to the life of the school. When the latter happens and teachers feel unable to live their values out in their work, they can experience a range of emotions such as frustration, anger, sadness, depression, conflict, pointlessness, being a pawn in a game, detachment, rejection, isolation and powerlessness. Reflection-on-practice offers teachers a chance to work together to (re)discover, develop and use the intellectual and emotional power within themselves to try to improve their situation. It has the potential to empower teachers because it is about helping them become more effective agents of educational improvement.

Empowerment, through the use of various reflective practices, is an important outcome. It is also an important characteristic of the discourse in some schools. But there is no one accepted meaning of the term (Johnson and Redmond 1998). For some, empowerment is linked with enhancing human possibility (McLaren 1989). This view sees teachers as confronted with social, political and economic forces which limit what is possible. From the field of feminist studies, the focus is on the empowerment of women (Weiler 1988). Empowerment is about freeing women from oppressive patriarchal regimes and subordinate positions within schools, and having their work respected and recognized. Another view of empowerment is offered by writers such as Simpson (1990) and Snyder (1988), where it is equated with notions of professionalism and concerned with granting new respect to teachers by improving the conditions in which they work. In the literature on school leadership, teacher dissatisfaction, participatory decision-making and staff development, for example, expressions of empowerment can be found.

The use of the term empowerment has become both problematic and paradoxical: problematic because teacher empowerment is becoming yet another slogan of contemporary discourse used for diverse purposes and possessing a variety of meanings;

paradoxical because the meanings and 'blueprints' for teacher empowerment have escaped the meaning systems and social actions of the teachers in which they are embedded.

(Melenyzer 1991:6)

This raises two fundamental questions. The first is, 'So what does empowerment mean to you?' For some, their experience is that empowerment is something of a commodity. It is bestowed on or withheld from them. If you have it you are empowered, if not then you are disempowered. Becoming empowered is unproblematic; it is rather like being a passive recipient of a magic potion which can dupe you into thinking that being empowered happens overnight, and all of a sudden you have a greater sense of control over your professional life and powers of self-determination. If empowerment is seen as something bestowed upon you by those people who have it to give, rather than acquired through struggle and negotiation, then it might be better to regard it as just another form of control and oppression. For other teachers, empowerment has come to be known as a learning process when options that add value to the quality of teaching and learning are opened up, seized and acted on. Viewed in this way, empowerment is not an either/or condition, nor is it a commodity. It is a dynamic individual and collective state which is time- and context-dependent: empowerment is enabling (Garman 1995).

The second key question is, 'What do empowered teachers do?' In her work on teacher empowerment with 40 middle school teachers in the USA, Melenyzer (1991) concluded that empowered teachers:

- assumed leadership roles and sought opportunities to share leadership with other teachers;
- shared in making decisions that affected their lives at school;
- actively expanded their own knowledge base and shared knowledge with others;
- established and maintained trusting relationships and confidence in themselves and others;
- sought appreciation and recognition and in turn extended appreciation and recognition to others;
- sought a sense of caring, sharing and community and extended these things to others;
- established and maintained honest and open communications with all those in school;
- maintained high expectations for themselves and others;
- sought and extended collegiality;
- safeguarded what they regarded as important.

To this list could be added the following. First, that empowered teachers are able to convince themselves and others, through rational argument and action, that they are teaching something of value. Second, they recognize that the world of education 'out there' can be overpowering. They appreciate that through hegemonic conditioning people *are* organized into power relationships, but they do not accept that any alternative is impossible. They do not accept their professional predicament because it is in some way natural and unchangeable. They recognize the extent of those factors which constrain, marginalize and dis-empower them, and actively question the order of things. Third, empowered teachers are aware that critical reflection-on-practice might be perceived, by other teachers in the school, as cynicism and obstruction. Some teachers might describe it as 'rocking the boat' or 'sticking your head above the parapet'. Some teachers have to suffer taunts such as, 'You are not living in the real world!' Fourth, empowered teachers are 'critical' people capable of critical self-reflection and critical action (Barnett 1997). This critical disposition is an ability to size up the world in all its manifestations, to take it seriously, but not kowtow to it. Empowered teachers have the clarity of thinking and emotional strength to stand apart from what some regard as the 'real world' of teaching and show, in their actions, that there are other ways of understanding and teaching in this 'real world'. This is why some teachers do not relish having either empowered or critically reflective practitioners on their staff. They find these colleagues unsettling. Their actions can generate resistance.

Critical kinds of reflective practice can be seen as constructive action towards a better life. Teachers need to be open about what a better life looks like and, through debate and contestation, be prepared to justify what they value and do. Critically reflective practitioners do not look at their professional lives in terms of what they are allowed to do, but what they can and want to do to improve teaching and learning in the school. An empowering school culture is always in motion. It modifies and reconstructs itself in the light of changing internal and external influences. It places children's learning centre stage, and exhibits those cultural characteristics which continuously, not erratically, support teachers in the pursuit of shared and valued outcomes. Like the development of effective school partnerships, becoming critically reflective takes time, patience, openness and courage. Critically reflective practitioners are risk-takers, able to deal with the uncertainty and ambiguity that comes from exploring new ways of doing things. They flourish in schools where there is not a culture of blame when things appear to get worse before they get better, but rather a culture of pride – a pride that comes from knowing that there is a collective commitment to continuously strive to 'think again' and to improve the quality of children's educational experiences.

Reflections on the Whole: Thinking Again

Reflection-on-practice is an expression of a 'desire to think again' (Clandinin and Connelly 1995). Reflection is thinking again about teaching and learning. Some of the important attributes of this process are neatly summarized by Benita, a Canadian student teacher who wrote the following in her professional learning portfolio:

> I see myself as a reflective practitioner. I am a person who wonders and questions. I think about daily happenings in my classroom: what is going on with my students, how I am making sense of being a teacher, and how I am figuring out the curriculum.
>
> (Portfolio entry, 5 June 1992 (quoted in Clandinin and Connelly 1995:82))

'Thinking again' conveys the idea that reflection-on-practice needs to be seen as a continuous process of knowledge co-construction. It is also about wondering.

Thinking again: Adam's reflections-on-practice

Adam is a final-year primary student undertaking an eight-week school experience. As part of his course he has to conduct a piece of practitioner research into an aspect of teaching and learning. He has chosen to focus on the notion of 'being an effective teacher'. A central claim of his course is to enable him to become a reflective practitioner, skilled at interrogating his practice and learning from the evidence he gathers about his teaching. Adam keeps a reflective learning journal, and has asked his pupils to do the same. He has worked hard in his first week's teaching to explain to his class how they might make entries in their journals. He has discussed issues of honesty and confidentiality, and the reasons why he is asking them to do this. One of Adam's early entries is presented below. Adam writes:

> The scene is a fairly typical classroom in an urban primary school located in an area of Victorian villas and houses built in the inter-war period. Children of Spanish, Irish, Italian, British, and other nationalities attend the school.
>
> It is a bright, sunny Monday morning in the summer term. I enter Room 2 just before the lesson from assembly to break time is due to start. I feel cheerful, expectant and am looking forward to my class of Year 6 (10–11 year olds). Under one arm is my visual aid, an old roll of patterned wallpaper with a large diagram on the

reverse side showing the school in relation to a place in northern Queensland called Ravenswood. Under the other is my laptop, complete with an extension cable which I've wedged up under my armpit. In my right hand is my briefcase with photographs to help convey the notion of a gold rush and handouts for all the children in the form of four pictures, in sequence, that reflect the changing fortunes of Ravenswood through time. In the other hand I have a carrier bag. Inside is a battery-powered cassette recorder – too many plugs and cables on the floor is not good news with this group. My tape is ready to turn and at the right place, I hope. Also in the bag is a copy of my lesson plan – carefully thought through, I think – a mug, jar of coffee, some dried milk and my potato.

I feel rather like a salesman with all this paraphernalia, a little like an ambassador (I'm a student on final teaching practice), and certainly like an anthropologist as I endeavour to undertake a piece of classroom-based practitioner research (as part of my module called 'The Teacher as Researcher') that requires me to get inside this thing called school culture and explore how the children are making sense of their learning experiences with me. I want to know how effective they think my teaching is.

The bell goes, but there is no sign of the children. To fill the expanding silence I reach down into the carrier bag and begin to carve my initials on my potato. (Monday is potato day for staff. The potatoes go in the oven at break time and are devoured at lunch.) No sooner done than the children enter the classroom, cheerful as usual. They always seem to be engaged in such earnest conversation. But here I am, 'student anthropologist', slipping into my participant-observer role again. As usual, they are never short of something to say as they pass my desk. 'You've had your hair cut, sir', 'Sorry we're late but Mr Springer (the Head) made us sing the hymn again because he said we weren't singing the words clearly enough', 'Did you have a nice weekend, sir?' 'Watch him today, sir, he's in a bad mood.' As they glide past I run through my much-practised looks which convey a sense of amusement, interest, slight embarrassment, and a measure of surprise.

As they settle in their places I begin my well-used opening move. It is a good exemplar of what Mehan (1979) would call a co-occurrence relationship. 'Good morning, everyone. I hope you had a great weekend.' 'Good morning, sir. Hope you did too.' So the lesson begins. It is about Man's use of scarce natural resources. First I read a short story, then turn off the lights and play some atmospheric music. In no time at all we are up on our magic carpet, travelling through time and across space to northern Queensland in the 1860s.

After the lesson the student reminds the children of the procedures they have negotiated for writing up and sharing their thoughts and feelings about the lesson, through the medium of their individual reflective diaries. The student did this for the duration of his eight-week teaching practice. When he reflected on what his children wrote, he learnt many things about himself as a teacher. Some of the main things were as follows.

1. *Learning to see things from the pupils' point of view*
   I have learnt that my children are more than capable of reflecting on our work together. What they have written is very useful feedback on my teaching. Perhaps

the most powerful thing I have learnt is that classroom action has a certain purpose and meaning. It has meaning for the teacher and for the child, and the two are not always the same. What really matters is what the children are learning.

2. *Being comfortable with different opinions about my lessons*

    My lesson evaluations are just one view of things. My class teacher's is another. The pupils have lots of different views as well. For example, in the Ravenswood lesson Paul found the whole thing easy but Michael found it hard. Michael has difficulties empathizing and imagining while Abi found it easy and says why. Raj, on the other hand, thought the lesson was 'very good indeed', whereas Rachael thought it got 'more and more boring'. On reflection, I have learnt that there is not just one 'reality' but many realities. What I need to do is learn to grasp reality as my children know it.

3. *Appreciating that I often say one thing and do something else*

    I have learnt that if I value group work and children getting on, working things out for themselves, discussing, learning to compromise and see other people's point of view, then I have got to let go of things more, especially what I control and when. One of Joanne's journal entries really made me stop and think. She wrote, 'You tell us to get on with our work then every five minutes you stop us and tell us something. It's good in a way but we don't get much done if you keep talking.' This is something I need to work on. I want to hear the children talk, but I haven't learnt when to shut up!

4. *Acknowledging that children have clear views about what is a 'good' teacher*

    Comparing my reflections on my lessons with the pupils' view of things has been a really sobering experience! They have helped me to question why I have done certain things and my teaching itself. Some of the things that I didn't think were that important at the start of the teaching practice, I now see differently, and the children have helped me to appreciate this. I am now much more aware of the importance to children of explaining things clearly, of not breaking up the dynamics of group work when I think of something else to say, about writing in their books more legibly, of giving them reasons why I am asking them to do the activities I set them, the importance of using praise and of being consistent in my application of classroom rules.

Thinking again: Tony's reflections-on-practice

Tony is a primary school teacher, in the UK, who is undertaking a taught Masters degree in the spirit of continuing his professional development. What follows is an extract from a reflective piece of writing, where he is trying to make sense of his first years in the teaching profession. In particular, Tony is questioning the whole business of knowledge production and re-production, questioning the nature and role of 'theory' and juggling the diverse 'texts' of professional socialization as he tries to develop a coherent philosophy which will enable him to act competently in the classroom.

I was trained as a teacher with geography as my subject specialism. I left college after four years of study with a Bachelor of Education degree, supposedly equipped to teach children from 8 to 13 years of age. My first job was in a school in Leicestershire. It was a period of survival, but it was also a time of discovery. One of my major preoccupations of that time was a question, 'How can I support and facilitate my pupils' learning when I am somewhat bewildered and uncertain about what is actually happening in my classroom?' Some of my reflections on my practice went like this. They are a reconstruction based on my own lived experiences.

I left college thinking that I should have a healthy respect for those robust and complicated things called theories. Lengthy lectures about Ausbelian advanced organizers, Piagetian stages, Brunerian spirals, Gagné's types of learning, Rumelhart and Norman's information processing, about Freud and Jung, and so on, led me to believe that educational theory was related to educational practice, my practice. Additionally, because I believed that those bodies of knowledge were put together systematically and over time by respected academics, then they would have the power to explain what was happening in my classroom, I put a lot of faith and trust in them.

But very soon things started to happen which initially led me to think that something was seriously wrong with me, the children, the activities or, even worse, the whole learning milieu in my classroom. For example, I was finding that some children were very good at solving practical science-type problems when working on the topics of rocks and soils, but less good at understanding that places were located in both space and time. I found that some children were very good at creative writing when we were exploring the experiences of those living in hazardous environments, and yet they were still counting on their fingers when we were doing exercises requiring graphicacy and numeracy. I found that some children wanted the freedom to learn and to express themselves in their own way when we were exploring the neighbourhood, but wanted lots of structure and guidance in order to be able to write an engaging story.

And what about my own teaching? In short, when I appealed to theory and tried to relate it to what was actually going on in my classroom full of unpredictability, multidimensionality and simultaneity, I discovered two things. First, the theory did not fit my particular situation: even if I tried to force-fit it, it did not fit. Secondly, it did not help to explain my practice, to enable me to offer explanations for what was going on. As a newly qualified teacher I needed to feel confident that the profession, which had just acquired a new member, possessed educational theory which could relate directly to educational practice in classrooms. For the first five years of my career I had a crisis of confidence. All this so-called 'knowledge' seemed to have no direct relevance to my practical everyday pedagogical problems.

Later in his account Tony reflects on his practice and in so doing begins to make good sense of it. Reflection helps Tony to 'add value' to his existing understandings. He writes:

I want to extend and elaborate upon some of the things I claim I learnt from these early and very formative 'beginning' years as a teacher. I held a number of debilitating beliefs. First, I had too much respect for the knowledge generated by others. I did not question it. By implication, I devalued my own knowledge. I can remember asking myself the question, 'So why doesn't my knowledge count as much as yours?' I was beginning to learn that knowledge was 'positioned' (Hollingsworth 1994). There seemed to be a kind of high-status knowledge and then there was my knowledge. I felt that my knowledge did not count as much as that knowledge I was reading about in books and written largely by people working in institutions of higher education. Secondly, I did not believe that knowledge could be seen as a 'contested terrain'. Perhaps, rather naively, I thought knowledge from 'outside' was relevant and appropriate. If it did not appear to be so then the problem rested with me, not with the nature of this knowledge.

Thirdly, I believed that I could facilitate children's learning even though I could not claim to understand and enhance my own learning: this was misguided and presumptuous. Fourthly, I believed that because I felt able to explain things clearly to children, I could naturally talk clearly about my practice to other teachers. I was in fact very inarticulate and unable to explain my most sacred and cherished work patterns and values when called upon to do so. I was unable to transform contextualized experience into decontextualized discourse.

Finally, I believe that if I looked at my pupils I would understand what they were learning. On reflection, I needed to shift from looking and make more effort to listen to my pupils. The conflict I experienced between my beliefs and my practice gave me the motivation to continue my professional development by looking specifically at my values and my values-in-action, on the one hand, and the idea of coming to know my own practice, on the other.

In this book, apart from other things, I have tried to convey reflection-on-practice as a process of continuous knowledge co-construction. This has meant two things. The first is that teachers need to be regarded as active, creative individuals, with an ability to think through the possibilities and probable consequences of a line of action, for example, a lesson, in the light of their experience of teaching other lessons. Reflective practitioners are 'educators with a purpose, able to take control over their own futures...' (Calderhead and Shorrock 1997:16). Second, it means that teachers have an ability to co-construct a professional world that is meaningful to them. These understandings and insights are often 'local', and grounded in one classroom or school. They may also be fragmentary in the sense that we can never claim to 'know it all'. We can never claim to know ourselves and our teaching in a complete, consistent and uncomplicated way (Ghaye 1986). Reflection linked to this constructionist view is, hopefully, a liberating message. It means that reality is not fixed or given, but that teachers partake in its co-creation. Reflection-on-practice helps us to keep our options open, to seek fresh alternatives and consolidate our learning. But there is another message also. This is to do with commitment. It is a commitment, willingness and enthusiasm to question the knowledge that is created, to challenge personal and collective values, and to interrogate the contradictions and paradoxes that appear from the construction of teachers' professional knowledge.

I have also argued that at the heart of the reflective process is the reflective conversation. I have taken Schön's original idea (1983) and broadened it to include a strengths-based reflective practice. Originally Schön referred to reflection where professionals try to solve their re-framed problems. He described this process as a 'conversation with the situation'. In extending this idea the work of Freire (1972) and Whitehead (1993), amongst others, is very useful. Meaningful reflective conversations can sustain and nourish us. They can raise individual and collective consciousness. Above all else, they involve a discussion of values. This is at the heart of the improvement process. In this sense, reflective conversations are those of:

- *possibility*, if they contain reference not only to what was felt, thought and done but also to what might come to be in terms of valued outcomes;
- *confrontation*, if they serve to interrogate and question teaching and learning and avoid celebrating it uncritically;
- *hope*, if the valued outcomes are to do with trying to bring about relevant, principled and ethically grounded improvements in teaching and learning in schools.

Reflection-on-practice is the way teachers attempt to improve the existing order and pattern of things. It is a vital part of a teacher's meaning-making process. When so many are buffeted by the forces of change, reflection-on-practice can help us regain some sense of control over our professional lives. When accounts of teaching contain repeated reference to professional turbulence and chaos, reflection can help them discern some order and pattern within the chaos, for teaching and learning is a universe of patterns.

> Every night the stars move in circles across the sky. The seasons cycle at yearly intervals. No two snowflakes are ever exactly the same, but they all have a sixfold symmetry. Tigers and zebras are covered in patterns of stripes, leopards and hyenas are covered in patterns of spots. Intricate trains of waves march across the oceans; very similar trains of sand dunes march across the desert. Coloured arcs of light adorn the sky in the form of rainbows, and a bright circular halo sometimes surrounds the moon on winter nights … Patterns possess utility as well as beauty. Once we have learned to recognise a background pattern, exceptions suddenly stand out. The desert stands still but the lion moves.
>
> (Stewart, 1995:1–3)

Thinking again about a strengths-based reflective practice

This has been the single and most substantial addition to the second edition of this book. It has brought with it a challenging and new purpose for learning through reflection. One consequence is that it has changed the language that so many have become so familiar with: a language of deficit. I have tried to complement this with a language of strength. This problem-first mindset, and a view of reflective practice as a solution looking for a problem, has brought with it a sense of fear and failure.

Problem 'fixing' is often based on the need to avoid failure and to protect our self-esteem. This is about the extent to which we feel good about ourselves and feel valued by others. Protecting self-esteem is a very high priority for many people. Many strive to feel valued and affirmed by themselves and others. They go to great lengths to avoid disapproval – sometimes at great academic cost to themselves. Another important point is that much of our self-esteem tends to be based on cleverness and competence.

Generally, we feel a higher level of self-esteem when we demonstrate cleverness and competence and when this is appreciated by others. We feel a lower level of self-esteem when our cleverness and competence are questioned. The link many professionals make between their cleverness, competence and their self-esteem is critical, because it is this that makes them vulnerable when there is a risk that they might fail or a likelihood that problems and weaknesses are the only things that will attract attention.

And all sorts of other mechanisms kick in if we ask deficit-based reflective questions – for example, defensive pessimism. This is where we begin to set low expectations leading up to a performance or evaluation situation. By lowering the bar, by being pessimistic, we cushion ourselves from the blow of failure (if it should occur), or the sting of criticism that can emanate from deficit-based reflective conversations. Defensive pessimism is self-defeating behaviour because it puts the focus on our shortcomings and negative outcomes and sets standards that do not challenge or extend.

And all this can lead to the worst thing of all: that is, learned helplessness. This is one of the most self-defeating protection strategies we can use. It is to give up trying completely. When we experience deficit-based reflective conversations, repeated failure or poor performance, and see no way of avoiding failure in the future, what is likely to happen? We give up! That is, we learn to be helpless. Learned helplessness is self-protective because we do not put our cleverness or competence, gifts or talents, on the line, to be judged. Learned helplessness can be a way to avoid complete damage to our self-esteem. It is the ultimate form of self-defeating behaviour, and the worst outcome of a repeated use of deficit-based reflective practices.

When trying to make the case for a more strengths-based reflective practice, I have attempted to emphasize that the practices of reflection are not just about fixing what is wrong and working out a way to get shot of our problems. Reflective practices can and should be about nurturing, extending and developing strengths and what is best. They should be about amplifying creativity, courage, perseverance, determination, kindness and fairness, for example.

When it comes to a more strengths-based reflective practice, we should try to avoid getting stuck in the first stage. That is simply trying to discover what our strengths are. We need to work out how to move beyond this labelling stage and actually put our strengths to work. We also need to know how to build a kind of workplace for ourselves, where we use our strengths for most of the day. So I suggest the challenge now is to see how we can use a more strengths-based reflective practice so that we play to our strengths, most of the time. Regarding high-performance teams, they call upon their strengths more than 75 percent of the time (Buckingham 2007). Buckingham goes on to say, '…we simply need to learn how to take our existing job and each week, reshape it around our strengths – even in the face of interference from the world around us' (p. 16).

The title of the second edition of this book is *Teaching and Learning through Reflective Practice: A practical guide to positive action*. The positive action I am encouraging is a strengths-based reflective practice where the best of our job becomes most of our job; where we focus on amplifying those things that invigorate not deplete us, strengthen not weaken us. We must bust the myth that reflection on problems and deficits is the only way to better performance and more satisfying work. We need to speak up and talk about our strengths more often. This is not only essential; it is also very uplifting. What's stopping you from doing this? What needs to change for this to happen?

References

Ackoff, R. (1979) 'The future of operational research is past', *Journal of Operational Research Society* 30(2), 93–104.

Argyris, C. and Schön D. (1992) *Theory in practice: Increasing professional effectiveness*. San Francisco, CA: Jossey Bass.

Ashcroft, K. and Griffiths, M. (1989) 'Reflective teachers and reflective tutors: school experience in an Initial Teacher Education Course', *Journal of Education for Teaching* 15(1), 35–52.

Ashton, E. (1997) 'Investigating the nature of values: Agreed or transcendent?' Paper presented at the Conference on Values and the Curriculum, Institute of Education, University of London, 10–11 April 1997.

Barnett, R. (1997) *Higher education: A critical business*. Buckingham: Open University Press.

Baumeister, R. (1991) *Meanings of life*. New York, NY: Guilford Press.

Bengtsson, J. (1995) 'What is reflection? On reflection in the teaching profession and teacher education', *Teachers and Teaching: Theory and Practice* 1(1), 23–32.

Benner, P. (1984) *From novice to expert*. New York, NY: Addison-Wesley.

Bolton, G. (2004) *Reflective practice: Writing and professional development*. London: Sage Publications.

Boniwell, I. (2008) *Positive psychology in a nutshell: A balanced introduction to the science of optimal functioning* (2nd edn). London: Personal Well-Being Centre.

Borko, H. and Mayfield, V. (1995) 'The roles of the cooperating teacher and university supervisor in learning to teach', *Teaching and Teacher Education* 11, 501–18.

Boud, D. and Miller, N. (eds) (1996) *Working with experience: Animating learning*. London: Routledge.

Boud, D., Keogh, R. and Walker, D. (1985) 'Promoting reflection in learning: a model', in D. Boud, R. Keogh and D. Walker (eds), (1985) *Reflection: Turning experience into learning*. New York, NY: Kogan Page.

Boud, D., Cohen, R. and Walker, D. (eds) (1997) *Using experience for learning*. Buckingham: SRHE and Open University Press.

Bourdieu, P. (1994) *Reproduction in education, society and culture*. London: Sage Publications.

Bradbury, H., and Lichtenstein, B.M.B. (2000). 'Relationality in organizational research. Exploring the space between', *Organization Science* 11(5), 551–64.

Brookfield, S. (1994) 'Tales from the dark side: a phenomenography of adult critical reflection', *International Journal of Lifelong Education* 13(3), 203–16.

Brookfield, S. (1995) *Developing critical thinkers: Challenging adults to explore alternative ways of thinking and acting*. Buckingham: Open University Press.

Brookfield, S. (2000) 'The concept of critically reflective practice', in A.L. Wilson and E.R. Hayes (eds), *Handbook of adult and continuing education*. San Francisco, CA: Jossey-Bass.

Brown, A. (1995) *Organisational culture*. London: Pitman Publishing Company.

Buckingham, M. (2007) *Go put your strengths to work: Six powerful steps to achieve outstanding performance*. London: Simon & Schuster.

Buckingham, M. and Clifton, D.O. (2001). *Now, discover your strengths: How to develop your talents and those of the people you manage*. London: Simon & Schuster.

Buckingham, M. and Coffman, C. (2005) *First, break all the rules: What the world's greatest manager's do differently*. London: Pocket Books.

Burr, V. (1995) *An introduction to social constructionism*. London: Routledge.

Calderhead, J. and Gates, P. (eds) (1993) *Conceptualising reflection in teacher development*. London: Falmer Press.

Calderhead, J. and Shorrock, S.B. (1997) *Understanding teacher education: Case studies in the professional development of beginning teachers*. London: Falmer Press.

Campbell, A. and Kane, I. (1996) 'Mentoring and primary school culture', in D. McIntyre and H. Hagger, H. (eds), *Mentors in schools: Developing the profession of teaching*. London: David Fulton Publishers.

Carey, G. (1997) 'Moral values – The challenge and the opportunity'. Unpublished Paper presented at the Values and the Curriculum Conference, Institute of Education, University of London, 10–11 April 1997.

Carr, A. (2001) 'Understanding emotion and emotionality in a process of change', *Journal of Organizational Change Management* 14(5), 421–34.

Carr, D. (1992) 'Practical enquiry, values and the problem of educational theory', *Oxford Review of Education* 18(3), 241–51.

Carr, W. (1987) 'What is an educational practice?', *Journal of Philosophy of Education* 21(2), 167–80.

Carr, W. (1989) 'Introduction: Understanding quality in teaching', in *Quality in Teaching: Arguments for a Reflective Profession*. London: Falmer Press.

Carr, W. (1995) *For education: Towards critical educational inquiry*. Buckingham: Open University Press.

Carr, W. and Kemmis, S. (1986) *Becoming critical: Education, knowledge and action research*. London: Falmer Press.

Cassidy, T., Jones, R.L., and Potrac, P. (2009) *Understanding sports coaching: The social, cultural and pedagogical foundations of coaching practice* (2nd edn). London: Routledge.

Chaffee, P. (2005) *Claiming the light: Appreciative inquiry and corporate transformation*. Herndon, VA: Alban Books.

Chittenden, A. (1993) 'How can a pastoral care programme improve a school culture?', *Pastoral Care in Education* 11, 3.

Clandinin, J. (1995) 'Still learning to teach', in T. Russell and F. Korthagen (eds), *Teachers who teach teachers: Reflections on teacher education*, London: Falmer Press.

Clandinin, J. and Connelly, M. (1995) *Teachers' professional knowledge landscapes*. New York, NY: Teachers' College Press.

Clarke, J. and Nicholson, J. (2010) *Resilience: Bounce back from whatever life throws at you.* Richmond, Surrey: Crimson Publishing.

Coe, S. (2009) *The winning mind: My inside track on great leadership.* London: Headline.

Cooperrider, D. (2001) 'Appreciative inquiry: Releasing the power of the positive question'. Working Paper. Cleveland, OH: Case Western Reserve University. Available online at: http://appreciativeinquiry.case.edu/uploads/working_paper_AI_and_power_positive_question.pdf.

Cooperrider, D. and Whitney, D. (2005) *Appreciative inquiry: A positive revolution in change.* San Francisco, CA: Berrett-Koehler Publishers Inc.

Cucina, J.M. and Vasilopoulos, N.L. (2005) 'Nonlinear personality-performance relationships and the spurious moderating effects of traitedness', *Journal of Personality* 73, 227–59.

Cunnah, W., Phillips, R. and Richards, S. (1997) 'Counting the costs or realising the profits? Partnerships, politics and professional development', *British Journal of In-Service Education* 23(2), 145–61.

Curran, C. (1997) 'Whose needs first? An exploration of the value systems underpinning arrangements for Primary-Secondary transfer'. Paper presented at the Conference on Values and the Curriculum, Institute of Education, University of London, 10–11 April 1997.

Csikszentmihalyi, M. (1990) *Flow: The Psychology of Optimal Experience.* New York, NY: Harper and Row.

Day, C. (1987) 'Professional learning through collaborative in-service activity', in J. Smyth (ed.), *Educating eeachers: Changing the nature of pedagogical knowledge.* London: Falmer Press.

Day, C. (1991) 'Professional development and change in the 1990s: Issues for action researchers'. Opening address presented at the Collaborative Action Research Network International Conference, University of Nottingham, 19–21 April 1991.

Demarest, L., Herdes, M., Stockton, J. and Stockton, W. (2004) *The Mobius Model: A guide for developing effective relationships in groups, teams and organizations.* Minneapolis, MN: The MMI Group, LLC.

Denzin, N. (1997) *Interpretative ethnography: Ethnographic practices for the 21st century.* Thousand Oaks, CA: Sage Publications.

Department for Children, Schools and Families (CDSF) (2008) *New Induction Guidance and Regulations for Newly Qualified Teachers from September 2008 onwards.* London: DCSF.

Department for Education (DfE) (1992) *Initial Teacher Training (Secondary Phase). Circular 9/92.* London: DfE.

Department for Education (DfE) (1993a) *The Initial Training of Primary School Teachers: New criteria for courses. Circular 14/93.* London: DfE.

Department for Education (DfE) (1993b) *The Initial Teacher Training of Primary School Teachers: New criteria for course approval, Circular 16/93.* London: DfE.

Department for Education and Employment (DfEE) (1998a) *Induction for New Teachers: A consultation document.* London: DfEE.

Department for Education and Employment (DfEE) (1998b) *Teaching: High status, high standards, requirements for courses of Initial Teacher Training.* London: DfEE.

Dewey, J. (1933) *How we think: A restatement of the relation of reflective thinking to the educative process.* Chicago, IL: Henry Regney.

Dewey, J. (1973) *The Philosophy of John Dewey* (Vols 1 & 2, ed. J. McDermott). New York, NY: G.P. Putnam & Sons.

Diamond, P. (1991) *Teacher education as transformation.* Milton Keynes: Open University Press.

Dunne E. and Bennett, N. (1997) 'Mentoring processes in school-based training', *British Educational Research Journal* 23(2), 225–37.

Dutton, J.E. and Heaphy, E. (2003) 'The power of high quality connections', in K.W. Cameron, J.E. Dutton and R.E. Quinn (eds), *Positive organizational scholarship: Foundations of a new discipline.* San Francisco, CA: Berrett-Koehler Publishers Inc.

Edwards, A. (1996) 'Can action research give coherence to the school-based learning of experiences of students?', in C. O'Hanlon (ed.), *Professional development through action research in educational settings.* London: Falmer Press.

Elliott, J. (1987) 'Educational theory, practical philosophy and action research', *British Journal of Educational Studies* 35, 149–69.

Elliott, J. (1994) 'Clarifying values in schools', *The Cambridge Journal of Education* 24(3), 413–22.

Elliott, J. (1997) 'School-based curriculum development and action research in the United Kingdom', in S. Hollingsworth (ed.), *International action research: A casebook for educational reform.* London: Falmer Press.

Elliott, J., MacLure, M. and Sarland, C. (1996) *Teachers as researchers in the context of award bearing courses and research degrees.* Norwich: CARE and University of East Anglia School of Education and Professional Development.

Eraut, M. (1994) 'Indicators and accountability at the school and classroom level', in *Making education count: Developing and using international indicators.* Paris: Organisation for Economic Cooperation and Development, pp. 289–306.

Eraut, M. (1995a) 'Schön shock: a case for reframing reflection-in-action', *Teachers and Teaching: Theory and Practice* 1(1) 9–22.

Eraut, M. (1995b) 'Developing professional knowledge within a client-centred orientation', in T. Guskey and M. Huberman (eds) *Professional development in education: New paradigms and practices.* New York, NY: Teachers' College Press.

Fairclough, N. (1998) *Discourse and social change*, Cambridge: Polity Press.

Fosnot, C. (ed.) (1996) *Constructivism: Theory, perspectives and practice*, New York, NY: Teachers' College Press.

Fowler, K. (1997) 'Partners in the partnership: Evaluation of supervision of final school experience for students placed in schools in Hereford and Worcester who are in partnership with Worcester College of Higher Education'. Unpublished thesis, University of Coventry.

Fredrickson, B. (2001) 'The role of positive emotions in positive psychology: The broaden-and-build theory of positive emotions', *American Psychologist* 56(3), 218–26.

Fredrickson B. (2004) 'The broaden-and-build theory of positive emotions', *Philosophical Transactions of the Royal Society: Biological Sciences*, 359(1449), 1367–77.

Fredrickson, B. (2009) *Positivity: Groundbreaking research reveals how to embrace the hidden strength of positive emotions, overcome negativity, and thrive.* New York, NY: Crown Publications.

Fredrickson, B.L. and Branigan, C. (2005) 'Positive emotions broaden the scope of attention and thought-action repertoires', *Cognition and Emotion* 19, 313–32

Fredrickson, B.L. and Joiner, T. (2002) 'Positive emotions trigger upward spirals toward emotional well-being', *Psychological Science* 13(2), 172–5.

Freire, P. (1972) *Pedagogy of the oppressed*. Harmondsworth: Penguin.

Freire, P. (1994) *Pedagogy of hope*. New York, NY: Continuum.

Fullan, M. (1994) *Change forces: Probing the depths of educational reform*. London: Falmer Press.

Furlong, J., Whitty, G., Whiting, C. *et al.* (1996) 'Re-defining partnership: revolution or reform in initial teacher education?', *Journal of Education for Teaching* 22(1), 39–55.

Galton, M., Simon, B. and Croll, P. (1980) *Inside the primary classroom*. London: Routledge & Kegan Paul.

Garman, N. (1995) 'The schizophrenic rhetoric of school reform and the effects on teacher development', in J. Smyth (ed.), *Critical discourses on teacher development*. London: Cassell.

Ghaye, T. (1986) 'Pupil typifications of topic work', *British Educational Research Journal* 12(2), 125–35.

Ghaye, T. (ed.) (1995) *CARN critical conversations: A trilogy*, Vol. 3, *Creating cultures for improvement: Dialogues, decisions and dilemmas*. Bournemouth: Hyde Publications.

Ghaye, T. (2005) *Developing the reflective healthcare team*. Oxford: Blackwell Publishing.

Ghaye, T. (2007) 'Is reflective practice ethical? (The case of the reflective portfolio)', *Reflective Practice* 8(2), 151–62.

Ghaye, T. and Ghaye, K. (1998) *Teaching and learning through critical reflective practice* (1st edn). London: David Fulton Press.

Ghaye, T. and Lillyman, S. (2000) *Reflection: principles and practice for healthcare profession-als*. Salisbury: Mark Allen Publishing Ltd.

Ghaye, T. and Lillyman, S. (2006a) *Learning journals and critical incidents: Reflective practice for health care professionals, key management skills in nursing* (2nd edn). Salisbury: Mark Allen Publishing.

Ghaye, T. and Lillyman, S. (2006b) *Reflection and writing a reflective account*. RL Publications, CD-ROM.

Ghaye, T. and Wakefield, P. (eds) (1993) *CARN critical conversations: A trilogy*, Vol. 1, *The role of self in action research*. Bournemouth: Hyde Publications.

Ghaye, T., Cuthbert, S., Danai, K. *et al.* (1996a) *An introduction to learning through critical reflective practice*. Newcastle-upon-Tyne: Pentaxion Press.

Ghaye, T., Cuthbert, S., Danai, K. *et al.* (1996b) *Theory–practice relationships: Reconstruct-ing practice*. Newcastle-upon-Tyne: Pentaxion Press.

Ghaye, T., Melander-Wikman, A., Kisare, M. *et al.* (2008) 'Participatory and apprecia-tive action and reflection (PAAR): democratizing reflective practices', *Reflective Prac-tice* 9(4), 361–97.

Ghaye, T., Lee, S., Shaw, D.J. and Chesterfield, G.A. (2009) 'When winning is not enough: Learning through reflections on the "best-self"', *Reflective Practice* 10(3).

Gibbs, G. (1998) *Learning by doing: A guide to teaching and learning*. London: FEU.

Giroux, H. (1987) 'Educational reform and the politics of teacher empowerment', *New Era* 9(1–2), 3–13.

Gitlin, A. and Russell, R. (1994) 'Alternative methodologies and the research context', in A. Gitlin (ed.), *Power and method: Political activism and educational research*. London: Routledge.

Gleick, J. (1988) *Making a new science*. New York, NY: Heinemann.

Glickman, R. (2002) *Optimal thinking: How to be your best self*. New York, NY: John Wiley & Sons.

Glover, D. and Mardle, G. (1996) 'Issues in the management of mentoring', in D. McIntyre and H. Hagger (eds), *Mentors in schools: Developing the profession of teaching*. London: David Fulton Publishers.

Goldhammer, R. (1966) 'A critical analysis of supervision of instruction in the Harvard Lexington Summer programme'. Unpublished PhD thesis, Harvard University.

Goodson, I. (1997) '"Trendy theory" and teacher professionalism', in A. Hargreaves and R. Evans (eds), *Beyond educational reform: Bringing teachers back in*. Buckingham: Open University Press.

Gore, J. and Zeichner, K. (1995) 'Connecting action research to genuine teacher development', in J. Smyth (ed.), *Critical discourses on teacher development*. London: Cassell.

Gramsci, A. (1971) *Selections from prison notebooks*. New York, NY: New Left Books.

Great Britain, House of Commons (1997) *Excellence in schools (cm 3681)*. London: HMSO.

Great Britain Statutes (1988) Education Reform Act 1988, Chapter 40. London: HMSO.

Greene, M. (1986) 'Reflection and passion in teaching', *Journal of Curriculum and Supervision* 2(1), 68–81.

Habermas, J. (1974) *Theory and practice* (trans J. Vientall). London: Heinemann.

Hagger, H., Burn, K. and McIntyre, D. (1995) *The school mentor handbook*. London: Kogan Page.

Halstead, J. and Taylor, M. (eds) (1996) *Values in education and education in values*. London: Falmer Press.

Harre, R. and Gillett, G. (1994) *The discursive mind*. Thousand Oaks, CA: Sage Publications.

Haydon, G. (1997) *Teaching about values: A new approach*. London: Cassell.

Henry, C. (1991) 'If action research were tennis', in O. Zuber-Skerritt (ed.), *Action learning for improved performance*. Brisbane: AEBIS Publishing.

Henry, C. (1993) 'McDonald's, Republicanism and Botham's early departure: democratic education for a change?', in T. Ghaye and P. Wakefield (eds), *CARN critical conversations: A trilogy*, Vol. 1, *The role of self in action research*. Bournemouth: Hyde Publications.

Heppell, M. (2009) *Flip it: How to get the best out of everything*. Harlow: Pearson Education Ltd.

Higgs, J., Titchen, A. Horsfall, D. and Armstrong, H. (2007) *Being critical and creative in qualitative research*. Sydney: Hampden Press.

Hill, D. (1997) 'Equality in primary schooling: the policy context, intentions and effects of the Conservative "reforms"', in M. Cole, D. Hill and S. Shan (eds), *Promoting equality in primary schools*. London: Cassell.

Hodges, T.D. and Clifton, D.O. (2004) 'Strengths-based development in practice', In P.A. Linley and S. Jospeh (eds), *Positive psychology in practice*. Hoboken, NJ: Wiley, pp. 256–68.

Hollingsworth, S. (1994) 'Repositioning the teacher in US schools and society: Feminist readings of action research'. Unpublished Paper presented at the CARN International Conference, University of Birmingham, UK.

Hollingsworth, S. (ed.) (1997) *International action research: A casebook for educational reform.* London: Falmer Press.

Hollway, W. (1991) *Work psychology and organizational behaviour: Managing the individual at work.* London: Sage Publications.

Holly, M.-L. (1989) *Writing to grow: Keeping a personal professional journal.* Portsmouth, NH: Heinemann.

Hursh, D. (1992) 'Re-politicising pedagogy: developing ethically and critically reflective teachers within the liberal discourse of teacher education programmes', *Critical Pedagogy Networker* 5, 1–7.

Hurson, T. (2008) *Think better: Your company's future depends on it … and so does yours.* New York, NY: McGraw Hill.

Jackson, P., Boostrom, R. and Hansen, D. (1993) *The moral life of schools.* San Francisco, CA: Jossey Bass.

Johns, C. (2002) *Guided reflection: Advancing practice.* Oxford: Blackwell Science.

Johnson, R. and Redmond, D. (1998) *The art of empowerment: The profit and pain of employee involvement.* London: Pitman Publishing.

Johnston, S. (1988) 'Towards an understanding of the values issue in curriculum decisionmaking', *School Organisation* 8(1), 51–7.

Judge, T.A., Bono, J.E., Ilies, R. and Gerhardt, M.W. (2002) 'Personality and leadership: a qualitative and quantitative review', *Journal of Applied Psychology* 87, 765–80.

Kahane, A. (2004) *Solving tough problems.* San Francisco, CA: Berrett-Koehler Publishers Inc.

Kaiser, R.B. (2009) *The perils of accentuating the positive.* Tulsa, OK: Hogan Press.

Kemmis, S. and McTaggart, R. (1988) *The action research planner.* Geelong, South Australia: Deakin University Press.

Kolb, D. (1984) *Experiential learning: Experience as the source of learning and development.* Upper Saddle River, NJ: Prentice Hall.

Kouzes, J. (2008) 'Foreword', in T. Simons, *The integrity dividend: Leading by the power of your word.* San Francisco, CA: Jossey-Bass.

Lee, S. and Wilkes, J. (1996) 'The changing role of the school experience tutor', *British Journal of In-Service Education* 22(1), 99–112.

Lehane, T. (1992) 'Wet Tuesday afternoons at Shireton School: How can I enhance the everyday school experiences of children with profound and multiple learning difficulties and those who work with them?' Unpublished MEd thesis, Worcester College of Higher Education.

Lewin, K. (1946) 'Action research and minority problems', *Journal of Social Issues* 2, 34–46.

Lewis, T. (1993) 'Valid knowledge and the problem of practical arts curricula', *Curriculum Inquiry* 23(2), 175–202.

Loehr, J. and Schwartz, T. (2004) *The power of full engagement: Managing energy, not time, is the key to high performance and personal renewal.* New York, NY: The Free Press.

Lomax, P. (ed.) (1996) *Quality management in education: Sustaining the vision through action research.* London: Routledge and Hyde Publications.

Lomax, P. and Selley, N. (1996) 'Supporting critical communities through an educational action research network'. Presentation from the Kingston Hill Action Research Group for the BEMAS Research Conference, Cambridge. Kingston upon Thames: Kingston Hill Publications.

Lomax, P., Whitehead, J. and Evans, M. (1996) 'Contributing to an epistemology of quality management practice', in P. Lomax (ed.), *Quality management in education: Sustaining the vision through action research*. London: Routledge and Hyde Publications.

Loughran, J. (2006) A response to 'Reflecting on the self', *Reflective Practice* 7(1) 43–53.

Marchi, S. and Ghaye, T. (2011) *Appreciative reflection: How to feel positive and do good work*. Gloucester: New Vista Publications (forthcoming).

Mardle, G. (1995) 'The consequences', in D. Glover and G. Mardle (eds), *The management of mentoring: Policy issues*. London: Kogan Page, Chapter 9.

McCall, M.W. Jr and Lombardo, M.M. (1983) *Off the track: why and how successful executives get derailed*. Greensboro, NC: Centre for Creative Leadership.

McCormack, B. and Titchen, A. (2007) 'Critical creativity: Melding, exploding, blending', in J. Higgs, A. Titchen, D. Horsfall and H. Armstrong (eds), *Being critical and creative in qualitative research*. Sydney: Hampden Press, pp. 43–55.

McGill, I. and Beaty, L. (1996) *Action Learning*. London: Kogan Page.

McIntyre D. and Hagger, H. (1996) 'Mentoring: challenges for the future', in D McIntyre and H. Hagger, H. (eds), *Mentors in schools: Developing the profession of teaching*. London: David Fulton Publishers.

McKernan, J. (1996) *Curriculum action research: A handbook of methods and resources for the reflective practitioner*. London: Kogan Page.

McLaren, P. (1989) *Schooling as a ritual performance*. London: Routledge & Kegan Paul.

McNiff, J. (1991) *Action research: Principles and practice*. Basingstoke: Macmillan Education Limited.

McNiff, J., Lomax, P. and Whitehead, J. (1996) *You and your action research project*. London: Routledge and Hyde Publications.

McNiff, J., Whitehead, J. and Laidlaw, M. (1992) *Creating a good social order through action research*. Bournemouth: Hyde Publications.

McPeck, J. (1990) *Teaching critical thinking*. New York, NY: Routledge.

Mehan, H. (1979) *Learning lessons: Social organisation in the classroom*. Cambridge, MA: Harvard University Press.

Melander-Wickman, A. and Ghaye, T. (2010) *Building a personal positive portfolio*. Stockholm: Karolinska Institute.

Melenyzer, A. (1991) 'Teacher empowerment: narrative of the silenced practitioners'. Unpublished PhD thesis, Indiana University of Pennsylvania, USA.

Mezirow, J. (1981) 'A critical theory of adult learning and education', *Adult Education* 32, 3–23.

Miller, J. (1990) *Creating spaces and finding voices*. New York, NY: SUNY.

Miller, N. and Boud, D. (1996) 'Animating learning from experience', in D. Boud and N. Miller (eds), *Working with experience: Animating learning*. London: Routledge.

Moon, J. (2004) *A handbook of reflective and experiential learning: Theory and practice*. London: RoutledgeFalmer.

Morrison, D. (1997) 'Cultural values: Human rights, religion and the curriculum'. Paper presented at the Conference on Values and the Curriculum, Institute of Education, University of London, 10–11 April 1997.

Munby H. and Russell, T. (1995) 'Towards rigour with relevance: How teachers and teacher educators claim to know', in T. Russell and F. Korthagen (eds), *Teachers who teach teachers: Reflections on teacher education*. London: Falmer Press.

National Curriculum Council (NCC) (1991) *Curriculum Matters 5: Health Education*. London: NCC.

Neale, S., Spencer-Arnell, L. and Wilson, L. (2009) *Emotional intelligence coaching*. London: Kogan Page.

Newman, F. and Holzman, L. (1997) *The end of knowing: A new developmental way of knowing*. London: Routledge.

Nicholls, G. (1997) *Collaborative change in education*. London: Kogan Page.

Nixon, J. (1995) 'Teaching as a profession of values', in J. Smyth (ed.), *Critical discourses on teacher development*. London: Cassell.

Noffke, S. (1997) 'Themes and tensions in US action research: Towards historical analysis', in S. Hollingsworth (ed.), *International action research: A casebook for educational reform*. London: Falmer Press.

O'Hanlon, C. (1994) 'Reflection and action in research: is there a moral responsibility to act?', *Educational Action Research* 2(2) 281–9.

O'Hanlon, C. (ed.) (1996) *Professional development through action research in educational settings*. London: Falmer Press.

Office for Standards in Education (OFSTED) (1995a) *Framework for the inspection of nursery, primary, middle, secondary and special schools*. London: HMSO.

Office for Standards in Education (OFSTED) (1995b) *Partnership: Schools and higher education in partnership in secondary initial teacher training*. London: HMSO.

Olsen, J. (1992) *Understanding teaching*. Milton Keynes: Open University Press.

Parker, S. (1997) *Reflective teaching in the postmodern world: A manifesto for education in postmodernity*. Buckingham: Open University Press.

Parry, J. (2003) 'Making sense of executive sensemaking: a phenomenological case study with methodological criticism', *Journal of Health Organization and Management* 17(4), 240–63.

Paul, R. (1990) *Critical thinking: What every person needs to survive in a rapidly changing world*. Rohnert Park, CA: Center for Critical Thinking and Moral Critique.

Pendlebury, S. (1995) 'Reason and story in wise practice', in H. McEwan and K. Egan (eds), *Narrative in teaching, learning and research*. New York, NY: Teachers' College Press.

Peterson, C. and Seligman, Martin E. P. (2004). *Character strengths and virtues: A handbook and classification*. Oxford: Oxford University Press.

Pheysey, D. (1993) *Organisational cultures: Types and transformations*. London: Routledge.

Polanyi, M. (1958) *Personal knowledge*. Oxford: Oxford University Press.

Polanyi, M. (1962) *Personal knowledge: Towards a post-critical philosophy*. New York, NY: Harper and Row.

Pollard, A. (ed.) (1996) *Readings for reflective teaching in the primary school*. London: Cassell.

Pollard, A. (1997) *Reflective teaching in the primary school: A handbook for the classroom*. London: Cassell.

Pollard, A. and Triggs, P. (1997) *Reflective teaching in secondary education*. London: Cassell.

Prilleltensky, I. and Fox, D. (1997) 'Introducing critical psychology: values, assumptions and the status quo', in D. Fox and I. Prilleltensky (eds), *Critical psychology: An introduction*. London: Sage Publications.

Pring, R. (1988) 'Confidentiality and the right to know', in R. Murphy and H. Torrance (eds), *Evaluating education: Issues and methods*. London: Paul Chapman.

Qualifications and Curriculum Development Agency (2010) *Introducing the new primary curriculum: Guidance for primary schools*. Coventry: Qualifications and Curriculum Development Agency.

Raelin, J. A. (2001) 'Public reflection as the basis of learning', *Management Learning* 32(1), 11–30.

Rath, T. (2007) StrengthsFinder *2.0*. New York, NY: Gallup Press.

Ratuva, S. (1997) 'In search of common values: Construction of ethnicist values, disempowerment and civil society responses in Fiji'. Paper presented at the Conference on Values and the Curriculum, Institute of Education, University of London, 10–11 April 1997.

Ravn, I. (1991) 'What should guide reality construction?', in F. Steier (ed.), *Research and reflexivity*. London: Sage Publications.

Redwood, S., Goldwasser, C., Street, S. and PricewaterhouseCoopers LLP (1999) *Action management*. New York, NY: John Wiley & Sons.

Reina, D. and Reina, M. (2006) *Trust and betrayal in the workplace: Building effective relationships in your organization*. San Francisco, CA: Berrett-Koehler Publishers Inc.

Richardson, V. (ed.) (1997) *Constructivist teacher education: Building a world of new understandings*. London: Falmer Press.

RobertsonCooper (2008) *Well-being at work: The new view – The Business Well-being Network Annual Report*. Manchester: RobertsonCooper Publications.

Rolfe, G., Freshwater, D. and Jasper, M. (2001) *Critical reflection for nursing and the helping professions: A user's guide*. Basingstoke: Palgrave.

Rothstein B, (2000) 'Trust, social dilemmas and collective memories', *Journal of Theoretical Politics* 12(4), 477–501

Runnymede Bulletin (1997) 'A new vision for Britian', *Runnymede Bulletin* 306.

Sarland, C. (1995) 'Action research: Some British funded projects: A review'. Paper presented at the International Conference on Teacher Research, Davis, California, 13–15 April 1995.

Scarth, J. and Hammersley, M. (1993) 'Questioning ORACLE: an assessment of ORACLE's analysis of teachers' questions', in R. Gomm and P. Woods (eds), *Educational research in action*. London: Paul Chapman Publishing, in association with the Open University.

Schein, E. (1969) 'The mechanisms of change', in W. Bennis (ed.), *Planning change*. New York, NY: Holt, Reinhart and Winston.

Schön, D. (1983) *The reflective practitioner: How professionals think in action*. New York, NY: Basic Books.

Schön, D. (1987) *Educating the reflective practitioner*. London: Jossey Bass.

Schön, D. (ed.) (1991) *The reflective turn: Case studies in and on educational practice*. New York, NY: Teachers' College Press.

School Curriculum and Assessment Authority (SCAA) (1996) *The National Forum for Values in Education and the Community: Final Report and Recommendations. SCAA 96/43*. London: SCAA.

Scott, C., Jaffe, D. and Tobe, G. (1993) *Organisational vision, values and mission*. New York, NY: Crisp Publications.

Seligman, M. (2002) *Authentic happiness*. New York, NY: Free Press.

Seligman, M. E. P. (2006) *Learned optimism: How to change your mind and your life*. New York, NY: Vintage Books.

Seligman, M.E.P. and Csikszentmihalyi, M. (2000) 'Positive psychology: An introduction', *American Psychologist* 55, 5–14.

Sharples, M. (1999) *How we write: Writing as creative design*. London: Routledge.

Silcock, P. (1994) 'The process of reflective teaching', *British Journal of Educational Studies* 42(3), 273–85.

Simons, T., (2008) *The integrity dividend: Leading by the power of your word*. San Francisco, CA: Jossey-Bass.

Simpson, G. (1990) 'Keep it alive: Elements of school culture that sustain innovation', *Educational Leadership* 47(8), 34–7.

Sinclair Penwarden, A. (2006) 'Listen up: we should not be made to disclose our personal feelings in reflection assignments', *Nursing Times* 102(37), 12.

Smyth, J. (1991) *Teachers as collaborative learners*. Milton Keynes: Open University Press.

Smyth, J. (ed.) (1995) *Critical discourses in teacher development*. London: Cassell.

Snyder, K. (1988) 'Managing a productive school work culture', *NASSP Bulletin* 72(510), 40–3.

Stake, R. (1995) *The art of case study research*. London: Sage Publications.

Steinmaker, N. and Bell, N. (1979) *The experiential taxonomy: A new approach to teaching and learning*. London: Academic Press.

Stenhouse, L. (1968) 'The humanities curriculum project', *Journal of Curriculum Studies* 1, 26–33.

Stenhouse, L. (1975) *An introduction to curriculum research and development*. London: Heinemann.

Stenhouse, L. (ed.) (1980) *Curriculum development in action*. London: Heinemann Educational Books.

Stenhouse, L. (1981) 'What counts as research?', *British Journal of Educational Studies* XXXIX(2).

Stenhouse, L. (1983) *Authority, education and emancipation*. London: Heinemann Educational Books.

Stevens, R. (1996) 'Introduction: Making sense of the person in a social world', in R. Stevens (ed.), *Understanding the self*. Milton Keynes: Open University.

Stewart, I. (1995) *Nature's numbers: Discovering order and pattern in the universe*. London: Weidenfeld and Nicolson.

Stratton-Berkessel, R. (2010) *Appreciative inquiry for collaborative solutions: 21 strengths-based workshops*. San Francisco, CA: Pfeiffer.

Sumara, D. and Luce-Kapler, R. (1993) 'Action research as a writerly text; locating co-labouring in collaboration', *Educational Action Research* 1, 387–95.

Swan, E. and Bailey, A. (2004) 'Thinking with feeling: the emotions of reflection', in M. Reynolds and R. Vince (eds), *Organizing reflection*. Aldershot: Ashgate Publishing Ltd.

Taylor, I. (1997) *Developing learning in professional education: Partnerships for practice*. Buckingham: SRHE and Open University Press.

Teacher Training Agency (TTA) (1996/1997) *Open minds, open doors*. London: TTA.

Teacher Training Agency (TTA) (1997) *Invitation to bid for TTA INSET funds*, Annex B, November 1997. London: TTA

Thatchenkery, T. and Metzker, C. (2006) *Appreciative intelligence: Seeing the mighty oak in the acorn.* San Francisco: Berrett-Koehler Publishers Inc.

Thomas, D. (1992) 'Putting nature to the rack: Narrative studies as research'. Paper presented at the Teacher's Stories of Life and Work Conference, Chester.

Thomas, D. (ed.) (1995) *Teachers' stories.* Buckingham: Open University Press.

Thompson, M. (1997) *Professional ethics and the teacher: Towards a General Teaching Council.* Stoke-on-Trent: Trentham Books.

Tice, D.M. and Wallace, H.M. (2003) 'The reflected self: Creating ourselves as (you think) others see you', in M.R. Leary and J.P. Tangney (eds), *Handbook of self and identity.* New York, NY: Guilford Press, pp. 91–105.

Totterdell, M. (1997) 'The moralization of teaching: a relational approach as an ethical frame work in the professional preparation and formation of teachers'. Paper presented at the Conference on Values and the Curriculum, Institute of Education, University of London, 10–11 April 1997.

Tronto, J. (1993) *Moral boundaries: A political argument for the ethics of care.* London: Routledge.

Tsang, N. (1998) 'Re-examining reflection – a common issue of professional concern in social work, teacher and nurse education', *Journal of Interprofessional Care* 12(1), 21–31.

Tsui, A.B.M., Edwards, G. and Lopez-Real, F. (2009) *Learning in school–university partnership: Sociocultural perspectives.* New York, NY: Routledge.

Tye, K. (1974) 'The culture of the school', in J.I. Goodlad, M.F. Klein, J.M. Novotney and K.A. Tye (eds), *Toward a mankind school: An adventure in humanistic education.* New York, NY: McGraw-Hill.

Valli, L. (1993) 'Reflective teacher education programs: an analysis of case studies', in J. Calderhead and P. Gates (eds), *Conceptualising reflection in teacher development.* London: Falmer Press.

van Manen, M. (1991) *The tact of teaching: The meaning of pedagogical thoughtfulness.* Albany, NY: SUNY Press.

van Manen, M. (1997) *Researching lived experience: Human science for an action sensitive pedagogy.* New York, NY: SUNY Press.

Wagner, A. (1987) '"Knots" in teachers' thinking', in J. Calderhead (ed.), *Exploring teachers' thinking.* London: Cassell Education.

Weick, K. (1995) *Sensemaking in Organisations.* London: Sage Publications

Weil, S. and McGill, I. (eds) (1990) *Making sense of experiential learning: Diversity in theory and practice.* Milton Keynes: SRHE and the Open University.

Weiler, K. (1988) *Women teaching for change, gender, class and power.* South Hadley, MA: Bergin and Garvey Publishers.

Wheatley, M. (2002) *Turning to one another: Simple conversations to restore hope to the future.* San Francisco, CA: Berrett-Koehler Publishers Inc.

Whitehead, J. (1985) 'The analysis of an individual's educational development', in M. Shipman (ed.), *Educational research: Principles, policies and practice.* London: Falmer Press.

Whitehead, J. (1989) 'Creating a living educational theory from questions of the kind, "How do I improve my practice?"', *Cambridge Journal of Education* 19(1), 41–52.

Whitehead, J. (1992) *An account of an individual's educational development.* Bath: School of Education Action Research Group, University of Bath.

Whitehead, J. (1993) *The growth of educational knowledge: Creating your own living educational theories*. Bournemouth: Hyde Publications.

Whitehead, J. (1996) 'Living my values more fully in my practice', in P. Lomax and N. Selley (eds), *Supporting critical communities through an educational action research network*. Kingston upon Thames: Kingston Hill Action Research Group, Kingston University.

Whitehead, J. (1997) 'An original contribution to educational knowledge and professionalism'. A commentary on two Papers presented at AERA, Chicago, 1997, in P. Lomax (ed.), *Kingston Hill Research Papers* 1, 37–49.

Whitehead, J. (2008) 'Using a living theory methodology in improving practice and generating educational knowledge in living theories', *Educational Journal of Living Theories* 1, 103–26.

Whitty, G., Barton, L. and Pollard, A. (1987) 'Ideology and control in teacher education: A review of recent experience in England', in T. Popkewitz (ed.), *Critical studies in teacher education: Its folklore, theory and practice*. London: Falmer Press.

Woods, D. (1994) *Problem-based learning: How to gain the most from PBL*. Hamilton, Ontario: McMaster University Press.

Wu, J. (1998) 'School culture and its impact on the competence of Newly Qualified Teachers in Britain: Implications for China'. Unpublished doctoral thesis, University of Worcester.

Wyllie, A. (1999) 'Writing strategies', in M. Sharples (ed.), *How we write: Writing as creative design*. London: Routledge.

Wyness, M. and Silcock, P. (1997) 'Market values, primary schooling and the pupils' perspective'. Paper presented at the Conference on Values and the Curriculum, Institute of Education, University of London, 10–11 April 1997.

Young, R. (1992) *Critical theory and classroom talk*. Clevedon: Multilingual Matters.

Zeichner, K. and Liston, D. (1996) *Reflective teaching: An introduction*. Hillsdale, NJ: Lawrence Erlbaum Associates.

Zuber-Skerritt, O. (ed.) (1996) *New directions in action research*. London: Falmer Press.

Index